MYTHOLOGIES

Before you start to read this book, take this moment to think about making a donation to punctum books, an independent non-profit press,

@ https://punctumbooks.com/support/

If you're reading the e-book, you can click on the image below to go directly to our donations site. Any amount, no matter the size, is appreciated and will help us to keep our ship of fools afloat. Contributions from dedicated readers will also help us to keep our commons open and to cultivate new work that can't find a welcoming port elsewhere. Our adventure is not possible without your support.
Vive la open-access.

Fig. 1. Hieronymus Bosch, *Ship of Fools* (1490–1500)

MYTHODOLOGIES: METHODS IN MEDIEVAL STUDIES, CHAUCER, AND BOOK HISTORY. Copyright © 2018 by Joseph A. Dane. This work carries a Creative Commons BY-NC-SA 4.0 International license, which means that you are free to copy and redistribute the material in any medium or format, and you may also remix, transform and build upon the material, as long as you clearly attribute the work to the authors (but not in a way that suggests the authors or punctum books endorses you and your work), you do not use this work for commercial gain in any form whatsoever, and that for any remixing and transformation, you distribute your rebuild under the same license. http://creativecommons.org/licenses/by-nc-sa/4.0/

Translation published in 2018 by punctum books, Earth, Milky Way.
https://punctumbooks.com

ISBN-13: 978-1-947447-56-1 (print)
ISBN-13: 978-1-947447-57-8 (ePDF)

LCCN: 2018941289
Library of Congress Cataloging Data is available from the Library of Congress

Book design: Vincent W.J. van Gerven Oei

HIC SVNT MONSTRA

Dane, Joseph. *Mythodologies: Methods in Medieval Studies, Chaucer, and Book History*. Earth: punctum books, 2018.

Contents

Introduction: An Exercise in Bad Faith · 15

Part 1 · Noster Chaucerus

Chapter 1 · How Many Chaucerians Does It Take to
Count to Eleven? The Meter of Kynaston's 1635
Translation of *Troilus and Criseyde* ·29

Chapter 2 · Chaucer's "Rude Times" · 53

Chapter 3 · Meditation on Our Chaucer and
the History of the Canon· ·79

Coda · Godwin's Portrait of Chaucer· ·105

Part 2 · Bibliography and Book History

Chapter 4 · The Singularities of Books and Reading · · · · · · · · 113

Chapter 5 · Editorial Projecting · 135

Chapter 6 · The Haunting of Suckling's
Fragmenta Aurea (1646) ·165

Coda · T.F. Dibdin: The Rhetoric of Bibliophilia · · · · · · · · · · · 191

Part 3 · Cacophonies: A Bibliographical Rondo

Section 3.1 · Fakes and Frauds: The "Flewelling
Antiphonary" and Galileo's *Sidereus Nuncius* ············201

Section 3.2 · Modernity and Middle English ·············· 215

Section 3.3 · The Quantification of Readability ············223

Section 3.4 · The Elephant Paper and
the Histories of Medieval Drama························ 231

Section 3.5 · The Pynson Chaucer(s) of 1526:
Bibliographical Circularity ·····························243

Section 3.6 · Margaret Mead and the Bonobos ············257

Section 3.7 · Reading My Library························267

Bibliography ··· 271

Acknowledgments

I thank various institutions for providing materials and permissions: the Henry E. Huntington Library of San Marino, California; the William Andrews Clark Memorial Library, University of California, Los Angeles; Bowdoin College Library, Brunswick, Maine; University of Southern California Libraries, Los Angeles. I thank also Eileen Joy and Vincent W.J. van Gerven Oei at punctum books for seeing this through press. Special thanks also for help and support to Linda Carpenter, Percival Everett, Mary Farley, Karen Grindle, Linda Pence, Alexandra Gillespie, Seth Lerer, Sidney Evans, Michael Peterson and Michaeline Mulvey, Scott Staples, Laura Scavuzzo Wheeler, and David Yerkes.

List of Figures

1. Kynaston, *Amorum Troili et Creseidae* (1635) · · · · · · · · · · · · 28

2. Spurgeon, *Chaucer Criticism and Allusion,*
   3: Index, 10–11 · 74

3. Furnivall, *A Parallel-Text Edition of Chaucer's*
   Minor Poems · 84

4. Supposed portrait of Chaucer from William Godwin,
   Life of Chaucer · 104

5. Gruninger Terence (1499) with hand-written interlinear
   commentary · 122

6. Chaucer Soc. Publ. on my shelves · 141

7a. Classical Stemma · 148

7b. Cladogram by Hölldobler and Wilson, *Ants,* 25 · · · · · · · · · 149

8a. Title Page of Suckling, *Fragmenta Aurea* (1646) · · · · · · · · · 166

8b. Title Page of Suckling, *FRAGMENTA AUREA* (1646) · · · 166

9. The Flewelling Antiphonary · 200

Introduction
An Exercise in Bad Faith

For, brother myn, of me taak this motyf:
I have now been a court-man al my lyf,
And God it woot, though I unworthy be,
I have stonden in ful greet degree
Abouten lordes of ful heigh estaat;
Yet hadde I nevere with noon of hem debaat.
I nevere hem contraried, trewely;
I woot well that my lord kan moore than I.
What that he seith, I holde it ferme and stable;
I seye the same, or elles thyng semblable.
— Chaucer, Merchant's Tale, ll. 1491–1500

The proven best way in evolutionary biology, as in most of science, is to define a problem arising during empirical research, then select or devise the theory that is needed to solve it. Almost all research in inclusive-fitness theory has been the opposite: hypothesize the key roles of kinship and kin selection, then look for evidence to test that hypothesis.
— Edward O. Wilson, *The Social Conquest of Earth*

The best introduction can keep you from reading the book: it summarizes what it cannot present, and even indicates to other scholars what they can expect to cite in the chapters that follow. It presents a thesis, which the rest of the book will support (see Section 3.5 later in this volume). To write one here, as I am attempting to do, is to conclude or imagine that a project is complete, that there is unity in the project, whether abstract and intellectual or merely material. But that unity has always eluded me. Instead, I keep focussing on the important things: the necessary conditions for a book, the big number. In the days of typewriters, that meant the number of pages; now, it means the number of words. When I reach it, I can start revising, and in some senses, I am done.

This project began in a discussion with a particle physicist about differences, real and imagined, between the fields of science and humanities. This is a now standard argument, popularized in several books by Stephen A Gould, E.O. Wilson, and even Steven Pinker, that bête noir, I see, of many humanist acquaintances. We argued about politics, a book on bundling from the nineteenth century, diet, the proper way to share expenses, automobiles, public transportation, dress codes, the correct way to conduct oneself in department meetings. The ashes of those discussions are scattered here (particularly in the final section) and remain active in conversations not recorded here: the chivalric deference I show to those who can work out difficult abstruse math problems I don't understand, the tolerance by both of us for the less convincing rants of the other. We both know that the attempt to find some common ground is futile, or, for fields as diverse as ours, despairingly describable (with some despair) as a search for the "least common denominator" (if I have this metaphor right); we cannot communicate in any way except on the most general or obvious of principles; and we realize that finding what those principles are, and attempting to build on them (that is, to find our way back to the areas that really interest us — the way books are constructed, editions are defined, or the way subatomic particles behave or if they behave and exist at all) — all this is an instance of *petitio principii*: we find a starting point that is so banal and obvious it is almost embarrassing to mention it. (Did you ever notice, for example, that Physics and English are housed in different buildings on a college campus?)

The thesis or purpose of this book is a bit more abstract, but no less straight-forward: I am concerned here with the tenuous connection between what we define as evidence and what we construct as the narrative, scholarly or historical, that makes sense of that evidence, the gap between the impressive but often cryptic footnotes (which graduate students were once instructed to arrange first before writing) and the narrative they seem to be supporting. Chaucer vs. Chaucerians; book history as an event (the life of book copies) vs. book history as a field commonly known as bibliography. The principal problem here is not difficult or abstruse; doubtless we all claim to know it, but most of us ("us" meaning those I read and listen to) act, write, and edit as if we did not. I would like to think that our methods and ways of thinking are determined by the object that seizes our attention: literature, history, humanistic vs. scientific inquiry. But I can't find any convincing foundation on which to make that claim or to refute it. Scholarly method quickly merges into scholarly myth — thus the portmanteau word in my title.

Such considerations run throughout these studies. At minimum, my hope is that readers (at least some of them) come away knowing more about Chaucerian metrics than they did going into it, more about the annoying rifts in the logic and conventions of, say, basic cataloguing conventions in bibliography, and realize also that these apparently diverse subjects are related and that they are variants of similar problems in scholarly methods in all fields. I also hope they consider how we think about these and other things, how we find or invent problems and imagine we have solved them. I would like us to be more comfortable with the imperfect knowledge we have of any of the subjects we deal with or claim expertise in.

Myths of Evidence

On considering the matter of evidence in the humanities, I looked first to a recent and self-declared premier source on this topic: MLA *Literary Research Guide*.[1] The *Library Journal* blurb, quoted on the MLA website, in a classic case of transferred epi-

---

1 James L. Harner, MLA *Literary Research Guide: An Annotated Listing of Reference Sources in English Literary Studies,* 6th edn. (New York: MLA, 2014).

thet, describes this as follows: "Animatedly, energetically, enthusiastically, and vigorously recommended." Moved as I was, I was skeptical: this work has over 800 pages (the fifth edition, of 2008, had 826); these consist of annotated entries for reference books and articles, and there are only three pages devoted to research methods, as if these were self-evident. The *Research Guide* thus seems less a guide to doing research, than a storage base for the construction of book-lists, footnotes, and Works Cited; 823 of its pages exemplify what it promotes, manifesting that amorphous and undefined excellence of kind that is the basis for success in other venues established by this institution, for example, the Submission Guidelines for its journal, included in every issue ("The ideal PMLA essay exemplifies the best of its kind, whatever the kind").

Alas, even the above sentences are speculative: this magisterial MLA Guide remained inaccessible to me. To take advantage of the advertised "Free Trial" proved beyond my computational competence and I would not part with the $700 to make this work "available to a university library." I turned instead to some of the works I assume were referenced in this more important one, these readily available at no cost on-line: I was interested in what it would take to define the evidence I have invoked repeatedly here. I began with the most basic of distinctions: primary versus secondary.

From BMCC Library in the Borough of Manhattan:

Humanities:
> Primary sources: original first-hand account of an event or time period. Usually written or made during or close to the event or time period. Original, creative writing or works of art; factual, not interpretive.

> Secondary sources: analyzes and interprets primary sources; second-hand account of an historical event; interprets creative work.

Sciences:
 Primary: report of scientific discoveries; results of experiments; results of clinical trials; social and political science research results; factual not interpretive.

 Secondary: analyzes and interprets research results; analyzes and interprets scientific discoveries.[2]

From the Library Guides at Princeton:
 A primary source is a document or physical object which was written or created during the time under study. These sources were present during an experience or time period and offer an inside view of a particular event. Some types of primary sources include: original documents…letters, interviews news, film footage, autobiographies, official records, creative works, relic or artifacts. A secondary source interprets and analyzes primary sources. These sources are one or more steps removed from the event.[3]

Other guides distinguish "tertiary sources": almanacs, bibliographies, dictionaries and encyclopedias, indexes.[4]

The distinctions are time-honored, but the difficulties with them are obvious even in these brief and uncontroversial descriptions. The statement regarding scientific sources fosters the notion almost universally discredited that there exist indisputable facts; secondary sources and only secondary sources interpret those facts. But there are no facts in the scientific papers I have read: there are accounts or narration of observations, an experiment that may be reproducible, or a series of equations. These experiments are unlikely to be tested or exactly repro-

---

[2] "Primary vs. Secondary Sources," BMCC Library, http://lib1.bmcc.cuny.edu/help/sources.

[3] "Princeton University Library Guides," Princeton University Library, http://www.libguides.princeton.edu.

[4] E.g., "Primary, Secondary, and Tertiary Sources," English Department, University of Maryland, https://myelms.umd.edu/courses/1034941/pages/primary-secondary-and-tertiary-sources.

duced: you cannot get grants or publications simply by confirming results already obtained by others. The narration of scientist A leads more often to a completely different narration by scientist B.[5]

The humanities, despite the growing distrust contemporary humanists have for historical documents and the once-standard distinction between document and monument, is similar:[6] a primary source is an "original, first-hand description of an event." Even here, the notion of 'primary' has been removed from the so-called "event," which, at least in historical studies, might be considered the major focus — the thing that happened. "These sources or materials were present during an event or time period and offer an inside view." The phrase "inside view" seems to imply that what we suspect to be the least reliable source (one directly involved and thus potentially interested in the event) would be a primary source: but this is the opposite of the attitude this distinction is intended to foster. Wouldn't a disinterested account be more accurate? Or does "accuracy" mean something different here, where the notion of truth changes from an accurate description of facts to the ontological status of a scholarly or witness statement. And are not eye-witness accounts, as we are often told, at the same time the least reliable and the most persuasive of sources? "Closeness to the event" is not the same as "what happened" unless the subject matter is the account itself.

The difference between these types of sources is often one of focus more than material: I can study "Chaucer's meter" or "cata-

---

5 There is an amusing Tumblr devoted to this topic, "Overly Honest Methods": "there are two types of people in this world: those who can extrapolate from incomplete data." "Curves were drawn, and the data was plotted." "Samples 3, 15, and 23 through 41 were discarded due to suspected taco sauce contamination." "We forgot to photocopy some of the surveys double-sided so we only had data from odd numbered surveys." See https://www.tumblr.com/tagged/overly-honest-methods.

6 See Armando Petrucci, *Writers and Readers in Medieval Italy: Studies in the History of Written Culture,* ed. and trans. Charles M. Radding (New Haven: Yale University Press, 1995), 238, on Jacques Le Goff's denial of this once essential distinction.

loguing conventions." In some sense I could distinguish these as investigations into "primary sources" (Chaucer's text) and studies of "secondary ones "(the catalogues describing older books). But anyone who thinks of these two topics knows that the distinction is specious. Chaucer's meter does not exist apart from our discussion of it. And we cannot conceive of what a book is apart from the bibliographical language (sophisticated or banal) that allows them to be considered in the first place. There is no hierarchy or even fast distinction to be had in these cases.

When I decided to look into book history and bibliography, I had no opportunity for instruction, either in the material or in the methods to study them. I thus had no experience with "standard sources "or "basic studies" until I had already dealt with far more esoteric ones. By the time I looked at these (McKerrow's *Introduction to Bibliography for Literary Students,* Gaskell's continuation, and various "histories of printing")[7] I was in a position to read them with amusement rather than simply trying desperately to absorb whatever was there. I had been thrown into the company of those to whom bibliographical study seemed second nature: John Bidwell and the staff of the Clark Library, readers and staff at the Huntington. At first, it took a monumental effort on my part simply to nod at the appropriate places in a conversation. And the whole experience embodied fears shared by many of my academic friends: some day, one day, "they" (whoever they might be) will "find out."

I was lucky enough to be accustomed to that feeling. I have taught languages I couldn't speak and can barely read; I have, since my undergraduate days, breezed through examinations on books I haven't read. And as examiners became more sophisticated and their questions more pointed, I simply gerrymandered areas of interest in which none of my advisors could possibly know more than I did. I survived; bibliography was not in those days recognized in America as an important field or area

---

7   Ronald B. McKerrow, *Introduction to Bibliography for Literary Students* (Oxford: Clarendon Press, 1927); Philip Gaskell, *A New Introduction to Bibliography* (New York: Oxford University Press, 1972).

in literary studies or even in some cases a legitimate one; consequently there seemed less at stake. If you were an incompetent collator, or didn't know variants from virgules, no one outside of a very small coterie really cared. It was also rather easy to blur one area (Chaucer, in which my employers had pigeon-holed me) into this new one — two areas or interests that are reflected in the structure of this present study. Chaucer/Bibliography: I cannot determine whether the centers of those Venn circles have become more or less distant. Perhaps there is a larger area — humanistic studies — into which they comfortably fit.

These areas of interest are accidents. One is due to what I found in graduate school — no one available to help me through early Germanic philology, but excellent readers of Chaucer. The second is another accident of history — finding myself in Los Angeles, where libraries outlining critical history (say, nineteenth-century French literary histories) were few, but examples of early printing were plentiful. Because of these accidental interests (or because of my awareness of their nature), certain types of study and scholarship have completely eluded me. There is nothing quite so admirable in scholarship as a well-researched and beautifully argued book that proves an articulable point and provides an avenue for future scholarship. And nothing quite so precious as a beautifully cut gemstone, seen under a microscope. But the world we live in, whether it is one of books, bibliographers, artists, or Chaucerians, is not at all like that. And the books that argue otherwise seem to me (as a professed hater of all things Victorian) like a Byrne-Jones painting set in some contrasting and utterly cartoonish version of Victoriana — rickety houses, turrets, roofs that have been shingled three times, steel-cut engravings. My logic then turns out to be like the logic I criticise: *given* that I cannot write such beautifully constructed books; *therefore,* I won't.

My own methods, considered most generously, grow out of this thinking and experience. And the essays below result from two opposing methods that form or imply a methodology. One is what I have called the "heaps of books" approach, or what earlier I might have called the "heaps of texts." When

I first began to study material books, I thought a good place to begin was with Caxton (that seems naive to me now, but most things in our past do). I would just call up all his books that were available and look at them. Something would turn up, the way things had always turned up by shelf-reading in the bookstacks. I would be the Micawber of book-historians. Or so I thought. Until some librarians, less kindly than I had imagined they might be, intervened. Civilian library patrons cannot just "call up" these precious Caxtons. Before asking to see one, you must know in advance exactly what you are looking for. So I modified this purported method: I invented a fraudulent or make-believe project, complete with a thesis, that would enable me to see, not only those Caxtons, but thousands of early books. They would be requested in what appeared to be a logical order, but in fact as close to random as the suspicious librarian, now a friend, would permit.[8] I finally got my heap of books. My notes on them, thousands of hand-written descriptions and questions, are of course unsystematic and scattered. I thus finally threw them away, enabling me to begin this project (whatever it was) again. Although library policies have changed and are far less congenial than they were in those fine days, something will still, I think, turn up.

The second method, if we can call it that, is to rely entirely on what is known as secondary evidence. I may well have no idea what to say about the heaps of things on my desk, about the heaps of books and texts I have read, but fortunately, other scholarss are not so reticent. I can simply take what they say and place those statements against other statements or perhaps against the very evidence they themselves cite (or in some cases should have cited).[9] The approach is largely negative. And true, if everyone acted this way, the world might grind to a cynical

---

8 Detailed in my "The Red and the Black," in Joseph A. Dane, *Blind Impressions: Methods and Mythologies in Book History* (Philadelphia: University of Pennsylvania Press, 2013), 149–55.

9 Examples in Joseph A. Dane, *The Myth of Print Culture: Essays on Evidence, Textuality, and Bibliographical Method* (Toronto: University of Toronto Press, 2003).

and nihilistic halt. Fortunately, there is no chance of that happening. There will always be grand claims from humanists. And there will always be young scholars instructed in the construction and organization of book-lists. Perhaps if you could just get your sources in order and arranged correctly, or, as Henry Bradshaw claimed more than a century ago, your facts rigorously arranged, the actual work of researching and writing up that research (two completely different things, we desperately imagine) would simply do itself.

Concluding Statement

One of my favorite encounters when I began to work seriously in academia was with a young classicist. The first day I met him, we were discussing areas of interest; at the time, I was thinking about parody as a topic, and he responded, as if responding: "In the opening sentence of the fifth oration of Demosthenes, did you know that there is an apparently parodic reference to…?" I can't remember the particulars and I won't try to invent them. But I do remember thinking that this was why I went to graduate school, just so I could have conversations like this one. No matter how abstruse a topic or interest (mine was not; his was), it is always possible to use that as a basis of thinking or communication. Three years later, I ran into this slightly older man again. I had not seen him since my first week on campus. It was graduation. I made some reference to the cruel irony (another area of interest) that there were not enough fold-up metal chairs in the quad for us newly minted PhDs to sit. He nodded: "In the opening sentence of the fifth oration of Demosthenes, did you know…?"

You, my friend, will never read this. You have long forgotten my name and have no interest whatsoever in the fields I pursue. You have no idea who I am. But you perhaps have had time to learn who you are.

I choose this anecdote to introduce my concluding paragraphs here but I could have chosen, and at certain points did choose others. The "Flewelling" collection at USC (see Section 3.1 in this volume), the notion of "readability" (see Section 3.3 in this volume), Hoccleve (alluded to here, and completed in *Mythologies II* in an act of near plagiarism of a once brilliant student, or rather brilliant once-student). I could also have chosen a remark by one of my friends, who does not realize he has used it on many occasions. Reading and critiquing something I have written, he concludes: "What this book/article is really about is not X [(my own interest and subject]), but Y [(the subject of one of his recent studies])." I of course do the same thing to him. I learned to call this "The Elephant Conversation," but to understand that, you need to know what "An Elephant Paper" is, and for that, you need to read Ssection 3.4 below.

There are, therefore, three parts: the first two are on fields I have worked in in the past and ones that still interest me to some extent: Chaucer, and bibliography. I could have chosen other areas, areas in which I once claimed competence, to complete this quasi-autobiographical sketch, but for various reasons, I am done with them, and there remain only vague allusions to them here: medieval drama, allegory, and Old English. These two parts are followed by a series of inquiries, or what I call "Cacophonies" in the form of a rondo. In my mind, each of these could be expanded, and that likely will be what I will be asked by a reader at some point to do. To this, I have already formed my answer: "Thank you for your valuable input and notes, which I have read with great interest. Now, concerning that project I am engaged in *here*...." Some of the problems I deal with here are old and familiar, others are new, and some are of my own creation. I have not been able to solve any of them in a traditional sense.

I have finally come up with a thesis, one that is neither too confining nor constricting. I am critiquing the methods I encounter often in the humanities — our construction of a foundation long after the rickety superstructure has gained the aura and veneration of tradition. I am aware that my own thinking tends to fit the same grooved pattern of the past, and why not? It worked well once, why should it not work again? I have stated on more than one occasion that before I take on a subject, define it, or pick up a book in a library, I know much of what I will say before so much as glancing at the evidence. I am neither proud nor ashamed of that. It is just the way things are.

None of these essays has a listed collaborator, although that was hardly the original plan. Sometimes, you just don't have the time left to let younger colleagues catch up with you; they will have to do it on their own. Or perhaps, more accurately, the banalities that always convince me have never quite convinced them.

part 1

NOSTER CHAUCERUS

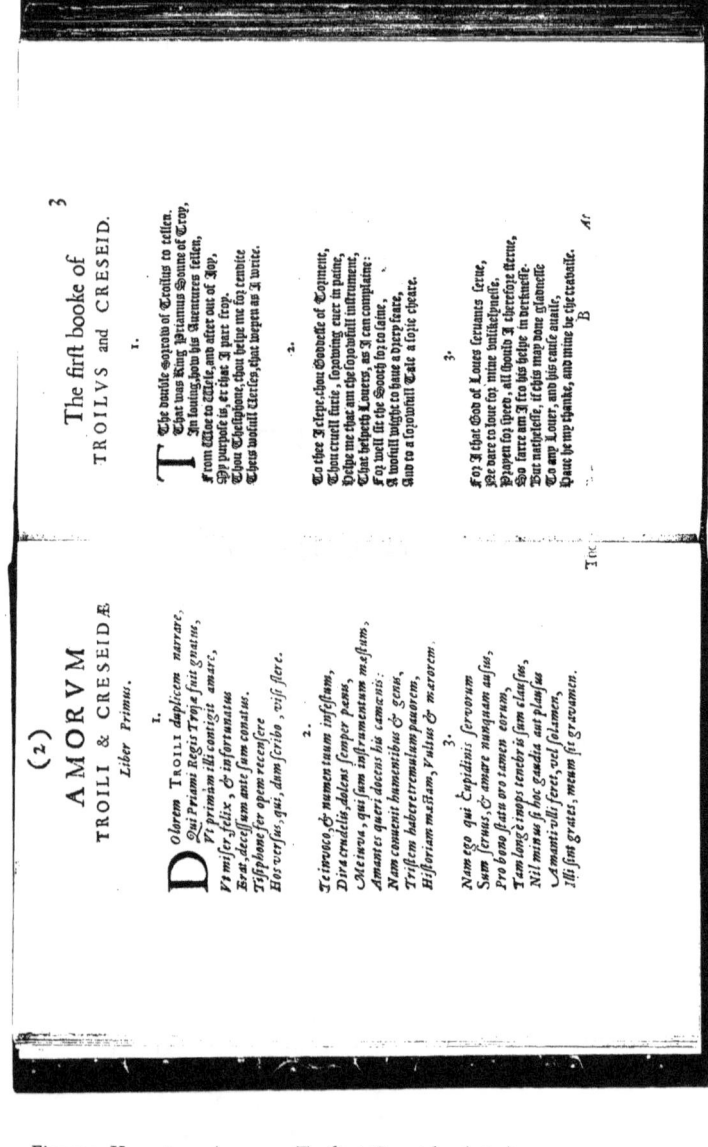

Figure 1: Kynaston, *Amorum Troili et Creseidae* (1635)

CHAPTER 1

How Many Chaucerians Does It Take to Count to Eleven? The Meter of Kynaston's 1635 Translation of *Troilus and Criseyde*

Among what are generally known as "curiosities" of Chaucerian reception history is the 1635 translation of the first two books of Chaucer's *Troilus and Criseyde* into Latin stanzas by Sir Francis Kynaston: *Amorum Troili et Creseidae libri duo priores Anglico-Latini* (Oxford, 1635; STC 5097). The Latin (printed in Italic) is on the left; the English (printed in black-letter) is on the right, in a manner familiar to budding and career Latinists from their experience with Loeb translations.

Kynaston completed, but never published, the remainder of the translation, and most of what anyone might want to know concerning the fate of this translation and Kynaston himself is now well-recorded. Spurgeon devotes several pages to Kynaston in *Five Hundred Years of Chaucer Criticism and Allusion*, although her selections include only the commendatory verses praising Kynaston and nothing from his own introduction or translation. The translation was the subject of a dissertation by Judith M. Newton in 1967, and there have been several articles on Kynaston since (the most important and succinct is by Richard Beadle in 1990).[1] The 1635 text is now readily available on

---

1   See Caroline F.E. Spurgeon, *Five Hundred Years of Chaucer Criticism and Allusion, 1357–1900* (1914–25), 3 vols. (New York: Russell and Russell, 1960), 1:207–15; Judith May Newton, "Chaucer's Troilus: Sir Francis Kynaston's Lat-

EEBO, and the rest of the translation is published in a modern edition by Helmut Wolf (an edition less accessible for some of us than electronic or even material copies of the original book!) and in a hypertextual edition by Dana F. Sutton.[2]

The most basic issues posed by Kynaston's work for Chaucerians are the quality of the translation and the nature of the verse. Here, I am concerned only with the second question, a question that seems to me the most basic and obvious of all: what verse form did Kynaston use? Surely the quality of translation (the concern of most Chaucerians) should depend on a clear answer to this question. I should say at the onset that the answer is (or should be) absurdly easy, and anyone with any knowledge of Latin verse and a few minutes of free time ought to be able to come up with it. Kynaston describes explicitly what he is doing; scholars quote his description and translate it correctly; and Kynaston does exactly what he says he will do. Yet for more than a century, those who studied this text have for some reason managed to ignore or repress all this (even their own explicit statements) and have instead offered what look to me like variations of the banalities taught us about versification in grade school: Kynaston, we are told repeatedly, despite what he explicitly claims, wrote accentual iambic pentameter. The fact that his verse cannot scan that way? That is apparently his problem, not ours.

---

    in Translation, with a Critical Edition of his English Comments and Latin Annotations," PhD diss., University of Illinois, Champaign-Urbana, 1967; and Richard Beadle, "The Virtuoso's *Troilus*," in *Chaucer Traditions: Studies in Honour of Derek Brewer*, eds. Ruth Morse and Barry Windeatt (Cambridge: Cambridge University Press, 1990), 213–33. See also Tim William Machan, "Kynaston's *Troilus*, Textual Criticism and the Renaissance Reading of Chaucer," *Exemplaria* 5, no. 1 (1993): 161–83, and Seth Lerer, "Latin Annotations in a Copy of Stowe's Chaucer and the Seventeenth-Century Reception of *Troilus and Criseyde*," *Review of English Studies* 53, no. 209 (2002): 1–7.

2 Helmut Wolf, *Sir Francis Kynastons Übersetzung von Chaucers Troilus and Criseyde: Interpretation, Edition und Kommentar* (Frankfurt am Main: Peter Lang, 1997), and Dana F. Sutton, *Sir Francis Kynaston, Amorum Troili et Creseidae Libri Quinque* (1639), http://www.philological.bham.ac.uk/troilus/.

How can the narratives of professional Chaucerians be so much more powerful than the evidence on which they claim those are based?

That Chaucerians and neo-Latinists have reached an apparent consensus on the wrong answer to this simple question is no great scandal and, in and of itself, of no great import: Chaucerians do not need to know a great deal about European versification in order to perform their basic functions. What is amusing to me is that something (literary training?) has made Kynastonians (if such persons can be said to exist) unable to perceive something as obvious as I am going to point out here. What is even more interesting about the reception of Kynaston's verse is that it seems to parallel a far more important issue in Chaucer studies concerning the description of Chaucer's own meter.

I will deal with several questions below: first, what is the verse Kynaston uses and what does this tell us about the seventeenth-century perception of Chaucer's verse? Let me state the case as directly as I can: on the specific question of the nature of Kynaston's versification, Kynaston's verse is what is called (not quite accurately) "isosyllabic verse"; it is a variant of the French and Italian models he cites. Scholars who claim otherwise (and that includes nearly all those referenced here) are mistaken. Second, and more important, are the inferences we can make as to what a learned seventeenth-century reader might have thought about Chaucer's verse and what our own perception of his translation might mean for us. What does the now traditional misrepresentation of Kynaston's verse imply about our own reception and prejudices concerning Chaucer's versification?

To discuss the second of these matters will involve my own view of the nature of Chaucer's versification. I realize my views on this subject (either what Chaucer's verse "is" or how it is to be described) are not shared by many Chaucerians and I won't try to persuade them here. I freely admit that, blinded as I am by my own theories, I find support for them nearly everywhere. My errors on a subject as complex as Chaucer's versification, however, are less surprising to me than are the errors of others on something as simple and uncontroversial as Kynaston.[3]

Descriptions of Kynaston's Verse

I begin with the first few lines of Kynaston's translation:

> Dolorem *Troili* duplicem narrare,
> Qui Priami Regis Trojae fuit gnatus,
> Vt primum illi contigit amare,
> Vt miser, felix, & infortunatus
> Erat, decessum ante sum conatus.
> Tisiphone, fer opem recensere
> Hos versus, qui, dum scribo, visi flere.
>
> Te invoco, & numen tuum infestum,
> Dira crudelis, dolens semper paenis
> … (lines 1–9)

A reasonable, but not entirely accurate translation of this might be the following:

> The double sorrow of Troilus to tellen,
> That was King Priamus Sonne of Troy,
> In loving, how his Aventures fellen,
> From Woe to Wele, and after out of Joy,
> My purpose is, er that I part froy.
> Thou Thesiphone, thou helpe me for tendite
> Theis wofull Verses, that wepen as I write.
>
> To thee I clepe, thou Goddesse of Torment,
> Thou cruell furie, sorowing ever in paine,
> …

---

[3] Joseph A. Dane, "Toward a Description of Chaucer's Verse Forms," *Studia Neophilologica* 81, no. 1 (2009): 45–52.

Anyone looking at this can see that Kynaston's Latin is a line-by-line translation maintaining the rhyme scheme of his original: the rhyme royale stanza familiar from contemporary French poets. What Latinists will also see almost immediately is that Kynaston's verse is not in classical Latin. Classical Latin verse is structured according to the quantity of syllables, not their accent. And Kynaston's lines are not written in any of the common quantitative models for lines of this length, not in classical iambic senarii, and not in various forms of, say, Latin hendecasyllables. Such classical verse forms posed no problems for Kynaston and his contemporaries: several of the commendatory verses in Kynaston's own book were composed in quantitative hendecasyllables. What modern Latinists seem to conclude from this, however, is that therefore it is written in accentual verse — a style of Latin versification that developed during the Middle Ages. But Kynaston's verse will not scan according to accentual principles either (or only will do so by the invocation of an unreasonable number of exceptions — try line 1 in the second stanza above). Anyone whose Latin is good enough to see that quantitative principles do not apply ought to be able to see that accentual principles do not apply either.[4]

The foundational principle behind Kynaston's verse is simple: these are eleven-syllable lines with a terminal accent on syllable 10. There is no need to provide visual scansion of the lines above: place an accent on the penultimate syllable; there will be one unaccented syllable following it and nine preceding

---

4 I should concede here that in versification, it is always possible to see any verse as a variant of any metrical system or template, just as in textual criticism any text can be seen as a variant of any base text, even "Mary Had a Little Lamb"; see my *The Myth of Print Culture: Essays on Evidence, Textuality, and Bibliographical Method* (Toronto: University of Toronto Press, 2003), 115–24. For example, line 1 in stanza two above could be scanned, with arbitrary elisions, as an accentual trochaic pentameter: TE in VOC et NU men TU min FES tum; perhaps an iambic one with trochaic inversions in the first two feet: TE in VO co et NU men TU min FES tum; or as an quadrimeter: T' inVO c'et NUmen TU min FES tum. Such exercises can be a source of intellectual amusement, but they say very little about the verse form itself.

it (you may have to invoke sometimes inconsistent rules of elision, as you would in Latin, French, Italian or even English, that is, dropping a terminal vowel when the following word begins in one).[5] They are modelled after well-known and uncontroversial rules regarding French and Italian verse (see note 22 below). This is precisely how Kynaston describes them in his brief Preface "Candido Lectori …":

> Cumque haec mecum meditarer, ecce novum scri bendi genus animum subit, iisdem enim syllabarum numeris, eadem metri methodo, consimilibusque Heptenariis vti, & rythmos etiam Prototypi, & ultimarum syllabarum symphoniam (quantum fieri potuit) exprimere decrevi.

> [And as I was considering all these things (how to clothe Chaucer in Latin etc.), a new kind of writing occurred to me: to use the same number of syllables, and the same meter, and the same seven-line stanzas, and I decided to express the rhythms of the original and the rhyme of the last syllable insofar as it was possible.]

Kynaston claims this is a "new form of writing." There is nothing here about accentual rhythms. There is nothing here about feet. Nothing about iambs in any sense. And when Kynaston later uses the word "pentameter," that has nothing to do with what English speakers mean by that term; it refers rather to the second line of a classical elegiac couplet. The term "iambic pentameter," commonly and incorrectly used to describe this verse, thus finds no support in anything Kynaston says here.

---

5   All lines in the above passage can be scanned this way, with the possible exception of line 8 (does Kynaston count *tuum* as one syllable?). He does not appear to use elision elsewhere in these lines. I concede of course, as do others arguing for different metrical schemes, that Kynaston uses elision inconsistently, and also makes many apparent mistakes, e.g., Book 2, lines 1818–19:
   Immo, inquit Troilus, diis propitiis faciam
   Epistola a Pandaro ad illum datur.

The consensus (an inaccurate one) on Kynaston's verse form is slow in developing. Thomas Lounsbury in his *Studies in Chaucer* (1892) simply quotes what Kynaston says: "It had the same number of lines in the stanza; the same number of syllables in the line."[6] This statement is correct, but I cannot tell from Lounsbury's extensive and amusing discussion whether he understands Kynaston's "ridiculous" meter or not, or whether he has any interest in understanding it. Falconer Madan in 1895 describes the verse-form as "a singular rhythmical rhyming meter, essentially decasyllabic iambics."[7] The qualifications "singular" and "essentially" (meaning here "not really") suggest Madan realized that this verse was not strictly accentual, despite what he seems to claim.

Saintsbury, in *History of English Prosody* (1906–1910) speaks of Kynaston in the context of late nineteenth-century Latin verse:

> That it may be possible…to establish an apparent concordat between accent and quantity, by selecting words which satisfy both systems, nobody can deny. It may be as legitimate a poetic amusement as any other prosodic tour de force — as pantoums and emperières à triple couronne, as poetical bellows and altars, as anagrams and lipograms and acrostics, as Sir Francis Kynaston's Latin rhyme-royal (to which it is very close) or Dr. King's Greek-gibberish macaronics.[8]

He discusses Kynaston again in *Minor Poets of the Caroline Period,* in his introductory notes to Kynaston's English poem *Leoline and Syndaris*:

---

[6] Thomas R. Lounsbury, *Studies in Chaucer: His Life and Writings,* 3 vols. (New York: Harper, 1892), 3:77.

[7] Falconer Madan, *The Early Oxford Press: A Bibliography of Printing and Publishing at Oxford, 1468–1640* (Oxford: Clarendon Press, 1895), 183, noted by Newton, "Chaucer's Troilus," 12n34.

[8] George Saintsbury, *A History of English Prosody from the Twelfth Century to the Present Day,* 3 vols. (London: Macmillan, 1906–10), 3:436.

> [Kynaston's] ultra-eccentric enterprise of translating *Troilus* into Latin rhyme royal, a venture in which he at least showed that he had thoroughly saturated himself with the rhythm.... There is a great charm, and also a not small lesson, in the way in which Latin, not too classically treated, adapts itself to modern measures.[9]

I believe Saintsbury is saying that Kynaston combines the principles of quantity and accent in *Troilus,* but the reference here is too casual to conclude much. Note the evasion "not too classically treated."[10] Note further the assumption that Chaucer's "rhythm" is unproblematic. I don't think it could be reasonably claimed that in 1910 this was the case, nor that a hundred years later we still share Sainstbury's confidence.

Saintsbury, Lounsbury, and Madan were all good turn-of-the-century Latinists — good enough to see that Kynaston's verse would not scan either by the principles of quantity or by strict principles of accent. But the qualifications and evasions in their descriptions are not found in the pronouncements of later scholars who speak with much more confidence on the nature of this verse. Judith Newton, in her 1967 dissertation, correctly translates the passage quoted above from Kynaston's preface: "a new kind of writing occurred to me, namely to use the same number of syllables, the same metrical patterns, and the same seven-line stanzas."[11] But a paragraph later she writes: "By writing in accentual, riming verse, instead of unrimed quantitative lines, Kynaston was endangering the success of his enterprise." And a few pages later: "[Kynaston] recognized Chaucer's meter as decasyllabic. The Latin would have to conform to the English

---

9 George Saintsbury, *Minor Poets of the Caroline Period,* 3 vols. (Oxford: Clarendon Press, 1905–21), 2:64.

10 Saintsbury is committed to the "foot" as a basic unit of verse, as noted by Alan T. Gaylord, Introduction to *Essays on the Art of Chaucer's Verse* (New York: Routledge, 2001), 7. But any foot-based system in my view makes Kynaston's verse unscannable.

11 Newton, "Chaucer's Troilus," 90.

pentameter pattern."¹² (The adjectives "decasyllabic" and "pentameter" are not synonyms.)

James W. Binns (1990) says specifically that the verse is neither quantitative nor rhythmic (that is, based on accent). But paradoxically, the fact that the verse does not conform to accentual principles seems to be evidence that it does:

> At first the result is somewhat disconcerting. The lines appear to have no shape in quantitative terms, nor do they seem to have any apparent rhythmic structure. The number of syllables (11, i.e., an attempt to reproduce the Chaucerian pentameter in a Latin guise) is however fairly constant, and if the lines are read with the strong iambic rhythm of the original in mind, they work fairly well.¹³

This is an interesting statement: even a late-twentieth-century scholar who recognizes the principle of the verse (eleven-syllable lines) is unable to resist superadding "iambic rhythm" and "pentameter." The same logical leaps are found in Dana A. Sutton's recent hypertextual edition. Sutton quotes the Binns statement above, then adds:

> Each verse indeed contains eleven syllables, but these have nothing to do with classical hendecasyllables. They are based on stress accentuation, and are more accurately described (in English metrical terminology) as iambic pentameters with feminine endings....Kynaston's rhyming stress-verses manage to impart an appropriately Chaucerian feeling....¹⁴

Lawrence V. Ryan in 1987 goes further, referring to Kynaston's stanzas as "senarii" (which he glosses, as "rime-royal stanzas"; I'm not certain what he means by this, since a "senarius" is a

---

12 Ibid., 90, 94.
13 J.W. Binns, *Intellectual Culture in Elizabethan and Jacobean England: The Latin Writings of the Age* (Leeds: Francis Cairns Ltd., 1990), 255, quoted both by Sutton and by Wolf, 14.
14 Sutton, Introduction, *Amorum Troili*.

line in six feet, not a stanza in seven lines).¹⁵ He claims that Kynaston's verse is "an equivalent of English accentual iambic pentameter in rhymed seven-line stanzas," adding with some condescension: "to attempt to reproduce the same metrical scheme in Latin, however, was indeed a novel enterprise."¹⁶

> The difference between monosyllabic English and polysyllabic Latin, with its preponderance of words having feminine endings, made it impractical for Kynaston to try to generate in the latter tongue decasyllabic iambic lines. His solution was to settle upon hendecasyllables containing five regular iambic stresses, effected by elisions and by frequent compression of certain types of disyllables into monosyllables or diphthongs, and justified upon the authority of such modern vernacular "classics" as Ariosto and Tasso.¹⁷

It is enough to note that this is absolutely incorrect, and Ryan unwittingly misrepresents in this short selection versification principles and practices of at least three languages.

Richard Beadle, in an otherwise excellent article of 1990, is a bit more circumspect: "The unusual but careful imitation of the rhyme scheme, and the ear for the rhythm of the original are strong clues."¹⁸ Here, as in nearly all these scholars, Chaucer rhythms (whatever those are) are characterized as unproblematic.

Wolf in his 1997 dissertation correctly translates Kynaston's passage above, as did Newton in 1967: "dieselbe Zahl der Silben, dieselbe Art von Metrum, die gleichen siebenzeiligen Strophen und den Endreim zu verwenden" [in orderto use the same number of syllables, the same type of meter, the same seven-line strophes, and the endrhyme].¹⁹ Yet his conclusion does not follow this: "Ohne Zweifel ist die Übersetzung ganz nach dem akzentu-

---

15 Lawrence V. Ryan, "Chaucer's Criseyde in Neo-Latin Dress," *English Literary Review* 17, no. 3 (1987): 288–302, at 290.
16 Ibid., 291.
17 Ibid., 291–92.
18 Beadle, "The Virtuoso's *Troilus*," 213.
19 Wolf, *Sir Francis Kynastons Übersetzung*, 114.

ierenden Prinzip gestaltet" [Without question, the translation is designed according to accentual principles]. Kynaston is said to see Chaucer's verse precisely as do twentieth-century Chaucerians, even though Kynaston himself gives no hint as to this prescient insight: "Chaucers Vers ist für Kynaston aus *fünffüssigen Iamben gebildet*" [Chaucer's verse is for Kynaston constructed from iambs in five feet].[20]

By the late twentieth century, the hesitations of Saintsbury, Lounsbury, and Madan are nowhere to be found. Qualifications give way to certainties. And nowhere is there any indication in any of this, as far as I can tell, that there is any question at all about the verse Chaucer used, no controversy whatsoever about "the rhythms of the original." The fact, of course, is that at no point in the history of Chaucer reception has his verse form or the rhythms overlaid on that form been uncontroversial.

That Kynaston is said to perceive exactly what we perceive (the "rhythms of the original") should cause suspicion. How could he have done this, since our views on Chaucer's meter (a product of late nineteenth-century Chaucerians) were not shared by anyone in the seventeenth century? Even Tyrwhitt's statements on meter in his 1774 edition, which modern Chaucerians claim to be the foundation for proper understanding of Chaucerian verse, are nearly 150 years away.

Kynaston and the Principles of Romance Verse

Most of what is said about Kynaston's versification is inaccurate. Kynaston's lines are not written in iambic pentameter (whatever that is); they cannot be scanned by quantity and only tortuously by accent. They are modelled after what Kynaston saw in Italian

---

20 Ibid., 115, 116. Wolf ends his brief section on meter with another invocation of the mysterious Latin word *senarius* (also used by Ryan), whose resonance likely blinds his readers to the fact that the statement in which it occurs is completely inaccurate: "Kynastons Vers ist also ein katalektischer iambischer Senar" (116). A catalectic iambic senarius is a verse of six-feet of iambs lacking the final syllable. It has nothing to do with Kynaston's verse.

and French verse and what he may well have seen in Chaucer's verse: seven-line stanzas, in rhyme royale, with lines of eleven syllables in length and a terminal accent in syllable 10 (anyone can apply this simple rule to his verse, although see qualifications above in footnotes 4 and 5). This is exactly how Kynaston describes them, and every scholar who has described and analyzed this verse has of course referred to the same passages in Kynaston's Preface.

> Visum est mihi consultissimum, illum nova lingua donare, & novato rythmi & carminis genere decorare
>
> [It seemed to me best to provide that in a new tongue and to decorate it in a new type of rhythm and song.]
>
> Non me praeterit, quanto facilius mihi fuisset authoris verba & sensus vulgaribus Latinis Hexametris & Pentametris reddidisse: sed cum recorder quod celeberrimi *Torquati Tassi,* atque elegantissimi *Ludovici Ariosti* opera (ut Gallos & Iberos taceam) hoc metri genere vere nobili & Enharmonico sint composita, & quod haec septennaria compositio non tantum Italis, sed & Anglis, Gallis, immo omnibus sit in deliciis, utpote melos quod aurem mirifico modulamine mulceat & delectet: Tentare mihi visum, quid Lingua Latina posset, & experiri, num grata forent carmina Idiomate Romano pacta & concinnata, quae in linguis derivativis & modernis, tantam obtinuerunt per tot secula sequiora existimationem.
>
> [I am not unaware how much easier it would have been to render the author's sense in ordinary Latin elegiac couplets. But when I remembered that Tasso and Ariosto (not to mention Spanish and French works) wrote in this kind of meter and that this seven-line stanza has been popular among Italians, English, and French it occurred to me to see what Latin could do ... in these same types of meters.]

He ends this preface with a reference to those who would condemn his verses as "Leonine" (rhyming accentual verse). That is, he condemns those who would describe his verse as late twentieth-century scholars do. Anyone so asinine, he says, obviously cannot distinguish the modulation of Neo-Latinists from the *faecutinos* (dreg-like [?]) rhythms of the monks. That bears repeating: the descriptions we find of Kynaston's verse in the twentieth century may be right; Kynaston himself, however, claims not only that those descriptions are wrong, but that those scholars who promote them are not competent to discuss the issue.

These statements do not seem to me to be ambiguous. Kynaston speaks of writing in a "new kind of song," and by this, he means not in a conventional Latin meter. He is translating Chaucer by using "the same number of syllables." He is not writing in quantitative verse (as every scholar recognizes) or rhymed accentual verse (as most scholars claim). He is, rather, following the precedent in verse by Ariosto, Tasso and in other romance languages. That is what he says. And most of his lines can be easily scanned accordingly.[21] All you need is the ability to count.

French and Italian verse is based on what is called isosyllabism: the foundational structure is determined by the number of syllables per line, where syllables are all of equal weight or value (regardless of quantity or accent). To this foundation are added rules regarding accent: line length is determined by the placement of a terminal accent. In both French decasyllables and Italian hendecasyllables, that accent occurs on syllable #10.

The development of the two languages is such that the nature of this line changes. In French, words tended to drop unaccented final syllables. Thus, many lines in French that we describe as decasyllables do in fact have ten syllables; others have eleven and are characterized as having feminine endings and rhymes (and a number of rules can be added regarding the deployment

---

21 I am not denying that some license needs to be allowed for the definition of what a syllable is and how elision is to be handled, and I suppose those who claim that his verse is iambic could argue that similar license would produce the five-foot iambic verse they see here.

of these types of rhymes). In Italian, these unaccented syllables are more persistent; the most common words retain a syllable after the final tonic accent, with the result that the most common line of this form in Italian has eleven syllables (the answer to the question "how many syllables does an Italian hendecasyllable contain?" is thus "from ten to twelve").[22]

Most French decasyllables (and all Alexandrines) have a fixed caesura, one that is regularly deployed in each poem. Italian does not have such a rule, despite some claims to the contrary.[23] And of course there are rules regarding elision and even what constitutes a syllable. There are in addition a number of conventions that apply to the deployment of accents or phrase breaks, but these do not affect the basic structure of a line (the difference between what might be called legal and illegal lines).[24]

---

22 See the excellent and detailed account in Martin J. Duffell, "Chaucer, Gower and the History of the Hendecasyllable," in *English Historical Metrics*, eds. C.B. McCully and J.J. Anderson (Cambridge: Cambridge University Press, 1996), 210–18, my more summary account in *The Long and the Short of It: A Practical Guide to European Versification Systems* (Notre Dame: University of Notre Dame Press, 2010), 37–61, and any basic work on the history of French versification, e.g., W. Theodor Elwert, *Traité de versification française des origines à nos jours* (Paris: Klincksieck, 1965; translation of *Französische Metrik*, 1961); L.E. Kastner, *A History of French Versification* (Oxford: Clarendon Press, 1903). See also, on the specific issues here, Martin J. Duffell, "'The Craft So Long to Lerne': Chaucer's Invention of Iambic Pentameter," *The Chaucer Review* 34, no. 3 (2000): 269–88.

23 See, e.g., Bartlett Giamatti, "Italian," in W.K. Wimsatt, ed., *Versification: Major Language Types, Sixteen Essays* (New York: MLA, 1972), 148–76; Bernhard Ten Brink, *The Language and Metre of Chaucer* (1884), 2nd edn., rev. Friedrich Kluge, trans. M. Bentinck Smith (London: Macmillan, 1901), 218. More recent scholars make similar claims: see, e.g., Duffell, "Chaucer, Gower, and the History of the Hendecasyllable," 216, and, following him, Donka Minkova and Robert Stockwell, "Emendation and the Chaucerian Metrical Template," in Donka Minkova and Theresa Tinkle, eds., *Chaucer and the Challenges of Medievalism: Studies in Honor of H.A. Kelley* (Frankfurt am Main: Peter Lang, 2003), 130. Given the strict (although quite different) definitions of "caesura" in French and Latin, I see no purpose in invoking the notion of a "flexible" caesura, which to me is not that different from "no caesura."

24 On phrase breaks (coupes), see, e.g., Jean Mazaleyrat, *Elements de métrique française* (Paris: Armand-Colin, 1974), 165ff.

And there is nothing in either verse form that corresponds to our notion of a "foot," a basic unit in most discussions of Chaucer's verse, including those cited here.

What makes Kynaston's verse "strange" and "curious" is not that he attempts to represent Chaucerian verse in Latin iambic pentameter, which he does not, but rather that he writes in Latin according to rules that apply to French or Italian verse. I doubt he is the only neo-Latinist to have done this, but I know of no other examples, and Kynaston, claiming this form is "new," does not cite any. It is worth noting here that this is a completely artificial way of writing Latin in the seventeenth or any other century. Kynaston's contemporaries had no difficulty in composing Latin according to standard classical meters (hexameters or hendecasyllables); the only reason I can imagine for Kynaston to compose in a non-classical meter (rhymed stanzas composed of isosyllabic lines modelled on Italian) would be that that was the form he saw in his original. Why else would he have done this? Kynaston's lines contain eleven syllables, as do the majority of lines in Ariosto and Tasso, and as do all French decasyllabic lines with feminine endings. And most, if not all of Kynaston's lines have a terminal accent on syllable 10, just as do all Italian hendecasyllables and all French decasyllables. Why would he have labored with this artificial form if he felt Chaucer had done something else?

Since Kynaston identifies the model of his verse as the verse of Tasso and Ariosto, it is difficult to see why scholars claim he writes in any other form. Those who have studied Kynaston seriously either have no familiarity with French or Italian verse (although that seems hard to accept, given some of the names here), or they are perhaps thrown off by Kynaston's word "Decasyllabon," which refers to a line type ("decasyllabic") not to a specific number of syllables in each line ("ten"); these are of course two different things. Perhaps too they are simply unable to get past the banalities of the ordinary ways of describing English verse (iambic pentameter), and read constantly as Binns advises "with the strong iambic rhythm of the original in mind"[25] — a clear case, I think, of *petitio principii*. If you are an English speaker and you look at a French decasyllable, you will quickly begin to "hear" a distinct iambic pattern (due to conventional accents on syllables 4 and 10) even though the rules of versification do not call for such a pattern.[26] From there, it is a short, but inaccurate step to assume that what we see or hear in any verse written according to these rules (whether in English or French) is in fact a flexible form of iambic pentameter; and that error happily conforms to what most of us were taught in grade school.

Implications for Chaucerian Metrics

To begin, I must make a concession. While my brief analysis of Italian and French verse is uncontroversial and its application to Kynaston fairly straightforward, where I differ from most Chaucerians is in my extension of these principles to Chaucer and even to other writers in English such as Alexander Pope. I could well be wrong here; but I will note that my own analysis of Chaucer's verse or even Pope's verse under these simple and basic principles does work, and I find few if any exceptions. If, on the other hand, you analyse any of this verse as accented iambic pentameter (whether Kynaston's, Chaucer's, or Pope's), you

---

25 It should be noted that Binns's regularly quoted statement, "If the lines are read with the strong iambic rhythm of the original in mind, they work fairly well" (*Intellectual Culture in Elizabethan and Jacobean England*, 253), is equivalent to saying that Kynaston's verses "are not iambic" (which is true); it also claims without argument that Chaucer's verses are iambic (which in my opinion is false).

26 Syllable 4 in most lines receives a tonic accent (exceptions involve what is called "lyric caesura" where the line break occurs after an unstressed syllable 4); syllable 10 invariably does. This in and of itself produces a real or illusory iambic rhythm. For French metricians, such "rhythm" is certainly a real, albeit variable feature of poetry. But it is part of what I have called style, not part of the versification system (Minkova's "metrical template"). See, e.g., Dane, *The Long and the Short of It*, 13, and the discussion in Mazaleyrat, *Elements de métrique française*, chap. 4, "Composants du Rythme," 109–40.

will find exceptions or deviations from the pattern in the vast majority of lines, exceptions that subsequently might be considered marks of the Poet's skill and (somewhat illogically) further evidence of the existence of the form or template that this same evidence shows the Poet violates. I am of course not denying iambic rhythms in Chaucer. I am only saying that such rhythms are not the basis of his versification, that is, not part of what Minkova and Stockwell refer to as his "metrical template." The analysis of such verse as iambic pentameter is far more complex than what is required, and the intricacies that result (whether of Chaucer's or your own making) are matters of style, not matters of basic versification.

Chaucer, like Kynaston, has not always written in iambic pentameter, and I am here referring not to the thing (how or what Chaucer wrote), but to the description of the thing (how Chaucerians have described what he wrote). Iambic pentameter is, as far as Chaucer is concerned, a modern phenomenon, not a medieval one. Even if Chaucer did write in iambic pentameter (that is, even if modern Chaucerians are correct), Kynaston in the seventeenth century would have had no knowledge of that and no reason to suspect it. Chaucer's "iambic pentameter" is a late-nineteenth-century discovery (or invention).

The modern consensus on Chaucer's verse, if it can be said to be a consensus at all, begins more than a century after Kynaston wrote, with Tyrwhitt's "Essay on the Language and Versification of Chaucer" in his edition of 1775.[27]

> The correctness and harmony of an English verse depends entirely upon its being composed of a certain number of syllables, and its having the accents of the syllables properly placed.[28]

---

[27] Thomas Tyrwhitt, ed., *The Canterbury Tales of Chaucer. To which are added, an Essay on his language and versification, an introductory discourse, and notes,* 4 vols. (London: Payne, 1775–78), 4:1–111. See esp. 4:83–109.

[28] Ibid., 4:88.

By the late nineteenth century, there are several competing analyses, most based on the notion that Chaucer wrote in some form of iambic accentual verse, that is, the emphasis is not on Tyrwhitt's "certain number of syllables," but rather "its having the accents of the syllables properly placed." The most important of these is probably by Skeat, although the details of his analysis in my view are only marginally intelligible.[29] The often cited analysis by Halle and Keyser in 1966 also assumes an accentual base, and there are many recent variants.[30] Even recent studies by Duffell, Stockwell, and Minkova emphasizing the close formal and historical relation between Chaucer and the French and Italian predecessors he used as models, place themselves within an unbroken tradition going back to Skeat and Ten Brink.[31] When push comes to shove, Chaucer wrote iambic pentameter, or, as characterized in Duffel, "the" iambic pentameter. What is described as the "metrical template" for Chaucer's verse is what we have all, at some point in our education, been taught: five feet of iambs.[32]

---

29 Walter W. Skeat, ed., "Versification," in *The Complete Works of Geoffrey Chaucer,* Vol. 6: Introduction, Glossary and Indexes, ed. Walter W. Skeat (Oxford: Clarendon Press, 1894), lxxxii–xcvii. See also Ten Brink, *The Language and Metre of Chaucer,* 213–22, relating it more closely to Italian models.

30 Morris Halle and Samuel Jay Keyser, "Chaucer and the Study of Prosody," *College English* 28, no. 3 (1966): 187–219. See also, the essays in Gaylord, ed., *Essays on the Art of Chaucer's Verse,* e.g., Stephen A. Barney, "Chaucer's Troilus: Meter and Grammar," on the "meter traditionally called iambic pentameter" (164).

31 Minkova and Stockwell, "Emendation and the Chaucerian Metrical Template," 129–30.

32 See, e.g., Donka Minkova and Robert Stockwell, "The Partial Contact: Origins of English Pentameter Verse: The Anglicization of an Italian Model," in *Language Contact in the History of English,* eds. Dieter Kastovsky and Arthur Mettinger (Frankfurt am Main: Peter Lang, 2001), 343. Minkova and Stockwell claim to be using as neutral terminology as possible ("Emendation," 129–30), but there is nothing at all neutral about this terminology if what is at issue (as here) is whether Chaucer actually wrote in or imagined something we describe as defined by iambs, feet, and the counting of foot-units by accent.

My view on these matters is that to describe as a template a fully-formed system of verse (accentual iambic pentameter) that was only described by modern metricians when we have, at least in Chaucer's translated works, a perfectly usable and workable alternative right before our eyes — the Italian (or French) models from which he borrowed stanza forms: this is absurd at worst, or historically misleading at best. In terms of the discussion above, Chaucer's template is a form or variant of romance syllabic verse, which might be represented as follows (I represent syllable 4 as accented here, but there are of course qualifications)[33]:

x x x X x x x x x X (x)

Accents are a part of this template; they are not something superadded from English. All that is left for Chaucer to do is insert the words. Whatever other patterns occur (or "seem to occur" — these may not be the same thing) are matters of rhythm or what can be classified as on the level of style.[34]

The problem with invoking iambic pentameter in this discussion and particularly in asserting it as a template is that to do so assumes "this is what Chaucer had in mind" (something we of course do not know, nor would any metrician claim we do), or that such a form is the foundation for Chaucer's verse. But it isn't (at least, not in the strongest sense), as even the re-

---

33 Italian does not have this obligatory accent, and French decasyllables contemporary with Chaucer occasionally use what is called a "lyric caesura," that is, an accented syllable 3, with caesura following syllable 4. See discussion in any basic work on romance metrics, e.g., all those cited in footnote 22 above.

34 The distinction found in many English scholars between meter and rhythm is exactly that found in French metricians. The difference is that, say, scholars committed to iambic pentameter consider accentual rhythm part of the basic rules or foundational aspects of meter (without rhythm, there is no iambic pentameter); a French metrician considers this strictly a matter of style, since rhythm is not part of basic versification rules. See above, footnotes 24 and 26.

cent scholars cited here occasionally concede.[35] The foundation, or less argumentatively "the origin," for Chaucer's verse in *Troilus* and in early poems modelled on French would seem to be what he found in his models, in the same way that his stanza forms are derived from those models. If the well-known and largely uncontroversial verse principles of the models that Chaucer imitated provide adequate descriptions of Chaucer's meter (although not necessarily of his style or rhythm), why invoke anything else? That is, what point is there in projecting back through time either the descriptive notion of iambic pentameter, or worse, the *res ipsissima*? Our allegiance to this verse form has befuddled students for decades, who know perfectly well that the English verse they are looking at does not follow anything like what they are taught iambic pentameter "is."[36]

Conclusion

The conventional language of meter, for better or worse, has direct bearing on the way scholars have viewed Kynaston. But Kynaston and what could be called his reception also has some bearing on this apparent consensus. Although most of the details of the modern metrical consensus on Chaucer post-date Kynaston, those same details have been used to describe Kynaston's verse. Kynaston, to Chaucerians, is a writer of iambic pentameter, which is also by implication the meter he somehow saw in Chaucer, just as we do. Yet as we know, the idea that Chaucer wrote accentual verse is late in arriving; why would we suppose Kynaston saw in Chaucer what it took two more centuries for professional Chaucerians to see? And why, if he did, was he silent about this? The answer, of course, is that Kynaston saw

---

[35] See, e.g., the occasional equivocation in Minkova and Stockwell, "Partial Contact," 340, where the "basic template" is described as "syllable count." Elsewhere in the same article, that template is said to be a form of iambic pentameter.

[36] I note the pedagogic implications of this in *The Long and the Short of It*, 2–4, 118.

nothing of the kind, nor is he in any way "like us" in his perception and representation of Chaucerian verse.

The failure to understand Kynaston's verse is not in and of itself of great import, although it does make high-toned stylistic analyses of his verse amusing: the "appropriate Chaucerian feeling," the "strangeness" of his verses, their singularity, ingenuity, in addition to all the technical language thrown at it (elision, synezesis, hiatus, *Taktumstellung*). My first thought confronting this was that the misunderstanding of basic principles of verse simply makes hash of all such sensitive and learned analyses. The fact that readers do not understand Chaucer's verse, or Shakespeare's, or Baudelaire's does not in and of itself invalidate their descriptions of its poetic beauties and rhythms; scholarly analysis of such verse in arcane technical terms or in relation to an inexistent abstract model — that's a different story.

Now, however, I think there may be more to this. Why do good scholars so often fail to see what is right in front of them?

One explanation in the present case surely involves the decline in Latin skills that we all have experienced in relation to our nineteenth-century forebears. Kynaston's once "strange" or "eccentric" lines grow more firmly "iambic" during the twentieth century (as fewer and fewer Latinists have the ability to read them) just as does Chaucer's own verse. Another source might be the uncritical adoption of the binary model of Latin verse: Latin verse is either quantitative or accentual.[37] Thus, as soon as scholars determine that Kynaston's verse is not quantitative (which even for amateur Latinists requires only a few minutes of frustration), the conclusion is that it must be accentual (even though Kynaston himself specifically denies this). This binary model of verse, whether applied to Kynaston's Latin or to Chaucer's English, excludes the form of meter with which

---

[37] See, e.g., Newton, "Chaucer's Troilus," 91–92, quoting F.J.E. Raby, *A History of Christian Latin Poetry*, 2nd edn. (Oxford: Clarendon Press, 1953), 20–22. Raby's argument is that early medieval Latin poetry was syllabic, and only later (in the eleventh century) developed into its accentual form. Raby's word for this is "rhythmical," which is equivocal, in that it could reasonably apply to any verse type.

Chaucer and Kynaston were most familiar (Italian and French verse, based on the principle of isosyllabism) and leads directly to the invocation of a type of verse that neither of them ever referred to. The great baggy monster of iambic pentameter, as I have elsewhere described it, simply cannot be expelled from the consciousness of modern English literary historians.

When Chaucer wrote *Book of the Duchess* or *Troilus,* he had directly before him or at least in his mind models in French and in Italian. He was imitating those models, just as Kynaston claims he was imitating Italian models in his translation. No one denies this. To translate what he saw, Kynaston rejected the obvious quantitative forms of verse that were available to him — hexameter, elegiacs, senarii, hendecasyllables — all of which any contemporary Latinist could have easily used in composition. He also rejected and ridiculed the very verse types he has been accused of writing: the "execrable Leonine verses of the monks" (Preface, "Candido Lectori …"). He invented instead a new form of writing Latin based on what he correctly saw in Tasso and which he may well (rightly or wrongly) have seen in Chaucer. The verse Chaucer used can in fact be described perfectly adequately using these models, that is, through the well-known and uncontroversial rules that apply to these French and Italian models. They may not give a complete account of Chaucer's style, of course, but Chaucer's lines, considered metrically, generally conform to them.

I conclude from this, however uncreatively, that Kynaston was right: that both Kynaston and Chaucer imitated the verse form used by the sources they were imitating, and that their verse can and should be most conveniently described according to the well-known and uncontroversial rules regarding these forms. After all, both borrowed non-English stanza forms (we don't attempt to describe rhyme-royale stanzas modelled on the French as some perverse form of English heroic couplet); why wouldn't they have imitated the versification form as well?

For Kynaston, this may be of little import. But for Chaucerians, more is at stake. Chaucerians who deny this are using some version of the following logic, which I will state in as extreme form as I can:

1. Chaucer wanted to translate a work in foreign verse written according to the well-known rules of isosyllabic verse;
2. in the process, he invented a new form of accentual verse organized in five feet that had no precedent in English;
3. when he wrote in this unprecedented verse, it sadly but forgivably did not strictly follow the rules of this new form of accentual, foot-based verse that he invented, but was riddled with exceptions;
4. by a completely irrelevant and negligible working of chance, his verse just happened to follow, with far fewer exceptions, the well-known and widespread rules of the French and Italian verse he had before him; furthermore,
5. this is mere coincidence.

Now all this may well be true, although no Chaucerian would admit to thinking this. The way to finesse this logic might well be by invoking what appears to be an unchanging fixed universal — iambic pentameter — one with which we are all familiar. But that is step 2 in the logical process outlined here. I see no way of avoiding steps 3 through 5.

And why not go further? Since Kynaston is said to see in Chaucer the very form of iambic pentameter described in the late nineteenth century, why should Tyrwhitt be given credit for discovering this? (which he did not). Why isn't "our Kynaston" credited with this insight more than a century earlier, even though he says nothing about it, nor can his translation be scanned accordingly?

Kynaston's translation is thus an important critique of this implied logic. When Kynaston looked at Chaucer in the seventeenth century, well before the consensus had been formed that Chaucer, like so many other English writers past and present, wrote in iambic pentameter, what seemed most important to him were not the accents of Chaucer (whatever they may have been), but the simple matter of syllable count (neither of which, of course, was perfectly represented in whatever printed book he used as his source — compare my transcription of his stanza 1 above with any modern edition). What is somewhat strange to me is that the much better informed and scholarly Chaucerians who followed him have proven unable or unwilling to see or consider this either in Kynaston's own verse (where the principle is obvious) or in Chaucer (where of course it is more problematic). Perhaps we shouldn't see a form of isosyllabism in either of them, and perhaps Chaucer did indeed invent iambic pentameter, with its "strong iambic rhythm," just as we were taught that form in middle school. But the fact that at least some Chaucerians cannot see an alternative verse form when it is staring them right in the face and when they are told specifically by the author what they are looking at — this does not give me a great deal of faith in other Chaucerians' ability to see it anywhere else.

CHAPTER 2

Chaucer's "Rude Times"

One of the most familiar, enduring, and amusing clichés in Chaucer reception is the notion of Chaucer's "rude times." I chose this topic years ago (or at least this title), not because I thought Chaucer's reception history was unique, but because I happened to be familiar with the anecdotal details of that history. I drafted the article, dropped it, then lost everything I had imagined or thought during a computer crash years ago, leaving me with that same sense of liberation I experienced in 1971, when everything I owned was incinerated in an apartment fire.

This critical myth serves and has served a number of functions, and this chapter will outline what those functions are. More important, it will reflect on my own understanding of this history, on why this topic appealed to me in the first place, why I did not pursue it almost two decades ago, and why I was blinded then to certain aspects of this project that seem obvious to me now.[1]

The phrase has now fallen out of favor: respected medievalists cannot really chide Chaucer, that sophisticated citizen of London, for his rudeness, whether they mean "rude" in a purely metaphorical sense, or hear vestiges of its presumably literal meaning 'rustic', 'uncultivated' (but there is that metaphor again). We cannot chide the medieval period for being less sophisticated than we are, or than Chaucer himself was. Such authorial rudeness, however defined, is something to be celebrat-

---

1   See my *Who Is Buried in Chaucer's Tomb? Studies in the Reception of Chaucer's Book* (East Lansing: Michigan State University Press, 1998).

ed, even though those likely most responsible for our notion of an "urbane" Chaucer — that is, Dryden and Kittredge — seemed to apologize for it.

Today, to invoke the contrast rudis/urbanus is to speak in metaphors, and perhaps this was always the case. In contemporary America, the meaning of these metaphors is entirely other than what it was in Dryden's day or in what seems to us that glorious past of old time America (the days when some of us grew up in mid-century, or perhaps a half or a full century earlier in the heady early days of the Chaucer Society). It is thus extremely difficult to communicate with our predecessors on such topics, and difficult as well for them to communicate with each other. Yet despite this (or perhaps because of it), the power and utility of the myth of rudeness persists.

One of the most full blown and effusive variants is in Thomas Warton's *History of English Poetry* (1774), a work that generally captures the full flavor of the Chaucerian clichés that enable us to understand Chaucer as well and as badly as we do:[2]

> Chaucer was a man of the world: and from this circumstance we are to account, in great measure, for the many new embellishments which he conferred on our language and our poetry....His travels...induced him to polish the asperity, and enrich the sterility of his native versification with softer cadences, and a more copious and variegated phraseology....At rude periods the modes of original thinking are unknown, and the arts of original composition have not yet been studied.[3]

> I have before hinted, that Chaucer's obscenity is in great measure to be imputed to his age. We are apt to form roman-

---

[2] Thomas Warton, *The History of English Poetry from the Close of the Eleventh to the Commencement of the Eighteenth Century*, 3 vols. (London: Dodsley, 1775–78). See Thomas R. Lounsbury, *Studies in Chaucer: His Life and Writings*, 3 vols. (New York: Harper, 1892), 3:244–53, on Warton, whom he respects but derides for relying on the opinions of those who knew far less about medieval literature than he did.

[3] Warton, *The History of English Poetry*, 1:341–43.

tic and exaggerated notions about the moral innocence of our ancestors. Ages of ignorance and simplicity are thought to be ages of purity. The direct contrary, I believe, is the case. Rude periods have that grossness of manners which is not less friendly to virtue thant luxury itself.[4]

We are surprised to find, in so gross and ignorant an age, such talents for satire and for observation on life; qualities which usually exert themselves at more civilized periods, when the improved state of society, by subtilizing our speculations, and establishing uniform modes of behaviour, disposes mankind to study themselves, and renders deviations of conduct and singularities of character more immediately and necessarily the objects of censure and ridicule.[5]

For Warton and those contemporaries who cared about Chaucer, "rude times" or any of its variants was a catch-all that encapsulated whatever topic literary historians wished to raise in regard to him: vices and virtues, distinctions of the subject from competitors, his relation to his competitors, poetic lineage. Warton's persuasive and self-assured rhetoric may obscure the illogic behind his particular claims: we think virtue is a function of pure ages, but gross ages produce it to the same degree. In fact, our ancestors were no less pure than we are, although perhaps we believe otherwise.

Warton pretends that we are "surprised" to discover that preceding ages are gross,[6] and furthermore, that whereas we *thought* Chaucer's virtue was a function of the absolutely pure age in which he lived, *in fact* his unquestioned virtue is to be praised *despite* the grossness of the age in which he lived. More likely, no serious reader of Chaucer ever formulated such a thought. It's just that we can be persuaded that we should have thought or actually did think that.

---

[4] Ibid., 1:431.
[5] Ibid., 1:435.
[6] A favorite phrase of Warton, e.g., 1:367: "We are surprised to find, in a poet of such antiquity, numbers so nervous and flowing...."

Early Variants (Fifteenth and Sixteenth Centuries)

What passes for the earliest criticism or evaluation of Chaucer is free from apology: Chaucer is simply the subject of praise. We know this because it is recorded in the now classic compendium of early Chaucer reception, Spurgeon's *Five Hundred Years of Chaucer Criticism and Allusion*.[7] It is now customary to call this a basic source, as if, rightly or wrongly, it were beyond criticism. I will be returning to the nature of this source and the implications of using it in my conclusion. The following are from Spurgeon, 1:10–66.

Gower (1390):
>Of Ditees and of Songes glade,
>The whiche he for mi sake made,
>The lond fulfild is oueral:
>Whereof to him in special
>Aboue alle othre I am most holde …

Lydgate (1400):
>Go gentill quayer, and Recommaunde me
>Vnto my maistir with humble affectioun
>Beseke hym lowly of mercy and pite
>Of thy rude makyng to haue compassioun

Lydgate (1401):
>Chaucer is deed that had suche a name
>Of fayre makyng that [was] without wene
>Fayrest in our tonge , as the Laurer grene.
>
>We may assay forto countrefete

---

[7] Caroline F.E. Spurgeon, *Five Hundred Years of Chaucer Criticism and Allusion, 1357–1900* (1914–25), 3 vols. (New York: Russell and Russell, 1960). E.g., Hope Johnston, "Readers' Memorials in Early Editions of Chaucer," *Studies in Bibliography* 59 (2015): 45–69: "The foundation for studies of Chaucer's reception is Caroline Spurgeon's classic, *500 Years of Chaucer Criticism and Allusion*."

His gay style but it wyl not be;
The welle is drie ...

Lydgate (1405):
    I symple shall extoll theyr soueraynte
    And my rudenes shall shewee theyr subtylyte ...

    And eke my master chauceris nowe is graue
    The noble rethor Poete of breteine
    That worthy was the laurer to haue
    Of poetrie

Hoccleve (1412):
    Of maister deere, and fadir reverent!
    Mi maister Chaucer, flour of eloquence,
    Mirour of fructuous entendement
    ....
    Althogh his lyfe be queynt, the resemblaunce
    Of him hath in me so fressh lyflynesse
    That, to putte othir men in remembraunce
    Of his persone, I haue heere his lyknesse
    Do make, to this ende in sothfastnesse,
    That thei that haue of him lest thought & mynde,
    By this peynture may ageyne him fynde.

Lydgate again (1412–20):
    The noble Rethor that alle dide excelle
    For in makyng he drank of the well
    Vndir pernase that the musis kepe
    On whiche hil I myght neuer slepe.

Lydgate (1426):
    The noble poete off Breteyne,
    My mayster Chaucer, in hys tyme,
    Affter the Frenche he dyde yt ryme
    Word by word, as in substaunce,
    Ryght as yt ys ymad in Fraunce ....

Hawes (1503):
> O, prudent Gower! ...
> O , noble Chaucer! ...
> O, virtuous Lydgate! ...

Others speak in the same vein. Skelton: "that famous Clerk"; Henry Bradshaw: "maister Chaucer"; Gavin Douglas: "My master Chaucer."

In my own condensed version of Spurgeon's selections above, there is nothing in Chaucer that requires apology or even qualification. He is simply a wonderful poet, and we come limpingly after him; we are not historians evaluating Chaucer with disinterest, but rather we ourselves are part of that history. To Lydgate, the only distance between "us" and "Chaucer" is one of quality: Chaucer was a great writer, we are worse. Our distance from Chaucer is not temporal, but literary. He shares the virtues of both the aristocracy (nobility) and clergy.

What appears to us to be the earliest criticism of Chaucer we could label as "modern" incorporates some notion of the historical distance we ourselves necessarily feel when discussing him: Chaucer's time and culture is in the past and irrecoverable. Caxton's famous preface to the second edition of the *Canterbury Tales* portrays a Chaucer whose text has been corrupted, not by his times, but by his scribes. It is interesting that Caxton uses this myth not only to excuse Chaucer, but also to excuse himself. He, Caxton, is not responsible for the corruption of Chaucer's text; rather, this is to be attributed to the badness (rudeness?) of a manuscript, which, like Chaucer's own pedigree, can only be corrected by an act of gentrification.

> one gentylman camn to me and said that this book was not according in many places vnto the book that Gefferey chaucer had made....Thenne he sayd he knewe a book whyche hys fader had and moche louyd that was very trewe ...

> Whereas to fore by ygnouraunce I erryd in hurtyng and dyffamyng his book in dyuerce places in settyng in somme thynges that he neuer sayd ne made....[8]

This sense of historical distance leads in the following centuries to many things: the creation of a biography that is largely fictional (at least in terms of what late nineteenth-century historiography believes constitutes a fact), monumentalization of Chaucer, best epitomized by his tomb in Poet's Corner or the series of complete editions begun in 1532 (or perhaps 1526), the ideological reinterpretation and modernization of him as a proto-reformist.[9] Chaucer is no longer the inspiration for particular writers (Hoccleve, Lydgate), but rather the origin of a history of writers.[10]

The earliest biographies of Chaucer seek to model Chaucer after writers in other traditions. Chaucer functions as does Dante, or Homer, or Alain.[11] That is, he is an abstract figure in literary history, not a poet familiar to other poets. His "meaning" has become more important than the words he wrote or the life he may have lived. And biographical assertions are a product of this cultural function, not mere records of historical fact.

---

8   The most easily available version is in W.J.B Crotch, *The Prologues and Epilogues of William Caxton*, EETS 176 (London: Oxford University Press, 1928). For my reservations on the use of this source, see my *Abstractions of Evidence in Manuscripts and Early Printed Books* (Aldershot: Ashgate, 2009), 132–37.

9   On these editions, see my *Who Is Buried in Chaucer's Tomb?*, Johnston, "Readers' Memorials"; and Kathleen Forni, *The Chaucerian Apocrypha: A Counterfeit Canon* (Gainesville: University of Florida Press, 2001). The notion of rudeness, which in earlier writers was simply a rhetorical *sermo humilis* attached to themselves, is historicized, and projected onto the historical context in which Chaucer stands out.

10 On this notion of "Father Chaucer," see Seth Lerer, *Chaucer and his Readers: Imagining the Author in Late Medieval England* (Princeton: Princeton University Press, 1993).

11 The most convenient summary of these early biographies is in Eleanor Prescott Hammond, *Chaucer: A Bibliographical Manual* (New York: Macmillan, 1908).

When John Shirley earlier discussed Chaucer in terms of class, nobility was attributed to his audience. This seems to correspond to what we know (or now know) of his background, all scrupulously recorded in *Chaucer Life Records*. Shirley in 1456 describes the *Canterbury Tales* as follows:

> First foundid, ymagenid and made bothe for disporte and leornyng of all thoo that beon gentile of birthe or of condicions by the laureal and moste famous poete that euer was to-fore him as in themvelisshing of oure rude moders englisshe tonge....[12]

Chaucer is a cleric (as he was for earlier writers) and the English language is given the attribute "rude."

The earliest biographers Bale, Leland, and Pitts literalize or transfer the metaphor of nobility. Chaucer is not a "noble rhetor" (as he was for Lydgate), but a "nobleman" period — a member of the aristocracy. In the introduction to the printed edition of 1532, William Thynne (or Brian Tuke) refers to Chaucer as "that noble & famous clerke Geffray Chaucer," the use of the word *clerk* shows that "noble" is still metaphorical.[13] But to Leland in 1545, it was not: "De Gallofrido Chaucero, Equite."[14] As these editions were reprinted and re-edited, that notion of nobility is established iconographically on the title page of 1561

---

12 On Prologue to *Knight's Tale*, quoted in Spurgeon, *Chaucer Criticism and Allusion*, 1:53–54.

13 This preface was one of the few major pieces of Chaucer reception not printed extensively in the two major scholarly works on Chaucer's reception in the early twentieth century: Hammond's *Manual*, and Spurgeon's *Chaucer Criticism and Allusion*. It was, according to Spurgeon, readily available in the EETS edition of Francis Thynne, *Animadversions Uppon the Annotacions and Corrections of some Imperfections of Impressiones of Chaucers Workes (1598)*, ed. G.H. Kingsley, rev. F.J. Furnivall (London: N. Trübner & Co., 1875).

14 Hammond, *Chaucer*, 87.

and most emphatically in the engraved author portrait in the 1602 edition showing details of his lineage.[15]

The notion of "Noble Rhetor" sets up an implied contrast with what came before: if Chaucer is noble, whether literally or figuratively, then others must be churls; if Chaucer's virtue is that he "embellished" the English language, then by contrast, English prior to Chaucer is unembellished. By the end of the fifteenth century, the main lines of Chaucer reception (or perhaps less grandly, the most common clichés in the reception of Chaucer) are well established. And it is easy (through Spurgeon) to multiply the examples shown above.

The themes of Chaucer's early reception are broad enough that any seemingly conflicting examples can be incorporated or explained away, and the commonplaces of the "noble" Chaucer and the embellishing of our tongue lead to a number of sometimes contradictory variants. For Robert Copland (1530), the printer saves Chaucer's language from the damage of time:

> And where thou become so ordre thy language
> That in excuse thy prynter loke thou haue
> Whiche hathe the kepte from ruynous domage
> In snoweswyte paper, thy mater for to saue
> With thylke same langage that Chaucer to the gaue
> In termes olde[16]

More commonly, Chaucer's language is not simply old (something to be preserved) but distinct from that of his contemporaries. The most tortured variant of this is perhaps in Thynne's Preface to his 1532 edition:

> For though it had been in Demosthenes or Homerus tymes
> whan all lernyng and excellency of sciences florisshed amon-

---

15 See also Berthelet's contemporary edition of Gower's *Confessio Amantis* (1532): "The whiche noble warke, and many other of the sayde Chaucers...." ("To the Reder").

16 *Lenuoy of R. Coplande boke prynter*; in Spurgeon, *Chaucer Criticism and Allusion*, 1:77.

ges the Grekes or in the season that Cicero prince of eloquence amonges latynes lyued, yet it had been a thyng right rare & straunge, and worthy perpetuall laude, that any clerke by lernyng or wytte coulde than haue framed a tonge, before so rude and imperfite, to such a swete ornature & composycion, lykely if he had lyued in these dayes, being good letters so restored and reuyued as they be, if he were nat empeched by the enuy of such as may tollerate nothyn, whiche to vnderstonde their capacite doth nat extende, to haue brought it vnto a full and fynall perfection.[17]

Even in Demosthenes' times, when learning flourished, it would have been a praiseworthy thing had Chaucer done what he did, and if he had lived in these times and avoided the envy of detractors, he might well have brought language to its full perfection. (But he did not, because he lived in his own times, and therefore had no chance of perfecting it.) Chaucer is a jewel set in "rude matter," just as in later centuries he would be "urbane" among his rude conmtemporaries. That seems the basis of Thynne's equally tortured praise of the King:

And deuisyng with my selfe, who of all other were most worthy, to whom a thyng so excellent and notable shulde be dedicate, whiche to my conceite semeth for the admiracion, noueltie, and strangnesse that it myght be reputed to be of in the tyme of the authour, in comparison, as a pure and fyne tryed precious or polyced iewell out of a rude or indigest masse or mater, none coulde to my thynkyng occurre, that syns, or in the tyme of Chaucer, was or is suffycient, but onely your maiestie royall, whiche by discrecyon and iugement, as moost absolute in wsysedome and all kyndes of doctryne,

---

[17] Geoffrey Chaucer, *Works* (London, 1532), STC 5068, ed. William Thynne, sig. A2v. On the ambiguity of the word "likely" and the modern attempts (starting with the Urry edition of 1721) to understand it, see *Who Is Buried in Chaucer's Tomb?*, 35–36.

coulde, & of his innate clemence and goodnesse wolde, adde, or gyue any authorite hervnto.[18]

Much of this is simply an acknowledgement of temporal change: that which makes us human rather than what we imagine it is like to be a god. It has to do with the growing unintelligibility of Chaucer's language and style, an unintelligibility that makes the claims of its virtues unassailable: there was a time when Chaucer seemed not strange at all, when scribes produced manuscripts of his work as if it were the most natural thing in the world. But no more. I read. I listen. I no longer understand what is in front of me. The effort I expend must be matched by the virtues of the text that requires it.

Rarely is this admitted: no purported literary scholar or dilettante says flat-out that Chaucer writes in a dialect that they no longer understand. Rather the strangeness of his language is paradoxically judged as hyper-modern. As such a hyper-modern author, Chaucer has lapses: his meter is unscannable, his words unintelligible, his spelling unorthodox. These apparent faults should be a product of chronological distance; but they are not. Rather, they are indications of an infectious "rudeness" in history. The chronological distance, which would easily excuse all this or make it hardly worth consideration (of course Chaucer is difficult to understand, because he wrote 200 years earlier), is ignored or rather displaced from Chaucer to his contemporaries. It is not that Chaucer is difficult; rather his "times" are rude. Chaucer, *noster Chaucerus* — he is like us; he maintains his "urbanity," which increases as those who can experience it, who can understand or appreciate it, become fewer and fewer in number. What begins as a diachronic view of history is scrapped in favor of a synchronic view (the transhistorical Chaucer, *noster Chaucerus*); and this Chaucer is then rehabilitated, or the myth of his greatness supported, by a readmission of the diachronicity: times have indeed changed; we have advanced culturally.

---

18 Chaucer, *Works*, 1532, sig. A2v–A3r.

In 1700, Dryden offers a more adequate interpretation of this linguistic situation, that is to say, one we consider modern: language simply changes, as we know from our Horace:

If the first end of a writer be to be understood, then as his language grows obsolete, his thoughts must grow obscure:

> Multa renascentur quae nunc cecidere; cadentque,
> Quae nunc sunt in honore vocabula, si volet usus,
> Quem penes arbitrium est et jus et norma loquendi.

When an ancient word for its sound and significancy deserves to be reviv'd, I have that reasonable veneration for antiquity, to restore it. … Words are not like landmarks, so sacred as never to be remov'd; customs are chang'd, and even statutes are silently repeal'd, when the reason ceases for which they were enacted.[19]

And the way is set for the philological Chaucer of the nineteenth century.

Modern Reception and Modern Chaucer

The history of Our Chaucer is amusing to trace and it is easy to proceed further. In the sixteenth century develops the notion of the reformist Chaucer, whereby Chaucer is first excused for "superstitious beliefs," then said not to have them. According to John Foxe in 1563, Chaucer wrote deliberately on such a dark allegorical level that the most inquisitory readers of all — the bishops — were completely fooled.[20] And this "Chaucer" was soon embodied in editions, with the elimination of the Retractions

---

[19] John Dryden, *Preface to Fables Ancient and Modern; translated into Verse, from Homer, Ovid, Boccace, & Chaucer* (London, 1700). Text from Spurgeon, *Chaucer Criticism and Allusion*, 1:272.

[20] Irene Basey Beesemyer and Joseph A. Dane, "The Denigration of John Lydgate: Implications of Printing History," *English Studies* 81, no. 2 (2000):

and the addition of obviously reformist texts such as the *Plowman's Tale*.

Yet as Chaucer is rendered familiar (a Protestant like us, with a language that through editions is evolving as we are), he is also growing distant. Kynaston's translation of 1635 shows that the ability to read Chaucer was not considered unusual among English speakers: readers needed a Latin version, not a modern English one. But within a half century, this seems to have changed.

> I soon resolv'd to put their Merits to the Trial by turning some of the *Canterbury Tales* into our Language, as it is now refin'd: For by this Means, both the Poets being set in the same Light, and dress'd in the same English Habit, Story to be compared with Story, a certain Judgment may be made betwixt them, by the Reader, without obtruding my Opinion on him.[21]

Bizarrely, the translator disappears; the real Chaucer (like the real Spenser) is the one obscured by his words.

Note however, that the myth of rudeness, having no particular function in the eighteenth century, remains constant, as Dryden: "With Chaucer the Purity of the English Tongue began."[22] What was once a response to the sudden obsolescence of Chaucer combined with ideological catastrophe, is now accepted as a given. Chaucer's "rude times," once invented and inserted into the canon of criticism, become inextricable.[23]

It would be easy to complete or at least extend this survey: the tradition of English translations, the first so-called modern edition by Tyrwhitt in 17754, complete with a scholarly preface and introduction. The philological work of the Chaucer Society

---

117-26; *Who Is Buried in Chaucer's Tomb?*, 79–86. Foxe's ingenious defense is of works that Chaucer did not write, e.g., *The Testament of Love*.

21 Dryden, *Fables*, quoted in Spurgeon, *Chaucer Criticism and Allusion*, 1:272.

22 Dryden, *Fables*, quoted in ibid, 1:273.

23 See also, the typographical variant of "rude letters," i.e., blackletter: Sian Echard, *Printing the Middle Ages* (Philadelphia: University of Pennsylvania Press, 2008), 21.

in the nineteenth century: Furnivall's extraordinary claim of an affinity between himself, Chaucer, and Tennyson, a claim that seems to be calqued from Dryden.[24] The invention of Chaucerian irony, which instantly transformed Chaucer into a modern poet (unlike his contemporaries), and readers of the mid-twentieth century into his most sensitive readers. But that goes beyond the principal sources that outline this history.

By Way of Conclusion

This was the kind of article I envisioned writing when I first ran into the strange 1721 edition of Chaucer by John Urry and its even stranger and (for Chaucerians) more embarrassing reception. At the time, it was the most disparaged and the least examined edition of all of them. So incensed were Chaucerians over the failings of this edition, they seemed to be rendered speechless, and thus had no recourse but to repeat, often word-for-word, the evaluations and opinions of their predecessors.[25]

I knew "rudeness" was a key concept in the development of our notion of Chaucer, and imagined it was one of the things Urry's roman type edition may have been trying to expunge from Chaucer. But that idea did not pan out. The roman type used to represent Chaucer was a purely economic issue, and not what Urry had intended.[26] In the end, I never analyzed or defined "rudeness" sufficiently. And there were other subjects that seemed to make my point better: the inscription of the tomb, typographical changes in Chaucer editions; the inscrutability and remaking of the past, our projection of our own prejudices back

---

24 "He comes closer to me than any other poet, except Tennyson": F.J. Furnivall, *A Temporary Preface to the Six-text Edition of Chaucer's Canterbury Tales,* Chaucer Soc. Publ., ser. 2, pt. 3 (London: N. Trübner & co., 1868), 3.

25 Joseph A. Dane, "The Reception of Chaucer's Eighteenth-Century Editors," (1989); rpt. *Who Is Buried in Chaucer's Tomb?,* 115–30.

26 See the detailed discussion of the publication history in William L. Alderson and Arnold C. Henderson, *Chaucer and Augustan Scholarship* (Berkeley: University of California Press, 1970), chap. 5.

onto Chaucer through such terms as "irony" and even "parody." The notion "rudeness" at the time just could not work, or rather, I could not make it work.

Obviously, neither Chaucer nor his times were rude in any meaningful way. Chaucerians created that myth; at least they did according to the argument sketched above, or more precisely, my version of the reception of Chaucer suggests that they did. Neither Chaucer's contemporaries nor the enthusiastic reformers were fools, nor were even the stuffiest of Victorian Chaucerians, and dismissing their claims as wrong would be pointless: "Aint it awful" that preceding Chaucerians were not as wise and sophisticated as we are; "ain't it awful" that they did not have the literary sensitivity we are blessed with today. Beginning, by contrast, with the seemingly naive assumption that they were right may help us see the function their claim had in Chaucerian history. Maybe Dryden was right: words have life, both Chaucer's and our own.

Or so I thought.

I return to the question of my sources.

The one source that at the time seemed to treat these critics as if they were right, that is, as legitimate witnesses to "the way Chaucer was," was Spurgeon's *Five Hundred Years of Chaucer Criticism and Allusion*. To use this work as a basis for studying reception never seemed problematic to me, no more problematic thant the differences between evidence types (see Introduction above). Everything in Spurgeon's book was "right," or at least "factual" in the nineteenth-century sense, and even the opinions registered there are "right," in the sense that they were intelligible variants or even versions of what we think of Chaucer today. Comments were reprinted, without serious mediation (so it seemed) from other historical sources; Spurgeon herself did not seem to second-guess, critique, or even feign amusement at any of them. No one advanced the claim that Spurgeon falsified history in serious ways, not even those who offered updates of her work or redid her work in more presumably accessible ways,[27] nor did anyone argue, as far as I know, that those who relied on it as I do and have was simply recycling what Spurgeon thought and imagined in the years before 1925.

Spurgeon's work was an embodiment of Henry Bradshaw's dictum to Furnivall: "Arrange your facts rigorously and let them speak...."[28] Bradshaw in this letter may have intended that as a mild admonition: no Chaucerian has falsified Chaucer more than Furnivall did and with greater effect, and no one was in better position to see that than Bradshaw. Yet even though Spurgeon claims that Furnivall's "spirit still lives in the work,"[29] she is following the presumably more sober Bradshaw, and in so doing, sets a high standard for a particular version of literary historiography: here are facts, arranged chronologically, and as such, they do not speak at all, until the scholar makes them speak with a second iteration.

Yet of course Spurgeon falsifies history in some way, just as I falsify history and her own version of it by discussing her here. Spurgeon selected these passages from an undefined corpus — published or printed comments including the name "Chaucer"(?), passages selected and collected by other Chaucerians(?), many chosen by serendipity(?) — and then edited those down to what she or others thought worthy to publish again in a more coherent collection that supported her view of history or contradicted it in what she thought were important or significant ways.[30] I in turn select from them. I have no idea whether I am distorting her history or confirming it, or perhaps misinterpreting completely what she considered the importance of the passages that eventually found their way into her book.

---

27 Derek Brewer, *Chaucer: The Critical Heritage,* 2 vols. (London: Routledge and Kegan Paul, 1978).

28 Bradshaw's "rigorously" is misquoted as "vigorously" in G.W. Prothero, *A Memoir of Henry Bradshaw* (London: Kegan Paul, 1888), 349, as I have repeatedly noted. Reviewers please take note.

29 Spurgeon, Foreword to *Chaucer Criticism and Allusion,* 1:vi.

30 She acknowledges her reliance on Hyder Rollins for *Troilus,* but does not detail, as far as I can see, her methods of collection. See her Foreword, 1:vi, for reference to those who "helped me in sending me references, in searching for references and in copying and collating."

Spurgeon's work was a massive extension of a genre that was once part of printed editions, that is, the "Testimonials" assuring potential buyers that the work was worthwhile. In Chaucer, these are found in Speght's edition of 1598 and again in Urry's edition of 1721. By the nineteenth century, such commentary is out of favor (or it is repurposed): testimonials are redefined as evidence of some kind, a Bradshavian set of facts; they are not statements about Chaucer (secondary sources), but rather facts of his reception (primary sources). These once testimonials, intended to compare Chaucer to his context (his verse is worthy of purchase) now function to isolate Chaucer from this context. Furthermore, they redefine everyone who writes or wrote about Chaucer as one of us — a modern scholar like us — with the same goals, ideals, and prejudices. Those who wrote these early testimonials were not blurb writers; they were critics, just as we are.[31]

But what is the alternative to these testimonials or to a compendium such as Spurgeon's? And how else can we begin to understand Chaucer reception, and thus perhaps Chaucer himself, without conducting a sober assessment of the presumed facts, that is, the language in which conversations about Chaucer are conducted? What better and more efficiently arranged compendium of those facts could there be than Spurgeon? Isn't this the same theory followed by textual-critical history? We study scribal and printing history in order to undo its pernicious effects, leaving us with the pure, unmediated original; and here, we study reception, in order to rid ourselves of its influence, ignoring, for the moment, that we ourselves are part of the reception we are attempting to undo.

Making the Facts Speak

As schoolchildren, we were repeatedly directed to dictionaries for spelling. These were amusingly referred to in the singular — "the" dictionary — as if they were authoritative without

---

31   See also my "Scribes as Critics," in *Who Is Buried in Chaucer's Tomb?*, 195–213.

being burdened by the inconvenience of authors. Yet as many of us whined behind the backs of our grammar school teachers (it would never have occurred to us to challenge them face to face), you have to be able to spell the word before you can look it up. So you cannot use a dictionary efficiently for this purpose until you have little need of it (it is somewhat alarming that this same difficulty with spelling reappears as one gets older). You also have to have confidence that a certain entity is in fact a word, as defined by "the" dictionary, before you can analyze or even assimilate its various meanings. How do you know that the definitions you see belong to the word you are trying to look up and not to a near homonym? I circle back to that spelling problem — how do I know the spelling of the word whose meaning I am seeking in "the" or in any dictionary? And all this before the even more vexing issues: the problematic assumption that primary and secondary meanings can be demarcated; that "the best writers," whoever they are, knew and respected these boundaries; that there is a coherent difference between a literal and a metaphorical use of a word. These assumptions are rational, even though they seem indisputably wrong. They are embedded in the conventions of lexicography, and the use of a dictionary can thus never challenge them.

I return to Spurgeon with these unhelpful thoughts in mind: it is no longer a question of the facts, which I have probably read or skimmed more than once. What concerns me is their arrangement, and the categories Spurgeon believes apply to them.

Vol. 1:ix lists the following sections:

1. An outline of the fluctuations of the literary reputation of Chaucer during the last five hundred years.
2. An examination of the criticisms and allusions themselves, roughly grouped and sorted.
3. The various classes of qualities ascribed to Chaucer.
4. The evolution of Chaucer biography.
5. A note on some Chaucer lovers and workers of whom we get glimpses through the centuries....

These first five sections concern what we would consider problems specific to Chaucer. Sections 6 through 9 are concerned with more general issues — for example, "the gradual evolution of new senses in the race" and "the evolution of scholarship."

Section 1 defines six apparent periods of Chaucer reception, variously named (I summarize these in part by running heads, in part by selecting from her discussion): I: Contemporary praise or "Enthusiastic and reverential praise by his contemporaries and immediate successors (Lydgate and Hoccleve)"; II. The Scottish Chaucerians through early editions, reformers, and those who condemned his "scurrilitie"; III: Elizabethans (1:x: "The critical attitude, which begins toward the end of the sixteenth century with the Elizabethans"); Francis Thynne; IV: The seventeenth century (editions 1602–87);[32] V: "Dryden and modernizations"; VI: "Scholarly study and appreciation" "revival of genuine appreciation" (Tyrwhitt and the Chaucer Society).[33] I think, although I am not certain, these categories can be mapped conveniently onto century divisions: I — fourteenth century; II — fifteenth; III — sixteenth; IV — seventeenth; V — eighteenth; VI — nineteenth. And that, I think, is roughly the organization of my inchoate article sketched above.

Grafted onto this chronological view is a list of "qualities" found in the reception of Chaucer.[34] (I do not see how sec. 2 really "analyzes and classifies" references; it seems rather a catchall, discussing "those who note that Chaucer 'refined' the language" and the relative popularity of texts.) This presumed uncritical (that is to say, unmediated) and unsystematized list of qualities in sec. 3 is distributed along the axis of chronology: (1) Chaucer is eloquent, ornate, (2) moral, (3) learned, and (4) jovial, facetious, merry. This seems to end with the seventeenth century.

---

32 This period, 1602–87, is defined as that period in which "the knowledge of his versification entirely disappears" (Spurgeon, *Chaucer Criticism and Allusion,* 1:x). Cf. my conclusions in Chapter 1 above.

33 There is certainly an article to be written about what "inauthentic" or "disingenuous" appreciation might be, at what period that was possible, and who would best exemplify it.

34 Sec. 3, in Spurgeon, *Chaucer Criticism and Allusion,* 1:xciiiff.

The following section is on the development of biography (sec. 4, Spurgeon, 1:ci). These categories and terms bother me: but that is likely because centuries (the basis of the organizational scheme above) are more a part of my thinking than the sometimes quaint literary critical terminology here.

The implication seems to be that serious (or "authentic"? or perhaps "modern"?) scholarship begins at the point where her survey ends: Spurgeon is thus a part of true scholarship and "genuine appreciation" that begins with Tyrwhitt, or perhaps with the magical date of 1800,[35] or perhaps with the creation of the Chaucer Society a half century later; she is not part of a tradition of flawed impressionistic "criticism and allusion" that begins in Chaucer's own lifetime. The growth and development of Chaucer studies moves toward discovering what he really is. At some point between the late-eighteenth and the mid-nineteenth century, we are in the realm of modern criticism, painstakingly recovering (or attempting to recover) the true Chaucer, in whom earlier readers had little interest. The familiar notion of *noster Chaucerus* is doubled in the notion of "Our Tyrwhitt," and from that moment on, we no longer read Chaucer criticism for its quaintness but for its truth (or perhaps more accurately, we ignore quaintness even in its most egregious manifestation, for example, in Furnivall). A scholar as good as Spurgeon, of course, would never put it this way.

I turn to the elaborate and sophisticated index, which according to Spurgeon is the "responsibility of Arundell Esdaile, without whose expert and invaluable help in recent years these volumes would, I fear, still be unfinished."[36] (There seems to be no reference to Esdaile in the Index itself.) Spurgeon's sometimes abstruse introduction seems breezy by comparison. For a few pages, everything proceeds in a pedestrian manner, fol-

---

35 See my "'Ca. 1800': What's in a Date?" in *Blind Impressions: Methods and Mythologies in Book History* (Philadelphia: University of Pennsylvania Press, 2013), 37–57.
36 Spurgeon, Foreword to *Chaucer Criticism and Allusion,* 1:vi. The Index appears now as the final section of Spurgeon's volume 3; it is paginated separately.

lowing conventions familiar to anyone who has made an index. Entries are alphabetized, and subheadings are organized not according to the alphabet or level of importance, but rather in the order of the first page reference given under that sub-heading.

But then, we arrive at the problem that every indexer sooner or later must address: the entry naming the main subject of the book, here Chaucer. The entry begins with a synopsis of the ten headings that follow: Biography, Criticism, Modernizations, Imitations, Illustrations, Manuscripts, Bibliography, Works, Chaucer (a character in fiction), Book titles taken from Chaucer. The order of these headings is neither explained nor is it clear (Spurgeon, vol. 3, Index pp. 1, 9–10). I turn to the most important section, sec. 2: Criticism, since that is announced subject of Spurgeon's entire work. The sub-headings and selected sub-sub-headings are as follows:

II. CRITICISM
a) evolution
b) general
c) language

The entry "language" contains ten sub-subheadings: 1. general; 2. monosyllables; 3. dialects; 4. pronunciation; and 5. "Held obsolete or rude" (including those who excuse while admitting the charge). For this sub-sub-heading, there are more than two columns of citations (Spurgeon, 31: Index, 15–16). This is followed by a brief 6. "Held not obsolete or rude"; 7. "C. praised for refining English"; 8. "C. corrupted English"; 9. "the importation minimised"; and 10. "the importation denied."

We are back to the first level of sub-heading:
d) verse.

This has ten sub-sub-headings: 1. thought irregular; 2. thought rhythmical; 3 thought only apparently irregular; 4. final -e discovered; 5. decried; 6. riding rhyme; 7. couplet; 8. stanza; 9. alliteration; and 10. miscellaneous
e) prose
f) particular qualities found in C.

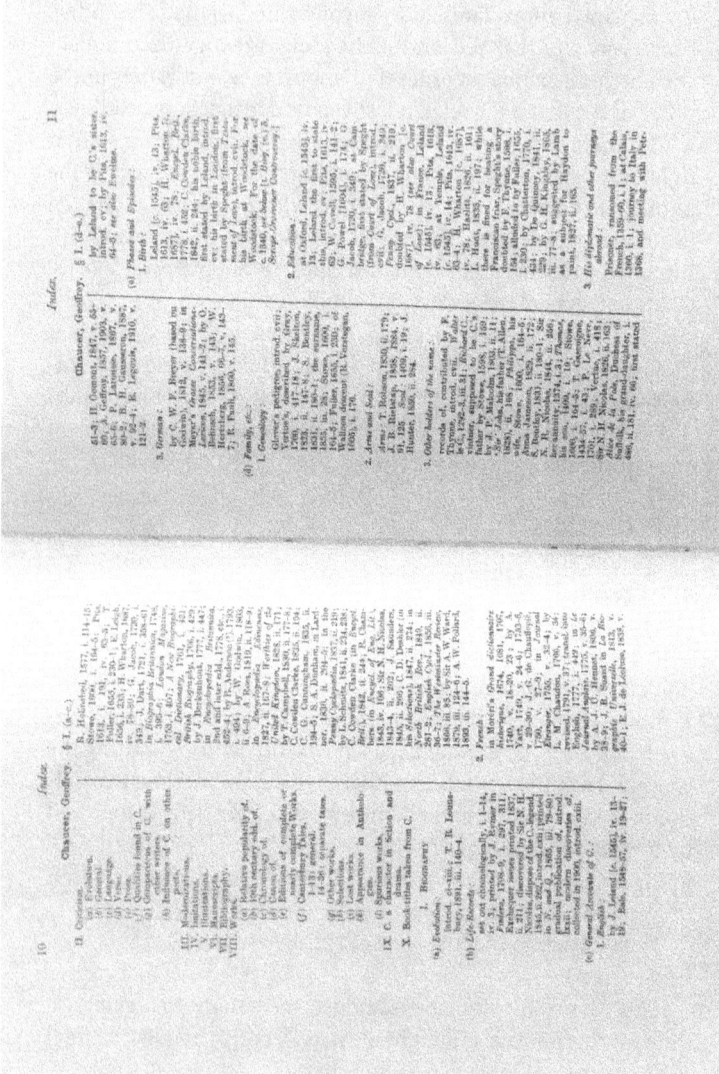

Figure 2: Spurgeon, *Chaucer Criticism and Allusion*, 3: Index, 10–11.

I believe I am still under the heading "Criticism," but it is very difficult, looking at a single page, to stay oriented in terms of the general outline.

Twenty-two sub-sub-headings follow. I believe these are under the sub-heading (f) "Particular qualities found in C." itself a sub-heading of II: Criticism:[37]

1. realism
2. observation of character
3. Humour : 'wit'
4. indecency frivolity
5. moral purpose: satire.
5. anticlericalism
7. piety
8. impiety
9. pathos
10. sublimity
11. want of sublimity or of seriousness
12. love of nature
13. happiness
14. learning
15. universality
16. prolixity
17. brevity
18. eloquence
19. facility
20. artifiality
21. heaviness
22. originality.

There must be a principle of order here, just as there must be in the ten sub-sub-headings under "Verse," but I look for a direct statement on it in vain. I had thought I understood the sections, even if they are somewhat arbitrary, but the order of these sub-sub-headings is a mystery. These are not arranged by any con-

---

[37] Spurgeon, *Chaucer Criticism and Allusion,* 3: Index, 16–17.

vention of indexing that I know: not alphabetically, nor by the number of references, nor by the date or first mention in which any of these things are found or asserted. Yet all of them look familiar; they look familiar because we know what nineteenth-century Chaucerians said, and we know what later scholars said based on what Spurgeon said.

Anyone in the late twentieth- or early twenty-first century who tried to speak intelligently about Chaucer reception without reference to Spurgeon would be grossly deficient as a scholar. Ignoring Spurgeon and the categories used by Esdaile that enable us to use Spurgeon is not an option for responsible, mainstream Chaucerians. And yet, anyone using Spurgeon is bound in some way to Esdaile's categories and the unsystematic or simply unintelligible way they are defined and deployed. Spurgeon had categories of thought to begin with: she knew what constituted a citation of Chaucer and also had or developed certain themes of reception, which are likely not the ones that would have been chosen at any other point in Chaucerian history. (Early Chaucer editors never had to organize their Testimonials; they simply repeated what was available.) Esdaile then overlaid this with his own detailed but abstruse organizations and Spurgeon must in some way have signed off on this, even though the two systems of organization do not seem to be the same.

I have used Spurgeon (by which now I mean the work in which both Spurgeon's and Esdaile's thinking is embodied) in various ways, usually reading from front to back, trying to avoid the restrictions of the categories and the history outlined in the index. I have done the same to the index alone. I have opened the various volumes and read passages at random — the Sortes Spurgeoniana approach to Chaucer reception — thinking or deluding myself that such a method was as good as any other. I would have no idea where in the volumes I was, and when I used the index in this way, I would have no idea how the entry I chose at random was classified. I have more diligently acceded to the apparent views represented in the finished book as it was presented to readers, beginning with a word in the index, trying to locate its various sub-headings, and following its guidance to the sources.

Yet whatever I do, I am still controlled by the assumptions I am trying to eliminate: Spurgeon's view of Chaucerian reception and even what literary reception is in the first place, her selection of passages, her editing of the passages she selected, and Esdaile's re-organization of her work in his index. Spurgeon never articulated the principles by which particular items were chosen and only rarely those for which some were rejected (see footnote 30 above). And neither Spurgeon nor Esdaile defined the conventions used for the extensive index. To determine even the basic principles of selection would require at least giving some attention to questions such as the following: In what way are these selections representative; and what is it they represent? How was the corpus defined? What constitutes an "allusion" to Chaucer? Does it have to involve his name? or a work he actually wrote or was assumed to have written? Is there a difference between "Chaucer" and "the Chaucerian" or is that a function of our conclusions and not involved in our corpus of evidence? If Chaucer's reputation and his very nature were determined in large part by works he didn't write, does this mean allusions to those works are part of our histories of reception? And does omitting them recast the history of Chaucerians in our own image? Were passages omitted because they were redundant? or because they did not cohere in any significant way?

I have no way of determining Spurgeon's thinking on these questions. I can only assume for better or worse that Spurgeon was more or less randomizing these selections more or less in accord with late nineteenth-century scholarship, which is sort of or kind of or to some degree the way we were taught to look at Chaucer in the mid-twentieth century, and that is sort of or perhaps the best I can do when looking at an overall pattern of reception (I cannot, say, confine my thinking to the grammar of a particular sentence in one of the texts that forms this reception). In other words, despite what I do, I seem locked into the (often quaint) assumptions of the nineteenth-century Chaucer Society, in whose series of publications Spurgeon's work first appeared. But even here, my views on "quaintness" interfere with what I am trying to do.

So I am entitling this chapter "Chaucer's Rude Times" and going about things the way I always used to, and to some extent still do: I take the most reputable or uncontroversial source, one that has to me proven useful in the past, and begin reading through it, pencil in hand. I check the index to make sure I have not simply read over something obvious. All is circular: variations of a theme, where the theme is so abstract (unlike a musical theme) that the discovery of evidence is merely a projection of the assumptions I formed when I began.

There may be a way around this, by beginning with a word rather than an abstraction: I would simply follow the use of the phrase "rude times" and see where we end. I would simply start with the word "Chaucer" and define that as constituting an "allusion to Chaucer" and exclude all else. But the method that seemed to work so well years ago — looking at the history of a word rather than the history of an idea — fails here. Even the name *Chaucer* does not work, and the index here diligently distinguishes allusions to the "real" Chaucer (the author?) from those to the "character" Chaucer (in a play?). What, after all, are "rude times"? Real ones? or the naming of them? The words for this idea (was it an idea?) seem so time-bound it is almost impossible to find a use of it after the seventeenth century. Does the concept end? Become concealed under a new, more modern phrase? Or, as Spurgeon seems to suggest, does history end in some Hegelian way once our most immediate ancestors come into view.

CHAPTER 3

Meditation on Our Chaucer and the History of the Canon

The development of the Chaucer canon is not a scholarly process of accretion (the slow unearthing of facts), but rather the development of theories defining evidence that supports preexistent conclusions. This history has been well studied; it is one that seems to end at the turn of the last century with the publication of Skeat's seven-volume Chaucer edition and Eleanor Hammond's still irreplaceable *Chaucer: A Bibliographical Manual* of 1908.[1] When I returned to this topic after many years away from Chaucer studies, I had forgotten most of what I knew about this history. I am neither a paleographer nor a codicologist, and thus I could not deal with the subject critically based on manuscript evidence; I turned instead to printing history. Wouldn't the printed editions of Chaucer (including as they do works by Chaucer, works about Chaucer, and works related to Chaucer) provide a good history of the canon and its development or mutations? And couldn't some simple question be constructed to demonstrate the history of this canon through print? So I asked that question: When did the works now in standard printed editions of Chaucer first appear in print? I assumed this would result in a reasonably coherent list that could then be adjusted or tweaked in accordance with the Growth and De-

---

1 Eleanor Prescott Hammond, *Chaucer: A Bibliographical Manual* (New York: Macmillan, 1908); Walter W. Skeat, *The Complete Works of Geoffrey Chaucer*, 7 vols. (Oxford: Clarendon Press, 1894–97) and *The Chaucer Canon, with a Discussion of the Works Associated with the Name of Geoffrey Chaucer* (Oxford: Clarendon Press, 1900).

velopment model associated with nineteenth-century literary-historical methods. I was surprised to find that such a list produced nothing of the sort: while the major works conveniently and expectedly were associated with early dates in print (the apocryphal works added to the *Canterbury Tales* made their way only into later printed editions), the more problematic "minor works" — the only works on which there is interesting controversy in terms of canon — most decidedly did not.

Here is a partial list based, I believe, on the order and discussion in the Riverside edition, along with the editions in which they first appear. 1532 refers to the Thynne folio edition, the first "Complete" edition:[2]

ABC: 1602
Pity: 1532
Mars and Venus: 1499 (Notary); 1532
Rosemond: first printed 1891
Womanly Noblesse: Skeat, 1894
Adam Scriveyn: 1561
Former Age: discovered by Bradshaw (Morris ed., 1866)
Fortune: Caxton; again 1532
Truth: Caxton; Pynson 1526; 1532
Gentilness: Caxton; 1532
Steadfastness: 1532
Lenvoy a Scogan: Caxton; 1532.
Lenvoy a Bukton: Notary 1499; 1532
Purse: Caxton; 1532
Proverbs: 1561
Against Women Inconstant: 1561
Complaynt d'Amours: 1888
Merceless Beauty: Percy Reliques 1767; Bell Chaucer 1854
Ballad of Complaint: discussed by Skeat, 1888

---

2 F.N. Robinson, ed., *The Complete Works of Geoffrey Chaucer* (Boston: Houghton Mifflin, 1933; 2nd edn. 1957); Larry D. Benson, gen. ed., *The Riverside Chaucer*, 3rd edn. (Boston: Houghton Mifflin, 1987).

Perhaps there is a coherence here. But I don't see it. There are many surprises: the number of works first printed in the nineteenth century, for example. Yet the dates these works first appear in print seem unrelated to the critical acceptance of those works into the Chaucer canon, what could be called the strength of the consensus. That strength is difficult to define, since most Chaucerians likely do not care overmuch about this list. Perhaps I could arrange these facts more rigorously and they would speak, but again, I hear only questions. Are works simply randomly associated with Chaucer until the philological theories of the nineteenth century straightened everything out? If so, what were the previous half-millenium of Chaucer readers and scholars for? Or is the formation of the canon, or (if we wish to call it that) the discovery of what Chaucer really wrote, a matter of particulars, with the history and being of each subject text and its reception so singular as to undermine any coherent critical statement that might be applied to it and to other texts?

I went back to this list and back, of course, to Hammond's *Bibliographical Manual*; the proper arrangement of facts — in this case, the printing history as it relates to the history of Chaucer canon — became ridiculously simple. Hammond simply arranges the table of contents of Thynne's 1532 edition against the lists of Chaucer's works found in the early biographies of Leland and Bale and from that list, it is obvious what conclusion could and should be drawn. The list of works included in Thynne (whether by Chaucer or not, and whether attributed to Chaucer in Thynne's edition or not) provided the basis of discussion of the Chaucer canon for at least as long as that edition was used in Chaucer studies (that is, until it was replaced by Urry's 1721 edition and Tyrwhitt's edition of the *Canterbury Tales* in 1775). Leland and Bale may supplement the Thynne list along with earlier evidence such as that collected by Spurgeon (citations by Lydgate, Hoccleve, or even Chaucer himself), but the Thynne list, coming as it does from the first self-declared complete works, seems the foundation for consideration of the

Chaucer canon for more than four centuries.³ With that as a starting point, it is easy enough to see how the printed canon evolves. The development of the Chaucer canon and its discussion are the same thing. And at least until the establishment of the Chaucer Society, the discussion of the Chaucer canon has been controlled by editing: the question of what is by Chaucer is equivalent to the question of what to include in a printed edition and how that is to be labelled. Separate categories for works labeled "spurious" and "often attributed to Chaucer" develop in the nineteenth century. It is not obvious why editing and canon-formation should be the same. Editing gets us back (theoretically) to what was written, not who wrote it. Any conflation of these two seems to me to involve an unavoidable circularity of reasoning, and an equally unavoidable series of assumptions we often claim to wish to avoid, for example, the greatness of the poet, the purity of origins.

The Power of Editions: The Chaucer Society and the Skeat Edition

The history I began to trace has several important moments. First, the series of blackletter folios and the 1721 Urry edition that follows them. Here is where the canon expands. (There will always be a reason to buy an edition that adds material to previous editions; it will be more difficult to sell an edition that advertises itself as containing less than previous ones). Any list will summarize this: 1532; 1542 (adds "Plowman's Tale"); 1561, adds short poems, largely from MSS; 1598, adds "Two Bookes

---

3 Joseph A. Dane, *Who Is Buried in Chaucer's Tomb? Studies in the Reception of Chaucer's Book* (East Lansing: Michigan State University Press, 1998), 51–74. Pynson's 1526 edition, now bibliographically three separate works (at least in STC), may have preceded Thynne in this. Each was consumed (or distributed?) in parts (see Section 3.5, "The Pynson Chaucer(s) of 1526: Bibliographical Circularity," later in this volume); although individual works printed by Caxton, de Worde, or Pynson could have been combined, and perhaps sold, as a "complete works," the first printed edition with a preface introducing a complete works is by Thynne.

of his, neuer before Printed": "Flower and the Leaf" and "Isle of Ladies"; 1602, adds "Jack Upland"; 1687; 1721, adds "Tale of Gamelyn."[4] This expansion of the canon stopped with Tyrwhitt, who was the first editor to question it. Since his edition included only the *Canterbury Tales,* he had less material interest in this matter than folio editors had had: he did not have to embody ideas editorially. With the exception of the "Plowman's Tale," and the "Tale of Gamelyn" (a tale never included in a printed edition until Urry), Tyrwhitt was able to separate the two questions of editing and canon in the same way that early biographers were able to: Leland and Bale also had no direct interest in their conclusions. Before Tyrwhitt, the question of the canon rested on what nineteenth-century Chaucerians would characterize as "external evidence": what was included in early editions, what biographers claimed was by Chaucer, what poems were attributed to Chaucer in manuscripts. Nineteenth-century Chaucerians opposed to this what their own printing technology and conventions enabled them to define as "internal evidence": evidence from and in the texts and variants that could be amassed in a series of pamphlets or produced together and formatted in parallel-text editions. Such editions were the very embodiment of the principle of the primacy of internal evidence.[5] At first glance, the method seems to allow for unmediated presentation of evidence: texts are simply placed side-by-side, without comment. But of course, there is no such thing as unmediated evidence. The most important editorial decisions regarding the authenticity or canonicity of the text are made prior to the printing and formatting of these texts. Furthermore, obvious failings of the method are reinterpreted as resulting from failings or anomalies of history. That is to say, when the method does not seem to work, that reveals not something related to the method, but

---

4 For a list of contents, see Hammond, *Bibliographical Manual,* 116–29.
5 See, e.g., F.J. Furnivall, ed., *A Six-Text Print of Chaucer's Canterbury Tales in Parallel Columns from the MSS,* Chaucer Soc. Publ., ser. 1, nos. 1, 14, 15 … (London: Trübner, 1869–77), and F.J. Furnivall, *A Parallel-Text Edition of Chaucer's Minor Poems,* Chaucer Soc. Publ., ser. 1, nos. 21, 57, 58 (London: Trübner, 1871–79).

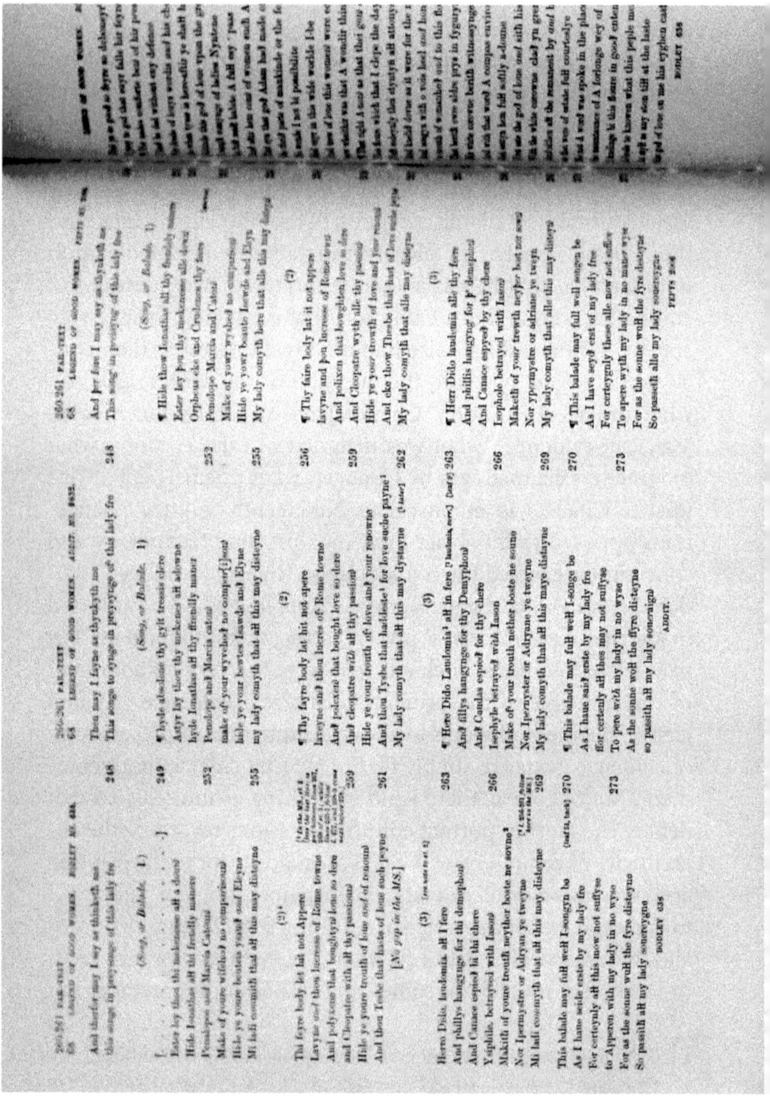

Figure 3: Furnivall, *A Parallel-Text Edition of Chaucer's Minor Poems*.

rather something of interest in the history it is applied to. Why history should be subject to or interpretable through the particulars of an arbitrary method of analysis is never questioned. To place two texts in parallel first requires the assumption that they are the same (an assumption that has been questioned in many texts, most notably in the case of *King Lear*). Once that assumption has been made, the texts need to be manipulated. Note in the illustration below, what appears to be a diplomatic edition involves reorganization of the lines of text (noted in the margin).

In extreme cases, the method fails completely. In the case of the *Legend of Good Women,* the method fails to answer editorial questions, and this failure led to hypothesized histories: two separate texts (Prologues F and G), a revision, and a history of Chaucer to satisfy these presumed facts. In the case of the *Canterbury Tales,* it reinforced editorial decisions that had been made earlier: the "best manuscripts" were the best authorities for the text and canon and presented in convenient parallel-text format. The presentation of evidence becomes itself a foundation for further discussion and thus in and of itself a new form of evidence.[6] The transcriptions produced by the Chaucer Society culminated in Skeat's edition of the 1890s, which included a seventh volume devoted to spurious works (*Supplement: Chaucerian and Other Pieces*). This was the first time that the canon had been embodied in a physical edition, with non-canonical works physically and materially separated from genuine works. (Stow's 1561 edition, by contrast, mixed canonical and non-canonical works together without physical distinction). Skeat's edition and the rigid separation of the genuine from the apocryphal thus became the foundation for all twentieth-century discussion of the Chaucer canon, and often the evidence for that discussion.

Skeat defined the canon as consisting of twenty-one texts plus three doubtful ones. That is, not surprisingly, the list one finds in

---

[6] Joseph A. Dane, "The Notions of Text and Variant in the Prologue to Chaucer's Legend of Good Women" (1993), in *Abstractions of Evidence in Manuscripts and Early Printed Books* (Aldershot: Ashgate, 2009), 25–40.

F.N. Robinson's edition of 1933. That is also the list one finds in Robinson's second edition of 1957. Somewhat more surprisingly, that is the list one finds in Benson's "Third Edition" of 1988 and in its own re-edition of 2008. And when it comes to the *Minor Poems,* that is also the list one finds in the Variorum edition of Pace and David (who certainly did some of the most solid editorial work in this now stalled edition).[7] None of the scholars who made these decisions hailed Skeat as the father of modern Chaucer scholarship. And although there is critical discussion of his methods, there is, on this question, less concern with his results.[8] If Skeat were unerring, there would be no need to continue: Skeat's edition is handy, comes in various forms, and more recent editions have tacitly conceded modern students are well served by annotations now over a hundred years old. The 1988 iteration of the Riverside Edition is a model of how modern editions make critical discussion difficult. Editors are assigned sections (as they were assigned sections in the Variorum Chaucer project), and their published conclusions obviously cannot differ from those of the general editors. Sub-editors seem encouraged to follow a template, and an overly critical attitude to the conclusions of the general editors or their predecessors is clearly unwelcome. Robinson, in 1957, repeated his notes of 1933, as if the central issues in Chaucer studies (courtly love, the question of sources, The Marriage Group) had not changed. Many of those notes reappear in the 1988 version.[9] On the canon, little

---

7   *Variorum Edition of the Works of Geoffrey Chaucer, 5: The Minor Poems, I,* eds. George B. Pace and Alfred David, (Norman: University of Oklahoma Press, 1982).

8   A.S.G. Edwards, "Walter Skeat," in Paul G. Ruggiers, ed., *Editing Chaucer: The Great Tradition* (Norman: Pilgrim Books, 1984), 171–89.

9   The Explanatory Notes and Textual Notes are written by different scholars, whose approaches vary widely. Compare the often belletristic Explanatory Notes to the Short Poems by Laila K. Gross (Riverside Ed., 1076–91) with, say, the Textual Notes to the Canterbury Tales by Ralph Hanna III (1118–35); Hanna opted to create what he calls an "edition of an edition" and thus sidestep (perhaps correctly) the practical implications of his own work. On Robinson, see, e.g., Richard Utz, "The Colony Writes Back: F.N. Robinson's *Complete Works of Geoffrey Chaucer* (1933) and the *Translatio* of Chaucer

changed, and on some texts, Robinson's earlier editions provide no chance of critical evaluation. They include a few "doubtful" works, but there is not enough context to evaluate the principles behind Robinson's choices. Other texts, on which Skeat had pronounced, are neither included nor part of the discussion. It is difficult to deal critically with "what is to be included" in an edition if users of that edition are not given examples of or even reference to "what is not to be included." An example is the "Isle of Ladies" (once known as "The Dreame of Chaucer" or, by Skeat, "The Assemblie of Ladies"). The "Isle of Ladies," first printed in the 1598 edition, was omitted (probably correctly) from the Chaucer canon by Skeat, and thus omitted without comment by most subsequent editions. I am conditioned to believe it is apocryphal, and I am not troubled by that stance. But the reasons Skeat has for omitting this involved evidence that Skeat did not acknowledge; not through external evidence (those extratextual facts such as attributions), nor for internal reasons (style, language, meter). The reason at least implied in Skeat is that it was written by a woman (that is, it has a female persona): "The authoress of the one was the authoress of the other."[10] No scholar today would deny authorship of a poem to a major English male author on this basis.[11] One would assume, then, that rejecting these ideological assumptions that to Skeat seemed self-evident would result in a growing skepticism about his pronouncements on the canon, but this has clearly not been the case. Philological evidence (did Skeat consider this internal?) happily supports

---

Studies to the United States," *Studies in Medievalism* 19 (2010): 160–203. See also Julia Boffey and A.S.G. Edwards, "'Chaucer's Chronicle,' John Shirley, and the Canon of Chaucer's Shorter Poems," *Studies in the Age of Chaucer* 20 (1998): 201–18.

10 Skeat, *Supplement*, lxii; Kathleen Forni, "'Chaucer's Dream': A Bibliographical Nightmare," *Huntington Library Quarterly* 64, nos. 1/2 (2001): 139–49. This poem is also responsible for Godwin's notion of Chaucer's residence at Woodstock. See Richard Osberg, "False Memories: The Dream of Chaucer and Chaucer's Dream in the Medieval Revival," *Studies in Medievalism* 19 (2010): 204–25.

11 I believe there is a similar attitude to canon in H.J.C. Grierson, *Poems of John Donne* (London: Oxford University Press, 1912).

ideological and social convictions that we do not share. And as long as our faith in Skeat's philology is greater than our faith in our own social, moral, and aesthetic principles, we're fine.

Nineteenth-Century Philological Tests

Skeat takes as a starting point Tyrwhitt's "Introductory Discourse" to his edition of 1775, and in so doing, casts Tyrwhitt as the beginning of modern Chaucerianism, a version of Chaucer reception that the preceding chapter suggests we still hold today. All previous versions of the canon had operated on the principle that the canon was to be expanded: if one work by Chaucer was good, the more Chaucerian works (however "Chaucerian" is defined) the better.[12] Tyrwhitt's reasons for identifying the canon were eclectic, including both internal and external evidence, although the definition of these terms was vague, as in the following passage, commenting on the early folio editions:

> The anonymous compositions which have been from time to time added to Chaucer's in the several Editt. seem to have been received, for the most part, without any external evidence whatever, and in direct contradiction to the strong internal evidence.[13]

Skeat applied a philological test, which, in a less well-defined sense, is likely what Tyrwhitt meant by "internal" evidence. If certain of Chaucer's works are incontestably his (the two major works, *Troilus* and *Canterbury Tales,* both, through a sort of *petitio principii*, stripped of their problematic and non-canonical additions),[14] then what is "by" Chaucer (or is indistinguishable

---

12 Skeat had two principle sources: Tyrwhitt, and the "heap of rubbish" that kept finding its way into editions, even in the innocuous edition of Moxon; see Dane, *Who Is Buried in Chaucer's Tomb?*, 175–83.
13 Tyrwhitt, Introductory Discourse, *The Canterbury Tales of Chaucer,* 5.
14 The tales of Gamelyn, "Plowman's Tale," Lydgate's continuation, and in *Troilus,* the "Testament of Criseyde."

from any work we claim is by Chaucer) can be determined by defining the language and style that corresponds to these works, insofar as that language and style can be recovered from the manuscript tradition and quantified philologically. (This is based on an unstated further assumption that the poem to be considered is the poem represented accurately in the manuscript). What is required is to define or discover some feature of style that can clearly distinguish Chaucer from later, uncontestably non-Chaucer works (for example, by Lydgate); what is also required is that such style be subject to clear definition. As demonstrated in these sometimes tortured sentences, just to state these deceptively simple principles correctly requires qualifications at every turn. The simplest and most important of these was the *-e/-ye* test, which Skeat and Furnivall attribute to Henry Bradshaw.[15] Chaucer regularly rhymes words that etymologically are disyllabic (from French, or from Latin *-ia*), but never rhymes them with monosyllabic *-y* (as in endings from *-lich*). Fifteenth-century writers who followed Chaucer do not distinguish these rhyme-groups, or more accurately, they consider them acceptable as rhymes. Thus, say, any work included in Stow's edition of 1561 that rhymed these terminations is "not by Chaucer" (although the word "Chaucer" here is again subject to qualification). These philological tests, particularly the rhyme test, were developed in large part to determine the authorship of the various sections of *Romaunt de la Rose*, and then extended to the rest of canon. Chaucer in his "best" or "mature" period would consistently distinguish sounds in ways that his successors did not. "Early" Chaucer or Chaucerian work would thus be ambiguous, since failure to conform to his mature style could indicate either non-Chaucer authorship, or youthful experimentation.[16] Such tests involve two distinct levels: one is purely

---

15 E.g., Skeat, *Canon*, 45, *Chaucer: Works*, 1:5. Bradshaw never presented this theory systematically, but alludes to it, e.g., in his "The Skeleton of Chaucer's Canterbury Tales," (1871), rpt. Henry Bradshaw, *Collected Papers* (Cambridge: University Press, 1889), 138.

16 For the *Romaunt of the Rose*, the reasoning was inevitably circular. See discussion and references in *The Romance of the Rose*, ed. Charles Dahlberg

stylistic (what Chaucer preferred to write, when other choices were available); the other is philological (what Chaucer and any of his contemporaries would have written).[17] The rhyme test is easy to check, and results in far fewer exceptions when applied to what is now considered the Chaucer canon than I originally had expected or hoped. (I am here considering only the canon proper and what could be called the "canonical non-canonical texts," that is, works not by Chaucer included in Chaucer editions). This is unsurprising, since it would be the case if (1) the conclusions on the Chaucer canon were true or (2) if the application of this principle were a matter of *petitio principii*: what is "Chaucer" or "Chaucerian" is "what is indistinguishable from what is defined as Chaucer or Chaucerian." In either case, there are many assumptions related to this test that Skeat did not express directly.

The distinction has a historical component. Later poets, even those imitating Chaucer, did not hear a difference in these rhymes (or at least, they wrote their poems as if they did not), and may not have been aware that Chaucer distinguished them. This, however, includes an aesthetic judgment: Chaucer is better than these later poets, so his rhyming is more nuanced and therefore superior. These conventions, both aesthetic and linguistic, are assumed to be stable (at least, once Chaucer reaches his "mature" period — that is, once Chaucer becomes "Chaucer"). And those rhymes, even had Chaucer lived until the 1420s, would have continued to distinguish him from those who did not respect these soon obsolete forms.

(Norman: University of Oklahoma Press, 1995), 6–7; Skeat, *Canon*, 70–72; and what is to me a still useful example, chap. 5 on the *Romaunt* in Aage Brusendorff, *The Chaucer Tradition* (London: Oxford University Press, 1925), 296–425.

17 For an overview of basic issues, see Dennis Freeborn, *From Old English to Standard English: A Course Book in Language Variation Across Time*, 3rd edn. (Houndmills: Palgrave Macmillan, 2006), and "Chaucer's Rhymes as Evidence of Changes in Pronunciation," *palgrave.com*, https://www.macmillanihe.com/resources/CW%20resources%20(by%20Author)/F/freeborn/pdfs/commentary/33_Chaucers_rhymes.pdf.

Ideally, various levels of evidence are distinguished: external (understood as attributions of works in manuscripts or by Chaucer himself), philological, and aesthetic. Yet in the end, these are often conflated: when Chaucer's style is raised to a philological level, it becomes external evidence insofar as the history of language is a field apart from "what Chaucer wrote." Philological distinctions are then returned to provide evidence of the history of Chaucer's style; that is, they are redefined as internal evidence.[18]

Chaucer the Philologist

In 2011, David Yerkes wrote a seemingly modest contribution to historical linguistics. The standard philological interpretation of Chaucer's vowel sounds (one we find in Skeat and other late nineteenth-century philologists, in all editions of Robinson, and to my knowledge never questioned in mainstream Chaucer studies of the twentieth century) is incorrect. It is not incorrect because of recent discoveries in linguistics. It is, rather, incorrect based on the evidence that Skeat and others cited as its foundation. Yerkes is not concerned with the most familiar of Skeat's tests (*-y/-ye*), but rather in the definition of vowels that is at the heart of other linguistic rhyme tests and the foundation for Chaucerian phonetics in general. In its simplest form, Yerkes shows that the evidence Skeat uses does not support the standard and elaborate system of vowel distinctions Skeat claims: where nineteenth-century philologists define three or more types of long vowels (e and o), Chaucer himself (at least in his use of rhymes) recognized only two.[19]

---

18 See George Kane, *Piers Plowman: Evidence for Authorship* (London: Athlone Press, 1965), on a third type of evidence, "Signatures": "The occurrences of the name are by my classification neither external evidence of authorship, since the name is an element of the text, nor internal evidence, since its existence is absolute, not contingent on identification by the critical faculty" (52).

19 David Yerkes, "Chaucer's Twelve 'Long' and 'Short' Vowels: The Evidence from Rhymes in *Troilus and Criseyde*," *The Chaucer Review* 45, no. 3 (2011):

> For more than 125 years all accounts of Chaucer's vowels in stressed syllables have assigned him the twelve monophthongs that are called "short a" "long a"; "short e," long open e," and long close e"; "short i" and long i"; "short o," "long open o," and long close o"; and "short u" and "long u."...But Chaucer did not have long and short vowels. What distinguishes Chaucer's vowels from each other is quality, not quantity; any differences in vowel length are allophonic, not phonemic.[20]

The implications of this article reach far beyond anything Yerkes claims directly. If we cannot sort out the simplest evidence before us (what vowels rhyme, and what vowel distinctions exist at all), we have little basis for using such evidence to answer more difficult questions: who wrote what?

There are a number of linguistic issues bound up in the relation of these philological issues to the canon of Chaucer, and Chaucer, as a poet, rather than a philologist, might legitimately have conflated or simply disregarded all of them. The first distinction is phonetic/phonemic. What are the values of these vowels, both in Chaucer's language and in the history of meaning, and do particular phonetic differences in sound (possibly functional ones in terms of style) constitute phonemic differences in meaning (for example, as in modern English word pairs such as bet/beet, lick/leek)? What non-phonemic differences might still be phonetic (the terminations -y/-ye)? It is also possible that vowels could be distinguished purely on the conventions of spelling, with no phonemic or phonetic difference. Differences on any of these levels could function stylistically and could do so inconsistently.

A related question is whether there is a functional difference in the way these potential phonetic distinctions apply to stressed/unstressed vowels and between long/short vowels, and to what extent this too is phonemic (MdE insight/incite). And

---

252–74.
20 Ibid., 252.

further questions are implicated in these: did Middle English at the time "carry" these differences such that they could potentially be realized in Chaucer, or perhaps ignored in Chaucer, but revived by a later poet? It is possible that Chaucer heard a difference and respected it, but did not use it to structure his verse. (This last argument seems to require that the evidence be in direct conflict with the reality that evidence is supposed to prove.)

Although Yerkes does not state this directly, the method he uses defines Chaucer as purely a poet — one who uses the phonetic material at his disposal coherently, but not in ways that are necessarily philologically correct. All we know is how he deployed that material; we do not know (or at least, we are not concerned with) what it is he, or any of his contemporaries, heard or understood. To Bradshaw and to Skeat, who were the first to define these questions in a systematic way, Chaucer was, by contrast, essentially a philologist: he excelled over other English writers in terms of his poetry (the Father of English Poetry), and he likewise excelled over them in terms of his philological knowledge. Unlike his lesser contemporaries and followers, he is like us, and his aesthetic virtues are directly related to this resemblance. If the history of the English language suggests a phonetic difference between two vowels, then that difference exists in (is known to) Chaucer even if it is not represented materially in a text or in the spelling in a particular manuscript. Thus Skeat's table of vowels, which is at times only minimally comprehensible, contains all vowels that could be differentiated philologically, that is, by respectable state-of-the-art studies in Anglo-Saxon and Middle English. And this state-of-the-art philology is at the heart of Chaucer's language.

Extracting Skeat's distinctions through a mere reading of Skeat can be as maddening as penetrating his metrical language to the theory of meter he claims underlies it. In his edition, Skeat uses at least three different symbols or systems of symbols distinguishing vowels in a mere four pages. The following distinctions are taken from Works, vol. 6, sec. 22 (Symbols):

> e short
> e final, unaccented (schwa)
> e long and open, or ee; (ae) or (èè).…This open e came to be denoted by ea, and the symbol, though not the sound, is commonly preserved in mod. English, as in heath.…
> e long and close, or ee; (ee) or (éé). Ex. weep (weep), or (wéép).

See also *Works,* 1: xxix on o:

> o short (o).…
> o long and open, or oo; (ao) or (òò)
> o long and close, or oo; (oo) or (óó)

And *Works,* vol. 6, sec. 25, "Rimes illustrating the pronunciation of long O and long E":

> Let us consider the case of the open and close o. These are distinguished by their origin.…Chaucer usually makes a difference between this sound (ao from lengthening of AS short o) and the former (ao) from AS long a. To keep up the distinction, I shall now write (òò) for the former open o, and (ò) for the latter.

This is not the same notation Skeat uses in *Canon,* secs. 65, 70–72, where long o and e are marked (inconsistently) with macrons, and a carat is used for a particular variety of e:

> Of course the most interesting examples are those which present some difficulty, as when we find the *third* variety of e involved.…This variety, arising from A.S. īe, Mercian ē, or from A.S. ǣ as due to gradation, is well exemplified in Fragment A; and I mark these vowels, as before, with the symbol ê.[21]

---

[21] Skeat, *Canon,* 72. See, also, secs. 45 and 49, referring to discussion in Skeat, Introduction, *Works,* xxv.

See in particular, the discussion in Canon, 50, on the "third variety of M.E. ē":

> But there was a third variety of M.E. ē which seems to have been intermediate between the other two; at any rate, words containing it rime with either of the above vowels indifferently. This ē has two sources [in Middle English]. This vowel, for the sake of distinctness, may be called the "neutral ē." All that need be said here is that, in considering Chaucer's rimes, it is simplest to *exclude* all cases in which ē arises from the last two sources. When this is done, we obtain the general rule, that words containing the open ē never rime, in Chaucer, with words containing the close ē.

But note:

> Examples of open ē (from oe [with macron, not on my keyboard!] or ēa): dèèd, lustihèèd, and of open ē (resulting from lengthening of A.S. e): wère, bère ... Examples of close ē: be ye....Examples of neutral ē (marked ê) riming with open ē: wêre, ère....Examples of neutral ē (marked ê) riming with close ē: shêne, grene.

Among the vowels distinguished here are: ē (long e), e (close e), è, èè (two types of open e), and ê. Unfortunately, the same terminology is used to describe a number of different things: vowels in Old English and in other dialects of English, generic vowels, and vowels as recognized in Chaucer.

Skeat's discussion in this section is a reflection of the state of linguistic study at the time. Although not necessarily confused, it is certainly unstable: there are no agreed upon conventions for describing the distinctions Skeat notes. Alexander J. Ellis, in his nearly contemporary *On Early English Pronunciation,* is, like Skeat, primarily concerned with philological-historical study — that is, the source of Chaucer's vowels rather than Chaucer's use of the vowel sounds at his disposal.[22] Furthermore, Ellis draws on earlier authorities, introducing into his own discussion their systems of phonetic notation. This is Ellis's distinction of vowels from his translation of F.W. Gesenius, *De lingua Chauceri* of 1847:[23]

> Part I. the Letters:
> Chaucer's e replaces several distinct ags vowels.
> Short e stands:
> for ags e short, in: ende 15....
> for ags. i, y, in: cherche....
> for ags. ë eá in: erme....
> for ags. ëo in: sterres
> Long e stands
> for ags. short e in: ere
> for ags. long e, more frequently in: seke....
> for ags. ae long: heres,
> for ags ëó as in: seke
> for ags. ëa and eá in: eek.

But these five sources of long e do not result in five different sounds or rhymes, at least as far as verse is concerned. From this, Ellis concludes:

> Nothing certain can be concluded concerning the pronunciation of these e's, which arose from so many sources. They all rhyme, and may have been the same. In modern spelling the e is now doubled, or more frequently reverts to ea.[24]

---

22 Alexander J. Ellis, *On Early English Pronunciation with especial reference to Shakspere and Chaucer, Part III: Illustrations of the Pronunciation of the XIVth and XVIth Centuries* (London: N. Trübner & Co., 1871).

23 Ellis, *English Pronunciation,* chap. VII, sec. 3: "F.W. Genesius on Chaucer," 664 ff. Reference is to F.W. Gesenius, *De Lingua Chauceri* (Bonn, 1847).

24 Ellis, *Early English Pronunciation,* 665. It is far from clear what the phrase "they all rhyme" means: it does not mean "they are indistinguishable in sound," as the following clause states directly. At no period would what poets consider acceptable rhyme provide infallible phonetic evidence.

Therefore, the difference in sound (reflected in a difference in spelling) is ignored. I think this must mean that Chaucer understood these sounds as different in quality, but nonetheless regarded the rhymes as acceptable. Ellis then, in a somewhat bracing passage, goes on to summarize and translate Moritz Rapp, who has roughly the same conclusion:

> For the vowels, Gesenius has come to conclusions, which are partly based on Grimm's Grammar, and partly due to his having been preoccupied with modern English, and have no firm foundation. The Englishmen of the present day have no more idea how to read their own old language, than the Frenchmen theirs. We Germans are less prejudiced in these matters, and can judge more freely.[25]

Rapp's notation (as represented by Ellis) is quite different, and includes such symbols as E (short e), schwa, ee (long e, I think). Ellis's commentary only makes things more difficult as in this sentence: "Rapp writes ê è but he usually pairs ê e ä è = (*ee* e EE E), the (*ee*) being doubtful, (*ee*, ee)."[26] See also where, like Gesenius, he sees only one long e:

> Long (*ee*) also replaces ags oe (h*ee*re, s*ee*, sl*ee*pe) hare, sea, sleep, and old long *éo* as (s*ee*ke, l*ee*fe l*ee*ve d*ee*pe tsh*ee*se) seek, lief, deep, chose, and finally the old long *éa* as (*ee*k) from (*éa*k), and similarly (gr*ee*te, b*ee*ne tsh*ee*pe) great, bean, cheapen. These different (*ee*) rhyme together and have regularly become (ii) in modern English.[27]

Ellis then transcribes these distinctions in his own notation:

---

25 Ibid., 674, quoting and translating (he claims) Moritz Rapp, *Vergleichende Grammatik* [of 1859] 3: 166–79.
26 Ellis, *Early English Pronunciation*, 674.
27 Ibid., 675.

> If in the above we read (ee, e) and (oo, o) for (*ee, e*) and (*oo, o*), and (e) for (E) which is a slight difference…the differences between this transcript and my own reduce to 1) the treatment of final e, which Rapp had not sufficiently studied,…4) the conception of (EE), an un-English sound, as the proper pronunciation of *ey, ay* as distinct from long *e*. It is remarkable that so much similarity should have been attained by such a distinctly different course of investigation.[28]

And further:

> The roman vowels (a, e, o, u) must be pronounced as in Italian, with the broad or open *e, o,* not the narrow or close sounds. They are practically the same as the short vowels in German … The final (-e) should be pronounced shortly and indistinctly, like the German final -*e,* or our final *a* in *hina, idea,*…It would probably have been more correct to write [upside down a, not a schwa!] in this places, but there is no authority for any other but an (e) sound.[29]

I concede that representing these passages on a modern keyboard using Microsoft Word is difficult, and I have doubtless made several errors, which may well be multiplied at press.

Bernhard ten Brink's discussion is equally confusing. He distinguishes three potential "quantities" of vowels: long, short, and variable. But his discussion seems to define these in terms of quality, as he distinguishes "long closed e" from "long open e" and fluctuation between open and "close long e."[30] The variation referred to by ten Brink is ambiguous: is he referring to an actual variation realized phonetically? His statement appears to be similar to Ellis's notion that there were two separate pronunciations of the same word and that Chaucer simply chose the one

---

28 Ibid., 677.
29 Ibid., 678.
30 Bernhard ten Brink, *The Language and Meter of Chaucer* (1884), 2nd edn., rev. Friedrich Kluge, trans. M. Bentinck Smith (London: Macmillan, 1901), 25.

that suited the verse.³¹ But the reasoning here is circular. How do we know that Chaucer heard two different sounds and selected one over the other if he left no evidence of that? And does this not require a theory of meter to support it, a theory of meter that in some cases is made up of whole cloth?³² Yerkes simplified this philological discussion and refocused it. Nineteenth-century philologists discussing Chaucer's language were interested in its relation to history (other Middle English dialects, Old English, etc.). But when they used that to form conclusions on the canon of Chaucer, they changed the topic of discussion, as well as what could be considered the evidence for that topic of discussion.

Yerkes looks only at the evidence in Chaucer (specific internal evidence, not the evidence from historical philology which is occasionally smuggled into this evidence), and does not speculate on what Chaucer may or may not have thought or sensed, nor on the sophistication of his philological knowledge or instincts, subjects about which we can know nothing until the evidence is compiled. Regardless of what Chaucer heard, spoke, or understood, when it came to structuring his verse, he did not distinguish or, perhaps better, he did not categorize vowels with the philological acumen of Skeat and his contemporaries. In other words, if we are talking about Chaucer's rhymes, we are only talking about stylistic matters (these might in turn bear on larger questions of authorship to be sure). We are not talking necessarily about philology, although there might be evidence that bears on that as well. We are talking about "Chaucer's English" in the sense of 'the language Chaucer used in his verse', not "Chaucer's English" in the sense of 'the dialect spoken by Chaucer and his contemporaries'. Most important, we can systematize this stylistic evidence without imposing nineteenth-century philological theories onto it.

---

31 Ellis, *Early English Pronunciation*, 641ff.
32 Yerkes, "Chaucer's Twelve 'Long' and 'Short' Vowels," 253, provides a table coordinating this language, and distinguishing in the language of early philologists three e's: short open, long open, long close.

Yerkes's summary is as follows:[33]

a: Chaucer did not distinguish long a / short a; he had just one a.
e: Chaucer did not have three e's long open, long closed, short (Skeat says this was open), but two: open e / closed e
o: Ch did not have three o's long open, long closed, short (to Skeat, this was open), but two open / closed

Thus, in stressed syllables, Chaucer had:

not Skeat's two a's — long a and short a — but just one a
not Skeat's three e's — long open e, long closed e, and short e (which Skeat says was open) — but just two e's: just an open e and a closed e
ditto for o

From a stylistic point of view, rhymes in Chaucer involving these crucial vowels form what Yerkes calls "two piles," open e, close e, and no other. There may be other sounds, and Chaucer may have heard and distinguished them, but he did not distinguish them for purposes of rhyme. In assuming that Chaucer distinguished long and short vowels (as in, say, Old English), earlier philologists introduced a phantom set of vowels into their tables: that set of short vowels variously marked (e o).

To nineteenth-century Chaucerians, Chaucer was not only a philologist, but a representative of the Growth and Progress model of a poet's career. According to Furnivall,

The chief interest of the investigation has been to me the watching the growth of the Poet's mind and power from his

---

[33] I am quoting here the summary Prof. Yerkes kindly provided to me. See also Yerkes, "Chaucer's Twelve 'Long' and 'Short' Vowels," 254: "Instead of three e sounds — 'short e', 'long open e', and 'long close e' — Chaucer had two e sounds plus, before r, an ae sound. Chaucer's two e sounds, 'open e and 'close e' … differ over quality, not quantity" — i.e., there is no "short closed e" in stressed syllables.

earliest effort to the greatest triumphs of his genius; and then its decline — in accordance with Nature's law — to its poorest, the begging Balade of the autumn before the Poet's death.[34]

And by that logic, nearly any argument concerning the authorship of, say, the *Romaunt* could find philological support. As a work of his youth, it would not have conformed perfectly to his mature use of rhymes. Furthermore, even a strict application of these tests would not produce unambiguous results. Any of us could write poems that would pass the rhyme test or any other philological test, just as we could write poems that do not. And the shorter these poems (as those in the disputed canon), the easier it would be to hide exceptions to apparent rules.

There were a number of other unstated assumptions involved in Skeat's notion of canon: the poem must be in Middle English; it must be included in a printed Complete Works edition of Chaucer or it must have been attributed to Chaucer by his near contemporaries. Under these assumptions, a new Chaucer piece is barely capable of discovery. The corpus of material had been set long ago, in this case, by the discredited printed editions, the blackletter folios from 1532–1602, to which nothing was to be added. As for the conservative nature of this canon, one only has to look at the remarkably stable lists of Chaucer's short poems during the twentieth century. In the sixteenth century, the canon meant: "A group of poems by Chaucer, said to be by Chaucer, and other related poems." Here, in the twentieth century, it is "a group of poems authenticated by late-nineteenth-century philology." In his 1561 edition, John Stow simply took what he was given and refined it, which to him meant: add.[35] Twentieth-century Chaucerians and twenty-first century Chaucerians do much the same thing — they start with a corpus (in this case, an unquestioned corpus of "The Chaucerian") and play variations

---

34 F.J. Furnivall, *Trial Forewords to my Parallel-Text Edition of Chaucer's Minor Poems for the Chaucer Society,* Chaucer Soc. Publ., ser 2, no. 6 (London: Trübner & Co., 1871), 5–6 .

35 Geoffrey Chaucer, *Workes* (London, 1561) (STC 5075, 5076).

on that. In so doing, they are a least in part trapped into repeating the banalities of their predecessors. The Victorian grand narrative of growth and progress continues to inform our Chaucer.

Conclusion

Not many Chaucerians today are interested in the kind of linguistic questions that were central to Chaucerians of the late nineteenth century. At least, the philological discussion (apart from the conclusions of that discussion) is no longer central to ordinary Chaucer studies. The late-nineteenth-century description of vowels seems old-fashioned and often self-contradictory (it is mirrored in many of the early grammar books which most of us born around mid-century used to learn Old English and Middle English). It is matched, as we saw in an earlier chapter, by an equally quaint and self-contradictory system of describing meter. And also by an equally flawed way of presenting textual evidence: the parallel-text method, and the definition and isolation of textual lemmata. Although no modern linguist or metrician would use this terminology today, the conclusions and sometimes working assumptions that were associated with such deeply flawed terminology remain: Chaucer the iambic pentametrist; Chaucer's unassailable canon; and finally Chaucer's texts — the *Canterbury Tales,* and the revised prologue to *Legend of Good Women.*

I have always wanted to avoid the influence of that legacy. Yet once again, I find it inescapable. It is impossible to communicate with modern Chaucerians without involving myself in the assumptions, methods, and conclusions of the nineteenth-century Chaucer Society, whose products I admire, but whose ambience and social substrate I find revolting. I go back, as responsible scholars must, to Skeat, to Bradshaw, to Furnivall; I go back to their dubious assumptions and often unintelligible language, which we later Chaucerians have too often accepted without serious comment or simply pretended to ignore.

In the end, "our" Chaucer seems unnervingly similar to "theirs."

Figure 4: Supposed portrait of Chaucer from William Godwin, *Life of Chaucer*.

CODA

Godwin's Portrait of Chaucer

Figure 4 comes from William Godwin's *Life of Chaucer*, 1803.[1] It is one of three engravings in this book. The first, in volume 1, is a familiar portrait of Chaucer, fingering what appears to be an amulet on his chest, actually a pen holder; his right hand is in the form of a "teaching" position. His left hand holds beads. This is a version of the engraving in the 1602 Chaucer — hand position, pen, and rosary beads.[2] A later version of this pose is in the portrait by George Vertue in Urry's 1721 Chaucer, which places Chaucer in a cameo; the beads are thus outside the frame. The frontispiece to Godwin's vol. 2 is of John of Gaunt, portrayed not as the Duke, but as "King of Castille and Leon." This would look fine on a pack of cards. The portrait of Chaucer reproduced here is variously placed in the copies I have seen.[3]

You can imagine a coherent history of illustrations of Chaucer, and all goes well until you come to this.

Godwin provides us no information on how he or his publishers expect us to interpret this. The caption tells us this is "supposed to be a Portrait of Chaucer" from a painting in "in the

---

1   William Godwin, *Life of Geoffrey Chaucer the Early English Poet*, 2 vols. (London: Davison, 1803).
2   A.M. Hind, *Engraving in England in the Sixteenth and Seventeenth Centuries: A Descriptive Catalogue with Introduction*, 3 vols. (Cambridge: Cambridge University Press, 1952–64); variously positioned in copies of Geoffrey Chaucer, *Workes* (London, 1602) (STC 5080, 5081).
3   In my copy, this is in vol. 2 preceding the Appendix; in a recent sale copy, it serves as a frontispiece, facing the title page of vol. 1, thereby authenticating it (Temple Rare Books, sale ending 20 Aug. 2014). It is omitted in the all copies I have seen of the smaller format, 4-vol. edition of 1804.

House where Cromwell was born,"[4] but doesn't tell us who supposes such a thing, or who is supposed to suppose that. Chaucer holds a sheet of paper, folded once. A staff. On his writing desk is a sheet of "paper"(?) with the writing "sas faire, was hs m up hle"? What does this say? Chaucer turns away — riding coat, stockings, birkenstocks.

Seeing this, I am reminded of the multi-layered verbal description of a minstrel in Thomas Percy's *Reliques of Ancient English Poetry* (1765). Percy describes a pageant for Queen Elizabeth put on by the Earl of Leicester in 1575:

> One of the personages introduced was that of an ancient Minstrel, whose appearance and dress are so minutely described by a writer there present, and give us so distinct an idea of the character, that I shall quote the passage at large.
>
> …His cap off: his head seemly rounded tonster-wise: fair kembed that with a sponge daintily dipt in a little capon's greace was finely smoothed, to make it shine like a mallard's wing…every ruff stood up like a wafer. A side [i.e., long] gown of Kendale green, after the freshness of the year now, gathered at the neck with a narrow gorget, fastened afore with a white clasp and a keeper close up to the chin;…His gown had side [i.e., long] sleeves down to mid-leg, slit from the shoulder to the hand, and lined with white cotton. His doublet-sleeves of black worsted: upon them a pair of points of tawny chamlet laced along the wrist with blue threaden poinets….[5]

I have quoted perhaps a third of this third-hand description. Note that by "character," Percy means the fictional character. I think. Percy notes: "The reader will remember that this was not a real minstrel, but only one personating that character: his or-

---

4   Godwin, *Life of Geoffrey Chaucer*, 2:584.
5   Thomas Percy, *Reliques of Ancient English Poetry: Consisting of Old Heroic Ballads, Songs, and other Pieces of our earlier Poets*, 3 vols. (London: J. Dodsley, 1765), 1:xix–xx.

naments therefore were only such as outwardly reproduce those of a real Minstrel."[6] What does it mean to "outwardly reproduce [the ornaments] of a real Minstrel"? Is this or is this not a description of a minstrel? And is Godwin's illustration, or is it not, a portrait of Chaucer?

Godwin has been much criticized in Chaucer scholarship, a unanimity of contempt parallel to that heaped on Urry's 1721 edition of Chaucer.[7] Much of this seems due to Nicholas Harris Nicolas's biography in the popular Aldine edition of 1866:

> In his ardour, Godwin has however both overlooked and mistaken some material circumstances: and his confidence in the fact not only induced him to case unmerited reproaches upon the learned Tyrwhitt for merely presuming to express a doubt on the subject, but to give the reins to his own imagining by describing Chaucer's motives for seeking the interview [with Petrarch], the interview itself, the feelings of the two Poets, and the very tone and substance of their conversation.[8]

Most of Nicolas's more strident criticism of Godwin comes early in his Memoir, where readers are more apt to be exposed to it.[9] Nicolas's opinions were confirmed by Thomas Lounsbury in

---

[6] Ibid., 1:xx, note.
[7] See Joseph A. Dane, "A Consensus on the Worst Edition: Urry's 1721 Edition," in Joseph A. Dane, *Who Is Buried in Chaucer's Tomb? Studies in the Reception of Chaucer's Book* (East Lansing: Michigan State University Press, 1998), 116–21.
[8] *The Poetical Works of Geoffrey Chaucer*, Vol. 1, ed. Richard Morris, with Memoir by Sir Harris Nicolas (London: Bell, 1866).
[9] Nicolas, Memoir, *The Poetical Works of Geoffrey Chaucer*: "If Godwin's extract from that Letter were a faithful version of the original, his argument would have weight" (11); "It would be profitless to follow Godwin farther through the web he has spun out of his own imagination on this subject, or to cite against himself his own equally baseless vision of Chaucer having first heard of the existence of the Decameron from Petrarch in 1373...." (15–16).

1892,[10] and they are now more or less canonized through Derek Brewer's Critical Heritage series.[11]

Godwin insists he has taken nothing second hand:

> Throughout this publication care has been taken to make no reference to any book, which has not been actually consulted, and the reference verified by inspection.[12]

But this narrative has nothing to do with evidence, however evidence might be characterized — first- or second-hand, internal or external, primary or secondary:

> It is likely that Thomas Chaucer stood by, and saw the remains of his father quietly deposited in the grave. it is likely that his funeral was attended by his nephew, Beaufort, bishop of Lincoln, and the brother of the bishop, the Lord Great Chamberlain of England. If these circumstances add nothing to the genuine honours of Chaucer, and if we confess the name of the poet to be greater than all the denominations which monarchs can bestow, yet the most fastidious philosopher may be gratified to see things as they actually were, and to be an attendant in imagination upon the herse of Chaucer.[13]

---

10 Thomas Lounsbury, *Studies in Chaucer*, 3 vols. (New York: Harper, 1892), 1:192: "It is perhaps the earliest, though unhappily not the latest or even the largest, illustration of that species of biography in which the lack of information about the man who is its alleged subject is counterbalanced by long disquisitions about anything or everything he shared in or saw, or may have shared in or seen. [These biographies] are not written to be read....Men with good intentions are always expecting to read them, but never find for it just the right time." See more recently, Richard Osberg, "False Memories: The Dream of Chaucer and Chaucer's Dream," *Studies in Medievalism* 19 (2010): 204–25.

11 Derek Brewer, Chaucer: *The Critical Heritage*, 2 vols. (London: Routledge and Kegan Paul, 1978), 1:237–47.

12 Godwin, *Life of Geoffrey Chaucer*, 1:xv.

13 Ibid., 2:559.

Now that I have finished my introduction, this is a section that should write itself. There is nothing really to "point out" to a reader who has even glanced at the Chaucer portrait, read even a paragraph or two of Godwin. I am wondering as I look at this portrait whether there is anything I really wish to know about it, or wish to formulate about it — what Godwin thought of this, or what he may have felt his readers should think of it, or what they did think of it, what the artist or engraver was thinking or whether they were thinking at all. And whether any of that is going to change what my own readers will think of it.

I could, of course, follow the usual path with this engraving. I could point out the difference between the engraving and the original — that is, how the engraving in the book is a sophistication and simplification of what it portrays. Or how the original is itself a sophistication and simplification of what it pretends to portray. Perhaps there is an irony in the original missed by the engraver, and mass production hides this detail. I could show also that Godwin's Chaucer (the Chaucer Godwin creates) is perfectly represented by this grotesquely anachronistic portrait.

I could investigate the difference between what is laughably obvious to us, or what we pretend is laughably obvious, and what finally is not. Shakespeare's anachronisms do not bother us, nor do those of Homer. We view these things through a dual perspective — on the one hand accepting the illusions completely, and on the other hand, perfectly aware of their stupidities, just as Samuel Johnson and Samuel Taylor Coleridge tell us we do. It is not the seamlessness of these illustrations we enjoy, but their failures.

But did that early-nineteenth-century reader, viewing this Tudor mock-up of Chaucer, see the same thing? I keep hearing Furnivall in all this — to us, the epitome of the Victorian scholar, his Chaucer "closer to me than any other poet, except Tennyson."[14] That unimaginable nexus of Chaucer, Tennyson,

---

14 F.J. Furnivall, *A Temporary Preface to the Six-text Edition of Chaucer's Canterbury Tales*, Chaucer Society Publ, ser. 2, pt. 3. (London: N. Trübner & Co., 1868), 3.

and Furnivall. What did those nineteenth-century readers think or see?

I could, more likely, follow through on my suggestion above, and show, as I have done with a number of other Chaucer works, that once a negative evaluation is proposed, there are few who bother to challenge it (see notes 9 and 10 above). By defining something as "outside" a tradition, a community of scholars simplifies that tradition and clarifies what it is; thus, if we are interested in Chaucer's biography, we need no longer refer to Godwin. Only a crank would seek to bring such works back in: Godwin's biography is not good, and there is nothing more to say. I could say, by contrast, Godwin's portrait is as accurate as any other of the time, except more sincere in its obvious anachronisms: it depicts precisely what stands between us and the history we seek.

Thomas Chaucer, reflecting perhaps on the end of things, as his father's body is lowered into the grave.

part 2

BIBLIOGRAPHY AND BOOK HISTORY

CHAPTER 4

The Singularities of Books and Reading

*The Canterbury Male Regle, taken on its own terms rather
than as a pale reflection of Hoccleve's "original," is a complete
and coherent poem with its own priorities...[and should be
read] as an extracted lyric with its own independent life, one
that is informed by its manuscript and cultural contexts.*
— Peter Brown, "Hoccleve in Canterbury"[1]

*Nous ne savons pas, dit Bouvard, ce qui se passe dans
notre ménage, et nous prétendons découvrir quels étaient
les cheveux et les amours du duc d'Angoulême.*
— Flaubert, *Bouvard et Pécuchet*

The following chapter concerns a number of familiar bibliographical entities: editorial versions, compilations or tract volumes, annotated works. These are the forms whereby books (the abstract repeatable things produced in editions) become transformed into or considered in terms of book-copies (singular, material entities with individualized histories), and the text (that abstract repeatable entity available to multiple readers) becomes a singular reader's experience of it. The generalities and universality that should be eliminated by focusing on the singular object are then smuggled back into the conversation: the

---

1   Peter Brown, "Hoccleve in Canterbury," in *New Directions In Medieval Manuscript Studies and Reading Practices: Essays in Honor of Derek Pearsall* (Notre Dame: Notre Dame University Press, 2014), 408–11, on Hoccleve's *Male Regle* in Huntington Library, HM MS 111.

singular object serves as a model for our understanding of other singular objects.

The popularity in scholarship of the material book has consequences. We can certainly understand the phrase "material books" without the qualifying "copies," but the phrase "material book" is misleading. Such a phrase ought to refer to a unique object: an individual book-copy. Yet scholars speak of this in a different manner, as if the phrase were "material Book" (whatever that might mean). Although I can disparage the portentous upper-case B and all its real and illusory implications, I recognize that the comforting notion of The Book allows for generalization, and that some form of generalization, even specious, is crucial to scholarly communication. Without it, the singularity of that book-object leads to the singularity of the scholarly utterance, and with that, scholarly contributions become scholarly performance, that is to say, art and art perhaps in the worst sense.

I will treat the books and our purported experience of them here as products of the same intellectual or scholarly act; in each case, the concepts or the objects that respond to them create what might be a secondary singular. We see an object in history; we abstract it (in all senses) by considering it on a linguistic or conceptual level; in other words, we make our singular object and our singular experience with it communicable. But our attempts to generate this abstract communicable entity act paradoxically to recover the level of singularity our very act of communication once seemed to destroy. We end, in our scholarly sophistications and machinations, with the same singular experience we began with, all the while seeming to follow D.F. McKenzie's appealing, but finally vacuous formulation: all printers, and by extension all their books and texts, are "alike in being different."[2]

---

2   D.F. McKenzie, "Printers of the Mind: Some Notes on Bibliographical Theories and Printing-House Practices," *Studies in Bibliography* 22 (1969): 1–75, at 63 (often reprinted), and my critique "Bibliographers of the Mind," in *Blind Impressions: Methods and Mythologies in Book History* (Philadelphia: University of Pennsylvania Press, 2013), 58–72.

Books and Book-Copies

We cannot hold a book, whether Shakespeare's First Folio, the Gutenberg Bible, or the first edition of Beckett's *Waiting for Godot*. We cannot see it, or experience any of those dilettantish smells and textures that only older book historians and scholars were permitted to mention, as they conflated the object they held or beheld with the abstract book of their histories. We can only imagine that "thing" referred to, say, in an STC entry, or in any entry written according to the principles of descriptive bibliography.³ It is an abstraction produced in our reconstruction of history, or in some sense what actually produces history and the objects of history. A writer, a printer — these people imagine what books are. A distributer, bookseller, scholar — these continue this fiction. As bibliographers (the role most readers of this chapter will likely adopt), most of our arguments are about such abstractions, that is to say, books and their descriptions, not the raw material we take as a given.

What we hold and see is a book-copy, a material object that can only become a book when we place it in history, whether the real history of the past we study or the future history, when, say, a printer imagines that book exemplified on booksellers' shelves: it is one of a group, a series, a collection, repeatable (or so we imagine), exemplary of that series or group and interchangeable with any other member of this series. We speak of a book or its literary analogue, the text, which others can experience simultaneously; what we hold and experience, by contrast, remains singular.

There is something unsettling and even irritating about this state of affairs; the thing we study (the book) seems inaccessible to us, but paradoxically accessible to anyone, at any time.⁴ I have no more claim on a bibliographical description in the English

---

3 In theory, but not in practice, such descriptions are not copy-specific, but refer to an abstract "ideal copy"; see Fredson Bowers, *Principles of Bibliographical Description* (Princeton: Princeton University Press, 1949), 113–17.

4 Cf. the notion of "accessibility" of David Scott Kastan, *Shakespeare and the Book* (Cambridge: Cambridge University Press, 2001), 4: "literature exists,

Short-Title Catalogue (ESTC) or even the images of a book in Early English Books Online (EEBO) than any other scholar, graduate student, or even undergraduate enrolled in a university that subscribes to these databases.

So I pick up that book-copy and try to imagine something else that will lend my own experience some privilege or advantage over other scholars. Another series, one that exists both in and apart from the material world. History. Use. Sales and losses. There are so many features of this thing I hold that place it within history. The binding, never part of the book until at least the eighteenth century. Stamps on the binding. Damage to the binding, never exactly repeatable. Even the paper might be unique, distinct from that in any other copy of the same book. The smell of the library that houses it. My own fingerprints on the pages. Ownership marks. The history of provenance, which connects only tentatively with other histories (other book-copies in the owner's library, shelf-marks, a rebinding plan). And finally the annotations and defacements I find in that book, personal, unique, redolent of history, it seems, but as I will show here, perhaps not. This copy exists in history, yet when someone else examines this unique copy, it will be something else.

Text: Preliminary Definitions

The literary equivalent of what I call a "book" is a "text"; books are distinguished from material book-copies in the same way texts are distinguished from their material variants. I realize this is a simple and restricted definition of the word text. I pose it here and I have relied on it in the past because I am wary of the way slippage in this term allows us to extend in a dubious and self-serving way our grand hermeneutical discussions: our metaphors congeal into objective realities — sub-texts, textuality, the web and woof of history.

---

in any useful sense only and always in its materializations;…only as texts are realized materially are they accessible."

My definition is based on the notion or verbal construction "literary text." A text so-defined is something that is perfectly repeatable and reproducible on whatever we consider a standard keyboard to be.[5] It has nothing to do with what that text implies, how it is constructed, what it can be linked to, what it means, what we can make it mean, and who makes it mean that. I am not disparaging the value of these things; I am only trying to find a language that will enable me to discuss them more clearly.

What you see in a book is ink on paper. What you see on a computer screen are marks produced by however marks are produced on it. Those are concrete material things and form book-copies or their equivalent. Because they exist in the real world, they are unstable, varying in temperature, humidity, positioning, ownership, cycled though the digestive systems of insects, dismembered, repaired. A text, by contrast, is an abstraction in the same way a book is. It is repeatable and replaceable. Considered as texts, those varying marks on the computer screen or in the book are at least potentially the same. A text is not lost because its material support is destroyed. And this last sentence as a text is the same whether seen by me on my screen or by you in a printed book. We can construct or repeat the text on a keyboard, even if some of those keyboards may be imaginary. And that text will be the same no matter what keyboard it is constructed on, or what font is chosen, or how the whole thing is laid out on a page or screen, or further, how many errors we make in each singular attempt to type it out.

This is a narrow definition of text. In literary-critical history, the word seemed to undergo a transformation about the time I was entering graduate school in the mid-seventies: perhaps it was recovering its etymological sense, which then complicated what was the bland metaphorical one. Textus — textile. Something woven. It gathered in another early medieval use: Textus

---

[5] See the once common distinction work/text, whereby "work" is the abstract verbal construct that is realized imperfectly through its variant texts or versions, e.g., in Paul Zumthor, *Essai de poétique médiévale* (Paris: Seuil, 1972), 70–75.

= the Bible, both the word of God and something of crucial importance and something to be interpreted; a hermeneutical object rather than this abstract product of mere repetition; something worthy of the scholar's attention rather than something produced by the scholar's attention. It could also be mystified by other terms such as Benjamin's *aura,* an association that would expand the scope of each of these.

There is thus a reluctance among us to give up all this for a more restrictive definition. We are unwilling also to give up the flexibility we find in words such as book, a flexibility that has been particularly exploited in French scholarship: nothing in English has quite matched the dizzying leaps of logic and subject matter enabled by Lucien Febvre and Henri-Jean Martin's use of "livre," "le livre," and "Le Livre" in their *L'Apparition du Livre* of 1958, although the phrase "The Book" in the proper solemn contexts occasionally comes close.[6] The new emphasis on materiality in bibliography leads to a denigration of what is opposed to it: Kastan's disparaging comments on the notion of a non-material entity in book history, where "ideal" is conflated with our nostalgia for "real presence" of Shakespeare.[7] What we communicate are not these materialities: what we communicate are ideas.

We can or do argue then that because something can be a literary text, therefore it *is* a literary text. Texts are things that "can be interpreted," and things that "are able to be interpreted" are "to be interpreted" pure and simple. Thus Brown's statement quoted at the head of this chapter, and Randall McLeod's even stronger dictum on the version of *King Lear* embodied in a text implied by the two quartos:

---

6 See Lucien Febvre and Henry-Jean Martin, *L'Apparition du Livre* (Paris, 1958), trans. David Gerard, *The Coming of the Book: The Impact of Printing 1450–1800,* eds. Geoffrey Nowell Smith and David Wooton (London: Verso, 1976), and my critique in *The Myth of Print Culture: Essays on Evidence, Textuality, and Bibliographical Method* (Toronto: University of Toronto Press, 2003), 21–31.

7 Kastan, *Shakespeare and the Book,* 121, 124.

The aim will be simply to detect whether, when we stand aside from editorial guidance, we find coherently differentiable aesthetic characteristics in Q and F.

The extent to which we can bears an inverse relationship to the confidence we should owe the theory that Q is merely a corruption of X.[8]

If such claims were accepted — that what can conceivably be interpreted ought to be interpreted — and if everything we and other scholars saw and experienced were equally interesting and compelling, as in the last few decades it sometimes is claimed to be,[9] there would be hardly a reason to study the past at all, since any banalities (even our own) would do as well.

Annotations as Text

Gabriel Harvey's annotations have been the subject of scholarship since the 1940s and were give a boost in 1990 with a now classic article by Lisa Jardine and Anthony Grafton, subtitled "How Gabriel Harvey Read his Livy." With articles such as this one, the responses of real historical readers came back to the critical foreground, joining those contemporary readers of the first reader-response theory of I.A. Richards (the actual responses, right or wrong, of his students), and supplanting those often imaginary readers created in the days of reader-response criticism.[10]

---

8   Randall Mcleod, "*Gon.* No more, the text is foolish," in *The Division of the Kingdoms: Shakespeare's Two Versions of King Lear,* eds. Gary Taylor and Michael Warren (Oxford: Clarendon Press, 1983), 157.

9   Roger Chartier, *The Author's Hand and the Printer's Mind,* trans. Lydia G. Cochrane (Cambridge: Polity Press, 2013), 152: "At the end of the twentieth century, when the obsessive theme of the infinite polysemy of texts invaded literary criticism, it led to interpreting every anomaly as the expression of a subtle intention, a voluntary error or a note of parody intended by the author."

10 Lisa Jardine and Anthony Grafton, "'Studied for Action': How Gabriel Harvey Read his Livy," *Past and Present* 129, no. 1 (1990): 30–78; Harold Wilson,

There are of course thousands of books and manuscripts with such annotations readily available in rare book library shelves, and even on our own shelves. For the most part, these have not yet been organized or analyzed in any significant way, and until recently, such annotations could only be studied by readers with convenient home addresses or on research grants to major collections.[11] Because of this limited access, the chances of scholars stumbling upon or focusing on the marginalia of the same book-copy in numbers sufficient to make critical discussion possible were small, and there has thus been little opportunity to construct a counter-argument to any but the most popular of articles bearing on these matters (in the case of Jardine and Grafton, such arguments have been made).[12] All is changing with the digitization of major collections: annotations are as readily available to scholars as texts once were (at least, to those whose home institutions subscribe to these databases); conferences are dedicated to them;[13] and critical discussion will flow, at

---

"Gabriel Harvey's Method of Annotating his Books," *Harvard Library Bulletin* 2, no. 3 (1948): 344–68. I.A. Richards, *Principles of Literary Criticism* (London: Kegan Paul, 1924).

11 Robert Alston, *Books with Manuscript: A Short Title Catalogue of Books with Manuscript Notes in the British Library* (London: British Library, 1994); Annotated Books Online: A Digital Archive of Early Modern Annotation, www.annotatedbooksonline.com; Carl Grindley, "Reading Piers Plowman C-Text Annotations: Notes toward the Classification of Printed and Written Marginalia in Texts from the British Isles, 1300–1641," in T*he Medieval Professional Reader at Work: Evidence from Manuscripts of Chaucer, Langland, Kempe, and Gower*, eds. Kathryn Kerby-Fulton and Maidie Hilmo (Victoria: University of Victoria, 2001), 77–91; Megan Cook, "How Francis Thynne Read His Chaucer," *Journal of the Early Book Society for the Study of Manuscripts and Printing History* 15 (2012): 215–44; and William H. Sherman, *Used Books: Marking Readers in Renaissance England* (Philadelphia: University of Pennsylvania Press, 2007).

12 Chris Stamatakis, "'With diligent studie, but sportingly': How Gabriel Harvey Read His Castiglione," *Journal of the Northern Renaissance* 5 (2013), http://www.northernrenaissance.org/with-diligent-studie-but-sportingly-how-gabriel-harvey-read-his-castiglione/.

13 Such as the Early Annotated Books in California Special Collections: An Exploratory Symposium, William Andrews Clark Memorial Library, Los Angeles, December 12, 2014.

least if some sort of canon could be established or determined: not *those* annotations, which are trivial, but *these*.[14]

With this newfound interest have come assertions that there is something uniquely modern or even postmodern about both the interest and the phenomenon: Chartier, for example, suggests that texts created materially by their authors are rare before the eighteenth century.[15] Yet even this simple statement depends on what we mean by "authorial" and whether the text of the marginalia we find in any particular book can be called "authored" — that is, whether it is produced by or copied by its scribe. It also somewhat mischievously defines away all contrary evidence in the invocation of "exceptionality." There seems little that is new or characteristically modern, in any sense of that word, about the composition of marginalia considered as the creation of the purely authorial text; and the notion of the marginal gloss overtaking the generating text is a well-worn and often parodied medieval cliché.[16] The question nonetheless remains as to whether the text of the marginalia or the new composite text formed of text and gloss are legitimate and interesting objects of study in a social sense, that is, not only interesting to me or to you, but rather to a community of readers.

Enthusiasts of print culture have argued that printing changed the earlier relation of gloss/text found in manuscripts or at least our view of that relationship. The printed text, now replicable, could be subject to different treatments, with the same text supporting different annotations. It would thus more

---

14 H.J. Jackson, *Marginalia: Readers Writing in Books* (New Haven: Yale University Press, 2001), on the notion of "value" of annotations; Jackson concedes the study makes "no claim to being exhaustive or representative or even statistically significant" (6).
15 "Before the mid-eighteenth century, authorial manuscripts are rare and were preserved for exceptional reasons" (Chartier, *Author's Hand*, 74). I am not sure how seriously Chartier intends this claim, since there are numerous medieval authors (e.g., Bede and Aquinas) whose hands have been identified, and the statement is almost meaningless in regard to anonymous texts.
16 Chaucer's "Nun's Priest's Tale" provides hundreds of lines of amusing and aimless commentary on Chaunticleer's simple dream.

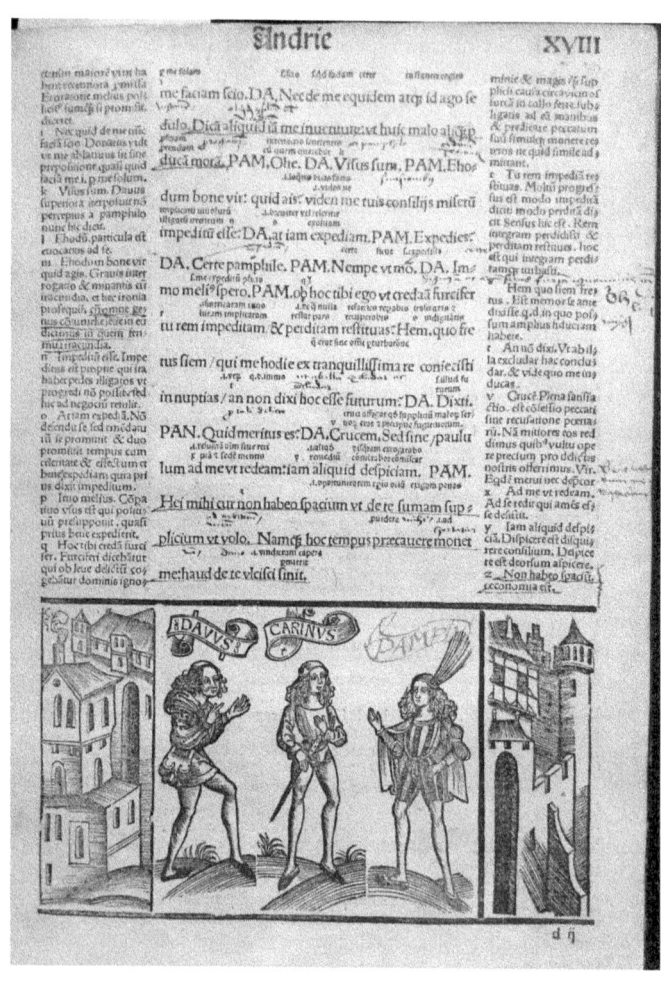

Figure 5. Gruninger Terence (1499) with hand-written interlinear commentary.

clearly embody something like textual reception than would a unique manuscript. The printed text, particularly one with what bibliophiles used to call "ample" margins, foresaw and demanded readers' particularized and singular annotations, which would be instantly distinguished from the text through the distinction print/scribe in a way that earlier annotations were not. Print changed everything, enforcing a split between printed, replicable text and unique, hand-written gloss even in the means of producing each. Such assertions may be true. But as is the case with many other appealing theses, I would rather argue against these than for them. In this copy of Gruninger's fifteenth-century Terence, the annotating student merely continues what is already begun in the printed text.

Such criticism, whether it involves historical readers such as Gabriel Harvey or contemporary ones, both real and imaginary, is based on singularity. That singularity can be generalized, if, say, we describe what authors were doing by allegorizing our own reactions to this literature: annotations and individual reactions constitute evidence, and they are thus valid indexes of features that could be or were once variously attributed to the author or to the personified text. But routine articles (that is, those not by Stanley Fish or Michael Riffaterre) often paid only lip service to the notion of universality when discussing marginalia or hardly dealt with it at all: the value was in the singular performance, not in communicable content, and there was little difference between such a performance and an article on "the structural integrity of this overlooked poem" from two decades earlier. Students and colleagues often admire these, not because they learn anything from them or about their own responses to literature, but rather because they see something that they dream of doing themselves.[17]

---

17 In 1986, Mark Schoenfeld, then a graduate student, reviewing a book by one of my former colleagues astutely noted: "Every graduate student should read this book; it will prove to them that anything can be published."

The Singular Reader

Kevin Sharpe's *Reading Revolutions* came out in 2001.[18] What followed this intimidating title were 600 pages not evidencing a revolution, but rather documenting what appeared to be ordinary annotations of a book by a William Drake (likely few of Sharpe's civilian readers had ever heard of him). On the face of it, Drake's annotations seemed to prove what most of us knew: (1) readers mark in books they own; (2) it's not always clear what they are annotating or why; and (3) some are more interesting than others. The very unsystematic and non-committal nature of these annotations could be used to support any conclusion one would like to form: in Sharpe's case, political ones.

Sharpe's study was not a critique: there was no one making a case that needed to be considered in depth, nor anyone claiming, for example, that William Drake did not annotate his books, or that Renaissance readers did not write marginalia or think about books they read. Sharpe's book was rather what medieval writers would have called a "Meditation," or what late nineteenth-century authors might have called an "Essay." It was a manifestation of its subject, where the gloss (Sharpe's) overwhelms the rather banal text (Drake's) serving as its origin. The revolution this book marks is one contemporary with Sharpe — a revolutionary way in which scholars could discover, define, and canonize texts.

The study of annotations in and of itself has long been a staple of bibliography, cataloguing, and librarianship. "Marks in Books" (the phrase is from Roger Stoddard) can tell you how books were corrected at press, who gave what book to whom, how much a book cost, who bound it, who sold it, or where it sat on early library shelves.[19] These are the standard details earlier

---

18 Kevin Sharpe, *Reading Revolutions: The Politics of Reading in Early Modern England* (New Haven: Yale University Press, 2001). See, also, Kevin Sharpe and Steven N. Zwicker, eds., *Reading, Society and Politics in Early Modern England* (New York: Cambridge University Press, 2003).

19 See Roger E. Stoddard, *Marks in Books* (Cambridge: Harvard University Press, 1985) and David Pearson, *Provenance Research in Book History* (New

found only in bibliographical notes or library catalogues; most professional literary scholars in the past would find them pedestrian. You can tell, for example, *what* Gabriel Harvey did while reading Livy: he wrote notes. But this does not tell you *how* Harvey read his Livy. You cannot determine what early readers thought important simply by looking at what they marked up in their books. Nor, until you begin to survey many book-copies like this one, can you tell whether Harvey's actions are generalizable — that is, whether what other readers did was in any way comparable to what Harvey did. Readers and even printers have a tendency to see significance where there very well may be none.[20]

I consider my own library. Nearly all of my ordinary scholarly books contain annotations of some kind. If they are books I read early in my career, or books I read late and was going to review, that marginalia consists largely of full sentences. I can summarize or dismiss an entire chapter, my notes tell me, with a single statement. I can condense an entire book by repeating what I mark throughout as "thesis" or sometimes "evidence." The indignant question marks tell me what I can cite, evincing exasperation or melodramatic despair at the current state of scholarship.

Yet these annotations — the text I create out of my personal copy of the book — say absolutely nothing that is not better expressed in my published note or review; that note or review may

---

Castle: Oak Knoll, 1998).

20 See Claire R. Kinney, "Thomas Speght's Renaissance Chaucer and the Solaas of Sentence in *Troilus and Criseyde*," in *Refiguring Chaucer in the Renaissance*, ed. Theresa M. Krier (Gainesville: University Press of Florida, 1998), 66–86, on the manicules or pointing fists in the 1602 Chaucer. Cf. my "Fists and Filiations in Chaucer Folios (1532–1602)" (1991); rpt. *Out of Sorts: On Typography and Print Culture* (Philadelphia: University of Pennsylvania Press, 2011), 105–17, demonstrating that these in fact originated as purely decorative printing marks, with no meaning whatsoever. A similar point is made by Peter Stallybrass and Roger Chartier, "Reading and Authorship: The Circulation of Shakespeare (1590–1619)," in *A Concise Companion to Shakespeare and the Text*, ed. Andrew Murphy (London: Blackwell, 2007), 49–52.

be coherent, my hand-written notes are not. Comparing both, you could argue that they chart how I reduced a complex book to incoherent notes and transformed those into a coherent albeit oversimplified review. But everyone knows that already and no one believes a review or citation gives a fair picture of a book. It is a re-statement, a re-use, a falsification, condensation — many words will do. Tracing its origins tells us nothing we want to know or need to know.

I have a student copy of Xenophon's *Anabasis* signed by my father when he was an undergraduate in the mid-1930s, and if you ever want to take up Greek, I highly recommend this edition. My father was the second owner; I am the third. There are pencilled annotations throughout Xenophon's first two books, with occasional elaborate notes on rules governing verb forms. There are also pencilled annotations on every verb and verb-form in the text. Looking over these today, I realize that I am looking at my own annotations when I (miraculously) had a one-year job in which I had to teach this text. Behind those notes are those of my father, and past those are the notes of the anonymous previous owner. The only thing these notes evidence is that both were much better Greek scholars as undergraduates than I was as a professor. Did I ever seriously doubt this?

Composite Texts and Modern Readers

For medievalists and book historians, the key terms in this area were defined in a series of studies by A.I. Doyle and M.B. Parkes on the notion of *compilatio,* and by Paul Needham on composite volumes, variously defined as *Sammelbände,* tract volumes, pamphlet volumes, or miscellanies. Doyle and Parkes were concerned with independent and autonomous texts (books) bound together in a single book-copy; Needham was concerned initially with printed fragments bound in as binding material in other books. Each considered the resultant composite volume as an historical entity, reflecting the literary practices of a particular period (medieval texts, early printed texts). Many studies have followed up on these notions, among them, two book-length studies that expanded the definitions in order to consider and interpret these works within their histories of reception. Jeffrey Todd Knight deals with books that are ready-made in history, deliberately combining autonomous literary texts; Arthur Bahr extends the notion of composite volumes or texts to include those compiled not only in history, but also in the attention of the modern reader. When I was asked to review one of these, I realized I was reproducing unconsciously the same scholarly method (a form of *petitio principii*) I would end up critiquing in both.[21]

Bahr's book selects topics that at first glance seem wildly diverse: the writer/compiler Andrew Horn (a civil servant), London (both justified by Ralph Hanna's *London Literature* of 2005),[22] the Auchinleck MS and Chaucer's *Canterbury Tales* (perennial subjects of English medievalists), and the Trentham MS of Gower. What is interesting about all these subjects is the simple fact of their association: they are all compilations in some sense, although not in the historical sense defined by Doyle and Parkes, and they can thus be imagined to belong to the same genre. Bahr thus does with his own subjects what he claims the

---

21 Arthur Bahr, *Fragments and Assemblages: Forming Compilations of Medieval London* (Chicago: University of Chicago Press, 2013); my review, *Studies in the Age of Chaucer* 16 (2014): 279–83; Jeffrey Todd Knight, *Bound to Read: Compilations, Collections and the Making of Renaissance Literature* (Philadelphia: University of Pennsylvania Press, 2013); A.I. Doyle and M.B. Parkes, "The Production of Copies of the Canterbury Tales and the Confessio Amantis in the Early Fifteenth Century," in *Medieval Scribes, Manuscripts and Libraries: Essays Presented to N.R. Ker,* eds. M.B. Parkes and A.G. Watson, 163–210 (London: Scolar Press, 1978); M.P. Parkes, "The Influence of the Concepts of *Ordinatio* and *Compilatio* on the Development of the Book," in *Medieval Learning and Literature: Essays Presented to R.W. Hunt,* eds. J.J.G. Alexander and M.T. Gibson, 115–41 (Oxford: Clarendon Press, 1976). Paul Needham, *The Printer and the Pardoner* (Washington, DC: Library of Congress, 1986). See also, among many studies, Alexandra Gillespie, *Print Culture and the Medieval Author: Chaucer, Lydgate, and Their Books, 1473–1557* (Oxford: Oxford University Press, 2006).

22 Ralph Hanna, *London Literature, 1300–1380* (Cambridge: Cambridge University Press, 2005).

compilers do with theirs; he combines them in a singular object that is interpretable. This genre is not confined to history, since it is of our own making: "a compilation as I define it relies on the perspective of its readers, who must ultimately determine whether to interpret its given assemblage of texts in compilational terms."[23] The only difference between his own text and his object texts is that the conventions of the genre in which Bahr works require a direct statement of the principle of coherence. Bahr explicitly performs the genre he is studying:

> This, then is my definition of a compilation: the assemblage of multiple discrete works into a larger structure whose formal interplay of textual and material parts makes available some version of those literary effects described above… metaphorical potentialities [and] resistance to paraphrase…. How those historical vectors inform and complicate the formal arrangements that together compose the visible compilation, I argue, constitutes both a potential source of aesthetic resonance and an invitation to literary analysis.[24]

Our reaction to these things, whose association is of our own creation, is finally what matters: "[our] delight in what I have called the literary can be found, and care for it nurtured, in the many ways in which codicological form and textual content create and complicate one another in particular medieval manuscripts."[25] These statements are all incontestable — some because they are vague, others because they are completely personal and singular. It is useless to argue about what causes delight.

I cannot read the pencilled details on a marginal diagram an early reader drew of Xenophon's line of battle. Apparently, in 1935, schoolboys were more interested in military formations than we are.

---

23 Bahr, *Fragments and Assemblages*, 11. So, also ibid., 247: a compilation is marked by "broad, structural, and thematic connections."
24 Ibid., 10–11.
25 Ibid., 257.

Knight's *Bound to Read* can be seen as an historicized version of the approach in Bahr. The construction of a compilation is not arbitrary, nor something unique to modern readers. Rather, our modern fascination with them is a legitimate reflection of something that existed within the period we are examining:

> [My] premise is the observation…that books have not always existed in discrete, self-enclosed units.… the printed work was relatively malleable and experimental.…Every bound volume was a unique, customized assemblage.
>
> [I] will argue first that books in early print culture were relatively open-ended…and second that the attendant practices of compiling and collecting came to have an important structural impact on the production of Renaissance literature.[26]

The familiar villain here is that *bête noir* of modern studies in book history and so-called "print culture" — fixity. Such "fixity" (always disparaged) is placed in opposition to whatever one is studying, whether that is a period, or rather a group of scholars.[27] Books, as we moderns understand them, are not books as understood by all scholars and even bibliographers of the past. They provide new contexts for individual scholars to develop or perform readings, for example, the *Sammelband* containing *Venus and Adonis* at the Huntington Library (HM MS 59000–59002): "Read against this already composite text, the Shakespearean portion of the volume — *Venus and Adonis* in particular — takes on a particular tone."[28] What this tone is, and who

---

26 Knight, *Bound to Read*, 4–5, 9.
27 See, e.g., Adrian Johns, Introduction, *The Nature of the Book: Print and Knowledge in the Making* (Chicago: University of Chicago Press, 1998), 1–47. For a recent case study of how such marginalia imply a "repurposing" of texts, see Laura Estill, "The Urge to Organize Early Modern Miscellanies: Reading Cotgrave's *The English Treasury of Wit and Language*," *Papers of the Bibliographical Society of America* 112, no. 1 (2018): 27–73.
28 Knight, *Bound to Read*, 74.

has access to it is not clear; nor does it seem that anyone could argue against its existence.

These two books take the same general type of subject matter: objects of concern that no longer obey the bounds of those neatly categorized objects we used to call literary texts or catalogued books. For Bahr, recontextualization is equivalent to rereading. And in this critical climate, there is no appreciable difference between the civil servant Horn, a manuscript of Gower we likely don't know at all, and one of the most canonical works in English literature:

> This book...contends that we can productively bring comparable interpretive strategies to bear on the formal characteristics of both physical manuscripts and literary works.
>
> I define compilation, not as an objective quality...but rather as a mode of perceiving such forms so as to disclose an interpretably meaningful arrangement....[29]

For Knight, those interpretive readings seem to be demanded by the materials we are looking at. We are thus privileged over early readers who wrongly projected their own prejudices onto their literary materials (the notion of the integral text); we rightly project our own.

My father's notes claim that the verb in Xenophon is a form of the verb "to send," not "to be." I pencil in (or once pencilled in) my gratitude, by adding that it is a second aorist.

Conclusion

The texts we once naively read (in all senses) were never stable, and we were perhaps uneasy with our tentative assumptions that they were. There were things like the order of tales in the *Can-*

---

29 Bahr, *Fragments and Assemblages*, 1, 3.

terbury Tales that were bothersome. Even the "fixing" of *Piers Plowman* in three states by Skeat in his edition of 1869 did not contain its fluidity, and soon, another form, the so-called Z version, appeared.[30] The more one studied any of these texts — *Piers Plowman*, the *Canterbury Tales*, the versions of *The Song of Roland* — the less that mouvance or fluidity seemed accidental, and the more it seemed essential; it was what finally made whatever we called "the text" untranscribable. All the once-standard groups and sequences of the *Canterbury Tales* (Kittredge's Marriage Group, for example) — these were mirages: real, as mirages go, but nothing that could be shared with anyone not suffering the same delusion. How could there be a Marriage Group in the *Canterbury Tales* when we knew so little of what marriage might have entailed or whether that had anything to do with what we call by the same name today?

This is the critical atmosphere into which Doyle and Parkes's article was inserted. The groups and fragments conventionally defined and discussed in Chaucer's Canterbury Tales gave way to groupings that were less ideational than material and codicological: the ones defined in the late-nineteenth century by Henry Bradshaw and quietly canonized in twentieth-century editions as A–I, or I–X.[31] Any of these intellectual or codicological groupings (the *Canterbury Tales* fragments, Hammond's Oxford group of manuscripts, Kittredge's thematic groups) provide us with fresh associations.

The term *compilatio* also makes intelligible a number of formerly neglected and often recalcitrant objects. It has the advantage of seeming to connect one branch of study (in humanistic context, the relatively "hard" fields of codicology, paleography, manuscript study) with another one (the "softer" field of literary criticism and appreciation). And it does so at a time when the

---

30 Now available, incorporating many of the problems of parallel-text editions in A.V.C. Schmidt, ed., *Piers Plowman: A Parallel-Text Edition of the A, B, C and Z versions*, 4 vols. (London: Longman, 1995–2008).

31 Henry Bradshaw, "The Skeleton of Chaucer's Canterbury Tales: An Attempt to the Distinguish the Several Fragments of the Work as Left by the Author" (1868), in *Collected Papers*, 102–48 (Cambridge: University Press, 1889).

rejection of familiar literary criticism in favor of so-called material culture seemed almost complete.[32]

I certainly am not the only scholar who went through a period of imagining that my career could consist largely of performing "readings" of canonical texts. Either I would read each text according to a particular critical school or method, or I would read one of them according to ten different schools or methods.[33] In the 1960s, there seemed an unlimited supply of material: "The Structure of X," an analysis of what was once thought a minor or failed work, now revealed as subtly or brilliantly coherent and exemplifying all the intellectual virtues defined by textbooks on criticism.

Doubtless these compilations, or what Knight terms assemblages, exist and are worth studying. Yet what forty years ago might have been termed perfect examples of Levi-Strauss's "bricolage" (interesting structures that just happened to come into being) are now provided with an imagined coherence or what might have once been described with the now-old-fashioned notion of intention. With our discovery of compilations and assemblages, we refresh our field of study with new legitimate objects of concern. We don't have to read the same old texts in different ways, because we can now mix and match even canonical texts to produce entirely new texts. There is now something new to do, or something apparently new: something that needs doing, something that is do-able, and something that must be done.

Legendum legendum est.

There is of course plenty a scholar can do who becomes absorbed in these compilations, miscellanies, tract volumes, or anything else that forces its way into the margins of a literary

---

[32] Armando Petrucci, "From the Unitary book to the Miscellany" (1986), and "Reading in the Middle Ages" (1984), in *Writers and Readers in Medieval Italy: Studies in the History of Written Culture,* ed. and trans. Charles M. Radding, 1–18 and 132–44 (New Haven: Yale University Press, 1995).

[33] For an example, see Peter W. Travis, *Disseminal Chaucer: Rereading The Nun's Priest's Tale* (Notre Dame: University of Notre Dame Press, 2010). See also, the often mind-numbing contributions in the MLA "Approaches to Teaching..." series.

text (annotations, contemporary politics, ideology, and so on). You can put them in some kind of array: if you look at a number of printed *Sammelbände*, for example, and even do a cursory examination of their histories when these are known or somehow accessible, you can easily categorize them into various types: authorial, readerly, or simply arbitrary. Each is unique, but each also resembles certain members of this group more than it resembles others.[34] Books and texts might be associated by genre, by title, by author, or by size. And by creating such an array, you can avoid saying at least a few uninformed things about them. You can avoid confusing an authorial compilation with an arbitrary one. You can avoid assuming that the texts bound together in a bindery ever were read together, interpreted together, or imagined to be a unit by anyone other than a modern librarian looking for a place to shelve it. You cannot know what your book-copy is, but you can place it on some sort of scale with others that at least gives you a place to begin. You can do the same with annotations: if you look at enough of them, you might be able to form a continuum or scale, in which various types could be defined: schoolboy annotations, scholarly, vetting for a printing press, childish markings, pointless doodling, critical.

In the early 1990s, R. Allen Schoaf, in a study that seems almost quaint today, invented what he called "juxtology."[35] Shoaf,

---

34 Joseph A. Dane, *What Is a Book? The Study of Early Printed Books* (Notre Dame: University of Notre Dame press, 2012), 171–78.

35 R. Allen Shoaf, "'For there is figures in all things': Juxtology in Shakespeare, Spenser, and Milton," in *The Work of Dissimilitude in Renaissance Literature: Essays from the Sixth Citadel Conference on Medieval and Renaissance Studies,* eds. David G. Allen and Robert White, 266–85 (Newark: University of Delaware Press, 1992), http://www.rallenshoaf.net/6.html (2013):

I coined the word juxtology in the 1980s and published my first essay on the topic in the late '

80s in a collection edited by Jonathan Culler on puns. The term was immediately useful to me in my teaching for conversations not only about books like Joyce's Ulysses but also about the poetry of Chaucer, Shakespeare, and Milton. Over the past two decades, as I have read and taught this poetry and continued to write about it, I have become increasingly persuaded that the term and its implications are very useful for interpreting late Medieval and Renaissance English poetry. Here are writers who not unlike the scholars here, did not care particularly what period these works came from since the thing he was studying was invariably and legitimately himself. Nor did he waste much time trying to justify his selections. Shoaf's self, interesting as it may be, remains irreducibly singular and nearly inaccessible. There is no arguing about what he might see in his juxtaposed texts, just as there is no arguing over what Bahr calls the delight produced by a particular set of texts or objects that he or history places together. We may, in accordance with the prevailing critical climate, privilege a material object, but that only increases the basic problem we have introduced: the singular object is not communicable, at least, not in a scholarly sense, nor is our particular experience with that object anything that can become the object of scholarly or critical discussion. What we communicate and what forms communities of scholars are those abstractions known as ideas, vague as they may be.

Marginal comment on "ouk acharista": "Lit.: 'not ungraciously' — ironically — prettily enough."

---

only juxtapose, they also make of juxtaposition an epistemology, as, for example, in Chaucer's "by his contrary is everything declared." And in my book *Shakespeare's Theater of Likeness*, I demonstrate how Shakespeare uses this utterly simple but also utterly indispensable word, *like,* to dramatize the crisis of self-knowledge and self-coincidence, in which, to paraphrase Catherine in *Henry V,* if we "do not know what is 'like me,'" we do not know who we are. Just so, today, in one of the most revolutionary discoveries of brain science yet, we have learned that there are mirror neurons by means of which we feel what others feel and therefore how to feel each of us himself or herself — as if we had found the neural basis of ancient homeopathy.

CHAPTER 5

Editorial Projecting

I find it most interesting how my memory fails me. There are gaps, holes in my past, which I must fill with a new stories and narratives that probably have little relation to the truth.
— my good friend, Nancy R.

One of the more imposing resources for literary scholars is the mid-twentieth-century etymological dictionary by Julius Pokorny, *Indogermanisches etymologishes Wörterbuch*.[1] In the following chapter, I will deal with the bibliographical and editorial variant of this issue: what I consider de-historicizing of texts through invocation of history, and the often mystifying creation of editorial terminology, particularly the notion of archetypes, and its variant levels "sub-" and "hyper-." Pokorny's *Wörterbuch* is a once state-of-the-art product of twentieth-century Indo-European linguistics. Its popular counterpart in student-level lexicography is the *American Heritage Dictionary*, a work that makes previous etymological resources (e.g., Skeat, or even the Oxford English Dictionary) seem amateurish.[2] At least, they will seem that way until a new method of classifying word origins (or even a new theory of what the word "origins" itself means) develops.

There is no end to the amusement of using this source. Relations between words can be laid bare. Earlier meanings can

---

[1] Julius Pokorny, *Indogermanisches etymologishes Wörterbuch*, 2 vols. (Bern: Francke, 1959–69).
[2] The *American Heritage Dictionary of the English Language* (Boston: Houghton Mifflin, 1969); Walter W. Skeat, *An Etymological Dictionary of the English Language* (Oxford: Clarendon Press, 1884).

be imagined or teased out. Often speculative readings can be provided with impressive philological support. All is based on the problematic but very useful theory that somehow the earlier history of word or morphemic units is contained within those units, either directly or subliminally, there to be expressed or cited by serious scholars against their adversaries, much the same as a vulgar reader or undergraduate of today might rant about a competitor's use of a certain word by citing what it means in "the dictionary."

Traditional etymological dictionaries were different. Medievalists are, or once claimed to be, familiar with Isidore's seventh-century *Etymologiae*. Isidore's theory is difficult to determine. It seems that original meanings of words are thought to be contained within the present meanings of words, although how that could be is mysterious. Modern scholars must interpret or read Isidore (whether rightly or wrongly) under the assumption that his theory is naive and incorrect, an early example of impressionistic etymology. The scholarly faults of the *Etymologiae*, paradoxically, make it especially useful: for real speakers and readers of a language, impressions may be far more important than historical truths, and these impressions can be or may be or potentially might be shared by an historical community (or so language historians can imagine). In this sense, a competent reader or speaker of a language would share such Isidorean (that is, historically false) associations of a word, and that in and of itself would make those associations a legitimate feature of any particular language or dialect. "I could care less," in fact, means, 'I could not care less'. "Literally" now famously means 'figuratively'. The meaning of the word "disinterested" is determined entirely by its context, and no competent speaker of English would be confused by its common use: "The casual way the left-fielder played his position showed he was disinterested in the outcome."

Pokorny's systematization of root-forms does not require that these units existed together, or even that they were words at all. These reconstructions are the end point of scholarship on recorded languages. Indo-European speakers, if they ever existed, did not pronounce or spell their units according to this system.

Furthermore, they did not have access to all these words. And there is no certainty that they ever used two of them together. Pokorny's theory thus constructs a history based on a theoretical competence that is well beyond that of any historical speaker.

Pokorny's *Wörterbuch* exemplifies the editorial problem I discuss below. What matters is not what has happened (how Indo-European languages evolved) but rather what exists now: state-of-the-art modern descriptions of those languages, particularly that base language — Indo-European — whose speakers are often only vaguely located in historical time and space, and who could not possibly have spoken or imagined a syntax-free language represented in a conventional spelling system familiar to twentieth-century western scholars. Speaking this Pokorny-esque language would be like trying to "see" a landscape through the description on an early printed page eaten through by bookworms. Or perhaps like seeing an authorial text through the 5% of the manuscript witnesses to that text which actually survive.

Editorial Ancestors and Progeny

The most impressive achievement of the past 150 years of Middle English scholarship has been editorial; at least, that is what most editors, as well as bibliographers such as myself, would claim. Significant editions include those of the Chaucer Society (the parallel-text editions of various texts and Skeat's multi-volume edition of the *Canterbury Tales*), the contemporary edition of *Piers Plowman* by Skeat, the later Athlone editions, and two electronic editions — The Canterbury Tales Project, and the Piers Plowman Electronic Archive. I apologize to other editors for not including their work, some of which is excellent (Derek Pearsall, Ralph Hanna, David Fowler — many others could be mentioned).[3]

---

[3] Principal editions discussed below include: Walter W. Skeat, ed., *The Complete Works of Geoffrey Chaucer*, 7 vols. (Oxford: Clarendon Press, 1894–97)

The representation of history in these projects, collectively and taken singularly, may well be correct — that is, the characterization of what Chaucer, Langland, Gower, or the author(s) of the *Pricke of Conscience* did, and even the modern transcriptions of texts that might, at some point, have been produced. (I am struggling to say what it is that editors do or attempt to do.)[4] Editorial procedures and the final histories described in all these editions seem to me generally reasonable, even when they contradict. What I am concerned with here are only the initial assumptions of these several projects and the preliminary language adopted, sometimes carefully, sometimes not. Is the representation of history at all like the history it claims to have existed? Or is it just an Isidorean-like representation of modern editorial imaginings?

Among the terms that bother me are the following: *text, version, recension, manuscript, reading, lemma, holograph, document,* and most important *archetype* and its many variants — that is, most of the terms basic to editorial procedures and reconstructions. Some of these refer to historical entities that have histories of their own (manuscripts, real and imagined). Others are purely editorial hypotheses (a manuscript group or classification). It may be basic editorial goals, and it may be editorial arrogance — the notion that the reconstructed text ideally is the author's text — that blurs what should be the quite different ontological status of these entities.

---

and *The Vision of William concerning Piers Plowman with Vita de Dowel, Dobet et Dobest, and Richard the Redeless, by William Langland,* 2 vols. (London: Oxford Univ. Press, 1885); A.V.C. Schmidt, ed., *William Langland: A Parallel-Text Edition of the A, B, C, and Z Versions,* 3 vols. (London: Longman, 1995–2008); George Kane and E. Talbot Donaldson, *William Langland's Piers Plowman: The B-Version* (London: Athlone, 1975). See also Piers Plowman Electronic Archive, http://www.iath.virginia.edu/seenet/piers/, and The Canterbury Tales Project, http://www.canterburytalesproject.org/.

4 On the Piers Plowman Electronic Archive, see my *Out of Sorts: On Typography and Print Culture* (Philadelphia: University of Pennsylvania Press, 2011), chap. 6, and on editorial goals more generally, see my *Blind Impressions: Methods and Mythologies in Book History* (Philadelphia: University of Pennsylvania Press, 2013), chap. 5.

Basic to the following discussion is my definition of *text* (I construct this only for convenience; I do not expect others to follow this, nor do I criticize them for adopting other meanings). What I call a text is an abstraction; it can be transcribed and reproduced. It exists in various supports, one of which is a manuscript. It can be imagined to exist in the mind of an author, a scribe, or even a reader. A manuscript, by contrast, is a real concrete entity that contains a text. This is the editorial version of a distinction that I have defined elsewhere as basic to book history: the difference between a book (an abstraction, usually equivalent to an edition) and a book-copy — the physical object you hold, generally referred to in common language as a simple book.[5]

Variation: Single-Text vs. Parallel-Text Editions

When Bembo and Politian transcribed the oldest surviving manuscript of Terence (now Vat. lat. 3226), they did so by transforming it into a series of variants copied into two copies of a contemporary printed edition of Terence (by Adam of Amergau, 1475).[6] Politian and Bembo were not interested in their printed "base text"; the edition was chosen only for convenience (likely it was the only printed edition for which two nearly identical copies were available). It made the transcription of the variants easier, and had no necessary effect on the final text that was implied, and both Bembo and Politian imagined their texts would be more or less the same as the text in the manuscript (they did not include accidentals of spelling or script, but did note colometry — that is, line length). The manuscript text, thus, is reduced to a set of variants, and from there, transcribable again as "the" text, even though Bembo's book-copy, Politian's book-copy, the Bembo manuscript, and the text of any of them — these are all

---

5 See e.g., Joseph A. Dane, *What Is a Book? The Study of Early Printed Books* (Notre Dame: University of Notre Dame press, 2012), 9–11.

6 The manuscript is as late as the fifth or sixth century, although Bembo believed it might be much earlier; see my "A Ghostly Twin Terence (Venice, 21 July 1475; IGI 9422, 9433)," *The Library,* ser. 6, 21 (1999): 99–107.

different things, and the two printed copies, although theoretically identical, themselves had variants.

Scholarly societies in the nineteenth century made many unfamiliar texts available in print without reference to or concern with editorial questions. For reasons of efficiency and convenience, many of the early club editions were simply transcriptions of whatever manuscript was available; under the influence of later editorial theory, some came to be described, wrongly, I think, as "best text" editions. Most of these editions had few if any editorial pretenses (for example, fabliaux collections, the many texts made available by François Michel in French, or the English editions published by Thomas Wright).[7] These books were meant to be sold to amateurs or members of literary societies, not used by scholars in edition-making.[8]

In the case of texts already available in printed editions, such variant single-source versions were printed as a first step in the editorial process that would eliminate their authority. For English medievalists, the most familiar examples are the editions and pamphlets produced by the Chaucer Society in the late nineteenth century. Nineteenth-century philologists thus provided for medievalists what early printers provided classicists. The dissemination of works led to the inescapable confrontation with variant versions of those works. And variant versions

---

7 See, e.g., the characterization of Thomas Wright's Chaucer editions as methodological precedent by late-twentieth-century editors of the Variorum Chaucer; Editors' Preface, *Geoffrey Chaucer: The Canterbury Tales, A Facsimile and Transcription of the Hengwrt Manuscript* (Norman: University of Oklahoma Press, 1979), xii–xviii, and in introductory sections of various editors in this project.

8 Statement by Roxburghe Club, founded in 1812: "Each member is expected to produce a book at his or her own expense for presentation to the other members"; see list of publications at http://www.roxburgheclub.org.uk/clubbooks. See the useful reprise of this tradition in Poiron's single-text edition of *Roman de la Rose,* with sections omitted by that manuscript added in brackets. The result is a cheap, serviceable edition (useful even for school use), that also provides sophisticated evidence for history, editing, and linguistics: Daniel Poiron, ed., *Le Roman de la Rose* (Paris: Flammarion, 1974).

led to the notion of a superior version.[9] But even that sentence (including the equivocal meaning of "superior") gets ahead of my point in this section—the definition and comparison of variants. The seamless history of editorial projects I seem to be constructing in this introductory section and which might well have been imagined by Chaucer Society editors was more chaotic in practice: those uniformly bound green volumes neatly

---

9   That mechanical features of print led to criticism in its strongest sense has been made in various forms: see, e.g., Anthony J. Grafton, *The Footnote: A Curious History* (Cambridge: Harvard University Press, 1999). My own view is that the nineteenth-century editorial practices were projected back onto the fifteenth century, which was recast in modern terms, and it was this period that was responsible for the editorial self-consciousness seen centuries earlier.

Figure 6. Chaucer Soc. Publ. on my shelves.

shelved in our libraries (or now in remote facilities) contrast sharply with the way they exist on my own shelves.

The Parallel-Text Edition

Parallel-text editions had or developed multiple and often conflicting goals. The first was to present evidence and thus lay the foundation for a standard edition (the Chaucer Society's *Canterbury Tales,* and several texts of the minor poems). To Skeat, these editions could in some cases make editing deceptively simple:

> The text of the present edition of the Canterbury Tales is founded upon that of the Ellesmere MS. It has been collated throughout with that of the other six MSS. published by the Chaucer Society....The text of the Ellesmere MS. has only been corrected in cases where careful collation suggests a desirable improvement.[10]

A second was to constitute an edition and to present variant versions as autonomous texts (e.g., Skeat's three-text edition of *Piers Plowman*).

The Chaucer Society editions seemed addressed only to scholars (unlike the Piers Plowman Archive and the Canterbury Tales Project, both of which claim their editions are useful for students and civilians). What they printed was not an edition per se, but rather the foundation for an edition, an edition later realized in Skeat's multi-volume edition of Chaucer.[11] Only in

---

[10] Skeat, *The Complete Works of Geoffrey Chaucer,* 4: xvii–xviii.

[11] See also, the Piers Plowman Archive edition of the supposed archetype for the B-version, called "Bx" — an edition that initially I thought was to be long deferred: "The B-Version Archetype," eds. John Burrow and Thorlac Turville-Petre, The Piers Plowman Electronic Archive, vol. 9, http://piers.chass.ncsu.edu/texts/Bx: "We shall argue that the readings of the B archetype (henceforth Bx) can be established with certainty in the majority of lines."

a few cases did a variant text become an autonomous one (the prologue to "Legend of Good Women" found in Cambridge University Library MS Gg. 4.27 and now printed in many standard Chaucer editions).

There are several paradoxes involved in this process. While on the face of it, the parallel-text method places unmediated evidence before the reader, its goal seems to be the opposite. It is not designed to retain evidence (that is, it does not serve the same function as the Synoptic Gospels, whose goal is to retain every trace of God's word), rather its goal is the same as that of the classical edition: to eliminate such evidence, and to provide the basis for scholars to rid themselves of the cacophony of manuscript variation.[12]

The nature of the parallel-text edition was also affected by a material consideration: the number of columns that could be printed in an ordinary book of "landscape" format, a constraint no longer applicable to electronic versions of these editions. That number was six. And that, it turns out, served extremely well for Chaucer's "Parlement of Fowls," "House of Fame," and even "Legend of Good Women," where the number of manuscripts was limited. It also was the origin of Furnivall's "Six-Text Version of the Canterbury Tales" — six being a very convenient number, since it also could be mapped onto an arbitrary notion of "important holdings": the then British Museum, university libraries, and "private owners." Evidence, in order to be evidence, fit the scholars' abilities to describe and to present it.

The presentation of evidence in this format is in some way duplicitous. Although evidence seems unmediated, many of the most interesting editorial decisions have been made before a word is printed. First, and most important, is that each of these (I'll call them texts) is a variant of the others, something that

---

12 See, also, the unselected parallel-text editing in the first EETS series by Zupitza and Koch, printing all variants of the "Pardoner's Prologue" and "Tale." Given the unrepresentative nature of links, it is not clear to me what editorial purpose these could have served. Julius Zupitza and John Koch, *Parallel-Text Specimens of all accessible unprinted Chaucer MSS: The Pardoners Prolog and Tale* (London, 1890–97).

seems more obvious and banal than it should. In order to make the two texts parallel (that is, to set them up for printing), they must first be defined as variants, and they must be modified through editing. Where one version, say, lacks lines found in the other, it is printed with a gap. Where the two versions have lines in a different order, the order of those lines must be changed (this is noted in the Chaucer Society editions in marginal print so fine it is difficult to read and reproduce; see Chapter 3, Figure 3 above). Lines and whole passages must be moved to create a text that duplicates as much as possible the text used as the basis of collation. Despite this, Skeat himself claimed his transcriptions were both: (1) identical to the manuscript evidence, and (2) somewhat paradoxically, superior to that evidence:

> In other words, my work is entirely founded upon the splendid "Six-text" Edition published by that Society, supplemented by the very valuable reprint of the celebrated 'Harleian' manuscript in the same series. These Seven Texts are all exact reproductions of seven important MSS., and are, in two respects, more important to the student than the MSS. themselves; that is to say, they can be studied simultaneously instead of separately, and they can be consulted and re-consulted at an moment, being always accessible.[13]

Such editions cannot be created without a logical *petitio principii*: the chosen texts are "the same," although the basis for that identity must exist in the editor's mind. In some cases, a parallel version can be defined as a different text (Piers C is not Piers B or A, even though sections can be collated and many lines are the same: in the case of *Piers,* the parallel-text method does not provide any of the evidence required to challenge such a claim). The most extreme form of this argument developed in the late twentieth century: each variant text (whether the product of an author or scribe) could be defined as an autonomous text, even

---

13 Skeat, *The Complete Works of Geoffrey Chaucer,* 4:xvii.

if the result of a reader's whimsy, ready for readerly analysis and appreciation.

Editorial Illusions: The Archetype

A staple of classical editing is reconstructing the sources (or re-imagining them) for extant copies, prints, or manuscripts. In genealogical editing, this (theoretically) can only be done after texts are conceived or declared as parallel, and after they are broken down into decontextualized *lemmata,* the identification and definition of which have received far less attention than they deserve.[14] A "text" (of a work?) is imagined to exist imperfectly in all its recorded or extant variants. The goal of editing is the reconstruct an earlier version of that text that accounts for differences in extant witnesses. This can be done either by ignoring certain witnesses (or declaring them irrelevant), or, more modestly, by reconstructing versions that will together explain or account for all the variants in the extant copies.

The goal might be various. Perhaps a Great Leap Backwards to the author's original: this was surely the goal of most classical textual criticism. The source of error was less important than the simple recognition that it existed. Or, in a method as-

---

14 See, e.g., John M. Manly and Edith Rickert, *The Text of the Canterbury Tales* (Chicago: University of Chicago Press, 1940), and the labored but largely unfiltered defense of their supposed methods by Roy Vance Ramsey, *The Manly-Rickert Text of the Canterbury Tales: A Revised Edition with a foreword by Henry Ansgar Kelly* (Lewiston: Edwin Mellen, 1994, 2010), esp. 47–91. Manly and Rickert's methods of transcribing these things on 60,000 cards received far more discussion than their actual choice of them. Lawrence Warner has criticized the editorial procedure of "lemmatization," but not in terms I fully understand; see Lawrence Warner, *The Lost History of Piers Plowman: The Earliest Transmission of Langland's Work* (Philadelphia: University of Pennsylvania Press, 2011), xiv. And on the red herring of Manly and Rickert's "basis of collation," see my "The Presumed Influence of Skeat's *Student's Chaucer* on Manly and Rickert's *Text of the Canterbury Tales*" (1993; rpt. Joseph A. Dane, *The Myth of Print Culture: Essays on Evidence, Textuality, and Bibliographical Method* [Toronto: University of Toronto Press, 2003], 114–24).

sociated with Karl Lachmann, a reconstruction of the history of such errors manifested in the textual tradition and the extant versions. At the heart of the genealogical method is the notion that while you cannot recognize truth, you can recognize error, and by constructing a clear and convincing genealogical history of these errors, say, of manuscript or textual readings (or any other field!), you can perhaps spiral in on the truth by stumbling upon or imagining readings that are irreducible: you can no longer account for them as errors. This is the *via negativa* of textual criticism, and common to all genealogical methods. Only in the twentieth century, and with the popularity of reception theory (in various practical and theoretical forms), was there an interest in this "erroneous history" as a subject in and of itself, spurred on by McGann's theories of the socialized text. This concern with texts and versions that were unauthorial then moved in even more radical directions to involve the banalities of individual readers' use, legitimate or not, of those texts (see Chapter 5 above).[15]

> The [Piers Plowman] Archive will be the supreme tool for carrying forward textual work on Piers Plowman....What the reader does is central, at least as a layered, collaborative, later process....The user will be able to assemble and disassemble the stages of such editions at will.[16]

Classification of Witnesses

Most editors, following the classical model, classify witnesses, generally manuscripts and manuscript readings, by construct-

---

[15] Jerome J. McGann, *A Critique of Modern Textual Criticism* (Chicago: University of Chicago Press, 1983), or Charles A. Owen Jr., *The Manuscripts of the Canterbury Tales* (Cambridge: D.S. Brewer, 1991).

[16] Andrew Galloway, "Reading Piers Plowman in the Fifteenth and the Twenty-First Centuries: Notes on Manuscripts F and W in the Piers Plowman Electronic Archive," *Journal of English and Germanic Philology* 103, no. 2 (2004): 232–52, at 232.

ing a stemma; or perhaps more accurately, the stemma is the virtual representation of the less well-defined classification scheme.[17] Other, more recent editors, have tried to get around this by using a presumably more neutral form of classification, one that takes witnesses as presenting individual readings classified without reference to their origins (Kane in particular.) A variant of this is what is occasionally called "rhizomatic" theory, or, more clearly, cladistic theory.[18] The first (Kane's theory) is to me a mere reconfiguration of the classical theory. The second (cladistic theory) does not seem to me as radically different as its practitioners claim, but can have the advantage of not materializing the entities critiqued here: the forks on a typical cladistic diagram do not demand a frustrating and futile imagining of, say, evolutionary "missing links" (the equivalent of the imagined textual-critical *archetypes).[19]

In textual criticism, a loose set of conventions applies to the notation used in these diagrams. In the classical diagram, the difference between an upper case roman letter and a Greek letter is a difference between a real and a hypothesized witness. Only attested manuscript or printed readings (represented by upper case roman) constitute "evidence" or "witnesses." The use of the word "witness" is problematic, however, in that it implies in a Platonic sense that such a witness must be a witness "of something." (That "something" is assumed to be an earlier or authorial reading, but such readings do not have the status of fact outside the editor's imagination).

---

17 "The stemma is not a tool for the editor but the product of the edition.... We differ from Kane and Donaldson in that we find no evidence that any manuscript offers readings derived from a putative pre-archetypal stage": Piers Plowman Electronic Archive, Introduction to the Electronic Edition of the B-Version Archetype of *Piers Plowman,* http://piers.iath.virginia.edu/exist/piers/restricted/crit/front/B/Bx/Front.

18 David Greetham, "Phylum — Tree — Rhizome," *Huntington Library Quarterly* 58, no. 1 (1995): 99–126.

19 Even fifty years ago, editors occasionally provided stemmata incorporating elements of both systems; see, e.g., E.R. Dodds, *Plato: Gorgias* (Oxford: Clarendon Press, 1959), 67.

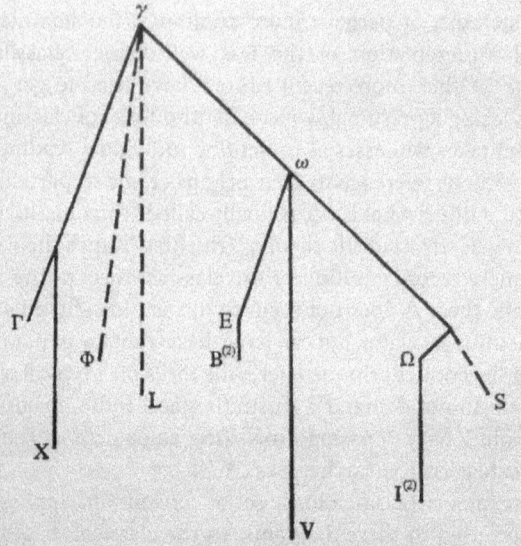

Figure 7a. Classical stemma.

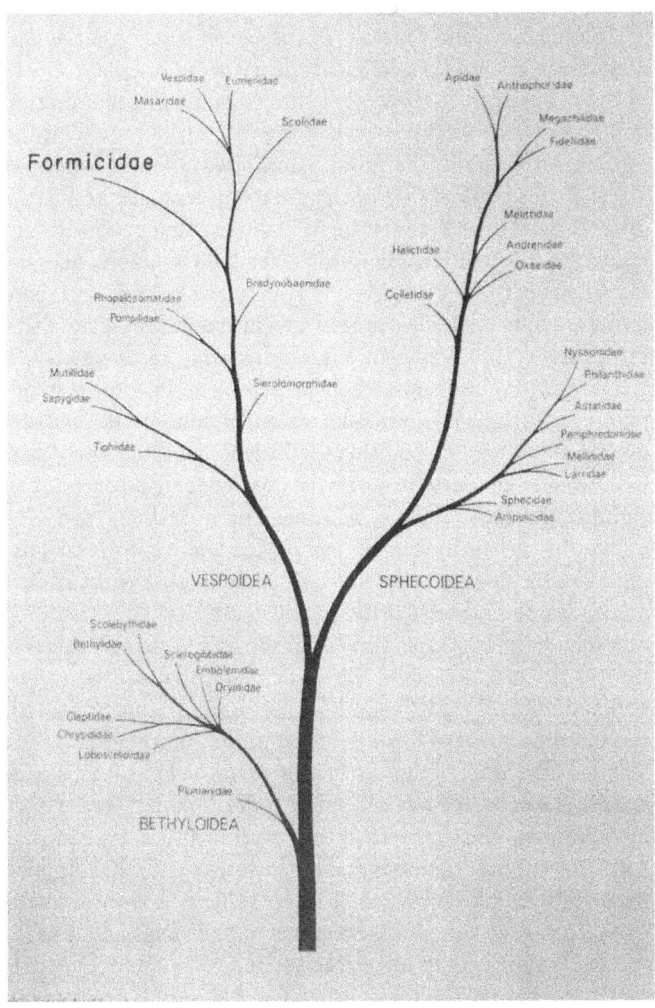

Figure 7b: Cladogram by Hölldobler and Wilson, *Ants*, 25.

The meaning and function of the Greek letter in a classical diagram is my concern here. In theory, it represents a source in the most abstract sense: some imagined text or manuscript, that is, a *res* that serves to explain the variants (all of them? the significant ones?) in the group considered a family below it? These might be direct descendants, or there might be further hypothesized texts between them. All these imagined texts are known as "hyperarchetypes" whatever their relations may be. Occasionally the word "subarchetype" might be used, but these terms are only distinguishable in specific contexts. Again, these things are editorial explanations, not historical facts.

Such hyper- and sub-archetypes intervene in some way between real witnesses (book-copies and manuscripts) and the imagined source of all of them, which is *the* archetype (*x or O') — that is, the imagined or hypostasized textual source of all variants in recorded texts of this imagined (or defined) text — or rather, the earliest imagined form that can be reconstructed using the genealogical method alone. Behind that editorial text might be the authorial original (whatever that is), something that may have existed in a material support (a manuscript version of the text preceding the earliest one that can be reconstructed from all extant variants), or abstractly (something that can be conjectured as having existed in the author's mind). The singular advantage of this distinction seems to be that O', like all texts, has errors (the one exception is the authorial text, which, by definition, must be perfect whatever form it is imagined to take). But the implication is that the historical authorial original, though by definition perfect, is never static and always subject to change. O', by contrast, is imagined to be a stable and thus reproducible text with its manuscript support. It exists at one time, in a way that the authorial original never could. This applies particularly to texts such as *Piers Plowman*, where Langland is constantly revising, or the *Canterbury Tales*, unfinished, and, according to Chaucerians, never achieving a final imagined form.

Notwithstanding its utility from an editorial point of view, there are many problems with this terminology. To begin with, it represents a more systematic process of composition and copying than may have existed: "what happened" cannot be quite the same as "what we describe as happening."[20] Modern editors (post-print) can reasonably speak of "publication" and can also reasonably consider the text in such an edition as stable, even given the unlikelihood of a print-run continuing start to finish error-free. Medieval textual critics can then extend this notion backwards, imagining that the production of a manuscript (or perhaps the author's signing off on the production of such a manuscript?) is itself a form of publication or, more abstractly and far more problematically, that the author imagined a form of publication similar to that of modern authors (that is, an authorial consideration that the text was ready to be put forth, despite the material state of such a text), and that this publication is itself documented or alluded to in the textual-critical history. This notion of publication is obviously different from print publication; it does not involve the production of hundreds of presumably identical copies or any of the steps in that process — for example, galley- or page-proofs. More important, there is, as far as I know, no convincing evidence that medieval authors ever conceived of their work this way. (Adam Scriveyn miswrites a work, but there is no certainty he will miswrite it in the same way again). Chaucer can speak of reactions to his *Canterbury Tales* in passages from that same work. But we have little evidence as to what those implied early forms of the tales were. And since the author's imagined "publication" is difficult to define or imagine, no less problematic are the abstractions that genealogical textual criticism creates in order to get there — archetypes, subarchetypes, and hyperarchetypes, whose ontological status changes as scholars describe them. This is especially but not exclusively true of texts whose variant versions are imagined to be authorial (Legend of Good Women and what I consider the purely scribal variant, Prologue G), or are prod-

---

20 For a critique of the self-contained nature of modern editing and the difficulties with its "semantic" value — that is, reconstructing real historical events — see my *Blind Impressions*, chap. 6.

ucts of continuing authorial intervention (the notion of "rolling revision" in *Piers Plowman*).[21]

*Archetypes

Now let us consider what an archetype, a hyperarchetype, or a sub-archetype actually is or is claimed to be (I will use the typeform *archetype to refer to these generally). An *archetype is an imagined text, one consisting of a series of substantive or significant readings that could account for the variants in its descendants (which may be other *archetypes or physical witnesses or manuscripts). These variants may be conjectured; they might include accidental variants, that is, specific spellings. They might be misreadings based on accidentals of spelling or even what I have called "subaccidental" extra-textual features (damage to a manuscript, inkblots, wormholes) that would in most cases not be indicated in any purely textual transcription.[22] The highest archetype, then, is that imagined text which contains (or in some way accounts for) all these readings, that is, all correct readings, and (except in extreme cases, which unfortunately are not rare in textual production) all erroneous ones as well.

As is the case with other basic editorial terminology, the more I try to make basic points such as these, the more obvious it is to me how difficult it is to say precisely what it is such editorial entities are or do.

The readings (or in some cases, features) imagined to exist in an *archetype do not constitute a complete linear text, even though they can be read as one, nor are they an accurate representation of what a manuscript or book might have contained. They are essentially a list. A Greek letter in a stemma might rep-

---

21 Ralph Hanna, *Pursuing History: Middle English Manuscripts and Their Texts* (Stanford: Stanford University Press, 1996), 222–23.
22 As far as I can tell, these are not really considered in W.W. Greg's often cited definitions of substantive/accidental: W.W. Greg, "The Rationale of Copy-Text," *Studies in Bibliography* 3 (1950–51): 19–36; rpt. W.W. Greg, *Collected Papers*, ed. J.C. Maxwell (Oxford: Clarendon Press, 1966), 374–91.

resent several generations of manuscripts, not just the last conjectured one. They are equivalent to the reconstructions of an Indo-European root — the most elegant imagined source for the descendant evidence, spelled according to a set of conventions that can be applied to all of them. There is no certainty that the various readings, correct and erroneous, attributed to imagined *archetype beta or gamma ever existed in a single manuscript any more than there is certainty that any Indo-European speaker actually used a number of Pokorny's reconstructed forms in a single coherent sentence, or, for that matter, even that those forms were contemporary and potentially usable.[23]

In a textual-critical sense, archetypal readings account for select and often decontextualized readings of real manuscripts, but may never have co-existed except in the editor's imagination and transcriptions. To my knowledge such "hyperarchetypes" or "sub-archetypes" that intervene between the real manuscripts and whatever is the final goal of the editor (either an authorial original or earliest conjectured manuscript O') have never been fully reconstructed or transcribed as complete texts even though they are described as if such transcriptions were completely unproblematic. If an editor provides a diplomatic transcription of an extant manuscript, together with an editorial version of the originary O' based on it through genealogical reconstruction, then every intervening *archetype the editor proposes (whether this abstraction represents one or several layers of versions) should be fully transcribable. I think that in a case where the editor imagines multiple manuscript generations or acts of copying here, a legitimate editorial transcription might not have to correspond to any one of them (even the last one); there is nothing theoretically unsound about that, although an editor, I think, might be loathe to concede it.[24]

---

23 I am not as confident about the validity of this statement as I would like to be. The archetype reconstructed to represent a series of manuscripts *might* have to represent the last in this series (but I am not quite willing to concede that).

24 An aspect of this analogy is that textual criticism imagines the norm as pure descent: accommodation or contamination are considered aberrations. In

An *archetype on any level is an idealization of the text it is supposed to represent, whether a scribal work or authorial one. Even though we know perfectly well from our own experience that with the exception of the shortest texts, there is no way we can keep our own works in a state of simultaneity, we speak of these texts/books as existing precisely in that fashion, such that they can be perfectly or imperfectly (as they seem to be) embodied in a support such as a book, typescript, or manuscript. And even in the most careful discussion, these abstractions very quickly become stabilized as they take material form.

However the editor proceeds, the difference between real historical versions (manuscripts intervening between the author and an extant manuscript) and editorial *archetypes is fundamental. Yet obeying this distinction is almost impossible for textual critics, who generally conflate the *archetypal text with the *archetypal support for that text (a manuscript or book). Note how in the otherwise excellent article by M.C. Seymour these editorial abstractions are materialized in a dazzling and dizzying combination of fact and pure conjecture:

> The extant text of LGW is now found only imperfectly in compilations and remnants of compilations. The "large volume...cleped the Seintes Legende of Cupide" would originally, without doubt, have been a separate publication, and the copy presented to Queen Anne was probably a handsome quarto with musical notation of ballade and lyric, each tale having an illuminated and possibly historiated initial set within a semi-vinet. The extant work (2,723 lines, i.e., 579 in prologue and 2,144 in tales) suggests that the completed work would have contained approximately 5,000 lines; at 30 lines to a page, with notation and illumination, its size would have been about 100 pages quarto (cf. the illuminated manuscripts

---

linguistics, contamination would obviously be the norm.

[of slightly later date] of Hoccleve's *Regiment*), and so might aptly have been described as a *large volume*.[25]

See also, this statement by Thorlac Turville-Petre, one of the main editors in the Piers Plowman Archive, where this editorial hypothesis materializes in a single sentence:

Establishing the archetype is one step on the way to a critical edition. Since even an archetypal manuscript, however accurate, will contain errors the critical editor must go further to introduce conjectural emendations to correct evident corruption.[26]

Skeat, *Piers Plowman*

For Chaucerians, the creation of these editorial theories did not much change their view of things. Editorial problems in Chaucer seem significant to those who have studied them, but for those who simply read Chaucer, they are largely irrelevant. Most of what has been said about Chaucer in the last hundred years or so could have been said on the basis of any text I have seen: Caxton, Thynne, Urry, Skeat, or the *Canterbury Tales* Project.[27] For *Piers Plowman* scholars and readers, the stakes are much higher. Using the same method used in the *Canterbury Tales* (the printing of multiple texts on the same open page), Skeat produced a

---

25 M.C. Seymour, "Chaucer's Legend of Good Women: Two Fallacies," *Review of English Studies* 37, no. 148 (1986): 528–34, at 530.

26 Thorlac Turville-Petre, "The B Archetype of Piers Plowman as a Corpus for Metrical Analysis," in *Yee? Baw for Bokes: Essays on Medieval Manuscripts and Poetics in Honor of Hoyt N. Duggan*, eds. Michael Calabrese and Stephen H.A. Shepherd (Los Angeles: Marymount Institute Press, 2013), 17–30. See also Warner, *Lost History*, ix where Bx is variously described as: "B archetype"; "archetypal B manuscript," a "document."

27 Ralph Hanna, *Introducing English Medieval Book History: Manuscripts, their Producers and their Readers* (Liverpool: Liverpool University Press, 2013), claims that the only textual-critical problem of interest in the *Canterbury Tales* is that of tale order (162).

three-text version embodying in a single work differences between the printed editions of Crowley and Whitaker, as well as manuscripts that agreed with neither of them.[28]

The three versions edited by Skeat represented three ideal forms of this text; "ideal" here means only 'abstract' — in textual-critical terms, the form of the text that could account for major textual variants in all versions of that text, versions which were themselves not perfectly, or at times even well represented in any single manuscript. Since there are manuscripts containing texts that conflate various of these forms (whether considered authorial or editorial), the distinction A/B/C/[Z] will not serve as a perfect classification of either physical manuscripts or the complete texts contained in them, but rather is an idealization that can classify sections or aspects of them. I don't see or propose any alternative to the editorial assumptions here. My only question concerns the nature of the things (whether one, three, or seventy) that scholars are reconstructing.

Skeat referred to A, B, and C as "Three Forms of the Poem" in the introductory section defining them. But within a paragraph, these are three "versions":

> In 1866, now twenty years ago, I printed a short tract (no. 17 OS EETS) entitled "Parallel Extracts from 29 MSS. of Piers Plowman with comments, and a proposal for the Society's Three-text edition of the poem." I believe I was the first to shew clearly, in this tact, that the number of distinct versions of the poem is really three, and not two only, as stated by Mr. T. Wright and others.[29]

Such language conflates two things: the history and creation of "the poem" in the fourteenth century, and the nineteenth-century classification of manuscripts and the texts they contain.

---

28 The characterization is from Skeat himself: *The Vision of William concerning Piers the Plowman,* 2:vii–viii. Skeat notes that the existence of a third version had been "suspected" earlier by Richard Price in a note to Warton's *History of English Poetry.*

29 Ibid., 2:vii.

In Skeat's edition, these three "forms" or "versions" are suddenly synchronic in a way that they never were claimed to be historically. In the theory of a revising author (Hanna's "rolling revision"), the synchronic nature of these texts was explicitly denied: Langland did not issue nor did he imagine three forms of the poem, even if we accept the notion of a medieval version of publication; rather, he cancelled one form through creation of the next. The modern scholar revises this history as a static corpus of evidence: three simultaneous versions of the text all included in Skeat's convenient edition.

We see much the same terminology in editorial projects contemporary with Skeat: John Gower's *Confessio Amantis* was revised in seemingly obvious ways, reflecting the regime change in England; G.C. Macauley, although presenting only one final text, uses the terms "forms" of the poem, "versions," "recensions," then "classes of manuscripts," as well as "partially revised copies of the first recension."[30] I think I can keep these straight, at least in a technical or theoretical sense: a version or recension of the poem is a text as published or issued by the author, or intended by the author. Of course it is an abstraction, but it is a product of a historical, fourteenth-century event, whether real or as imagined by a modern scholar. A "form" of the poem is I think closer in spirit to 'a class of manuscripts'. This is the abstract form that enables a modern scholar to claim that certain versions, that is, texts in various manuscripts, are the same. Note, however, that this discussion is not at all clear, and these terms, even in my own critique, blur almost as badly as they do in the editions I am critiquing. Macauley uses the word "recension" in his "Text and Manuscripts" section to refer to a version of the text, but a few pages later, it is a scheme for classifying texts in manuscripts. ("In producing the originals...partially revised copies of the first recension must have been used as a basis.")[31]

---

[30] G.C. Macauley, *The Complete Works of John Gower, edited from the Manuscripts with Introductions, Notes, and Glossaries,* 4. vols. (Oxford: Clarendon Press, 1899–1902), 2:cxxvii–cxxx.

[31] Ibid., 2:ccxxvii and cxxx.

The Editions of Kane-Donaldson and A.V.C. Schmidt

The Kane-Donaldson edition of *Piers Plowman* addressed these ambiguities by looking at manuscript relations in a different manner. What they saw were variants of individual lemmata and these variants served to classify manuscripts for each particular lemma and not for others. In other words, manuscript classifications were done on the basis of each individual lemma, not as an a priori means of classifying the variants and determining which ones were significant.[32] Or so it seemed. Kane-Donaldson used, then, not a classical textual-critical schema with holograph — archetype — manuscript form, but rather a classificatory system in terminology proposed by Greg.[33] They constructed not a history, but a synchrony of manuscripts whose readings exist simultaneously: for example, [(CrS)M] = Cr and S agree in a reading against M; Cr and S and M agree in a reading against other manuscripts.[34]

But their printing conventions are difficult to follow. It is not always clear what an upper case letter refers to (manuscript? or a reading within that manuscript?) — at least, it is not always clear to me.[35] I will represent in the following quotations bold upper case A as "boldA" and italic A as "italicA." I do this, because there is no possible way to avoid errors in my own proofreading and the introduction of further errors at press if I use any other convention. Thus:

---

32 In classical textual criticism, this leads to many cases of *petitio principii*, in that variants that do not conform to the manuscript classifications implied by other variants (defined as "significant") are regarded as "insignificant" or the product of a long list of scribal habits and accidents.

33 W.W. Greg, *The Calculus of Variants: An Essay on Textual Criticism* (Oxford: Clarendon Press, 1927).

34 The genealogical version of this might be: MSS Cr and S descend from manuscript gamma which together with M descends from a manuscript beta.

35 This is compounded occasionally by a purely typographical problem in that certain letters, upper-case G, seem to be printed in bold.

The text of that ancestor, the 'archetypal' boldB text, can generally be ascertained from the evidence afforded by the boldB manuscripts.[36]

This is a cumbersome system of annotation, but one I think Kane and Donaldson generally use consistently and correctly. It is difficult to find them in violation of their implied principles. But ambiguities in terminology like this are unavoidable. The following locutions imply a difference between, say, boldX and italicX, but I have no idea what that is: "material common to all three forms italicA italicB italicC"; "the text of boldAC"; "readings of the boldA and boldC versions"; "boldB archetype"[37] Is this implying a difference between an imagined text and a transcribable one? I just don't know. "Nevertheless where R is represented, F alone of the boldB manuscripts has about 100 readings...."[38] I believe "F" should never be used of a text, since it is a manuscript; rather the phrase should be "the text in F."[39]

Schmidt in his recent Skeat-like three-text edition returns to a more classical way of expressing manuscript relations, while amplifying the typographical conventions found in Kane-Donaldson. Schmidt does not use Greek letters for presumed archetypes. Upper case roman refers to an extant manuscript, as it does conventionally in classical textual criticism. Lower case roman refers, I think, to a group suggested by combinations of extant manuscripts. Italic lower case (I think) refers to the source implied by agreement in readings of implied lower-case groups. Bold lower case refers to the highest conjectured group of lower-case groups. Ax thus means the archetype for group A. BoldA refers to the entirety of Group A manuscripts? (I am not certain precisely how, in practice, this differs from Ax, which is based on and implies those variant readings). To these are added such ambiguous phrases as seen in the following: "the lost archetypal

---

36 Kane and Donaldson, *Piers Plowman: The B-Version*, 70.

37 Ibid., 71.

38 Ibid., 100.

39 See, also, "we have applied the practices followed in transcribing W to all the manuscripts" (ibid., 220).

159

manuscript of the **A** version, was, it seems likely, not the poet's holograph."[40]

The bold/roman distinction, generally followed in the Kane-Donaldson edition, is far more confusing in Schmidt and I have no confidence while reading that it is used consistently. The following come from the opening pages of his introductory section "The Manuscript Tradition":[41] "The text of **A** is only of variable certainty. Thus in about 7%, it has to be constituted from either **r** or **m**. ... The two independent copies made from Ax, **r** and **m**, both in turn introduced a number of errors." **r** and **m** are clearly imagined to be real manuscripts. "Two early copies are likewise presumed to have been made of **r**, which are here called **r**1 and **r**2. Another two were made of italic r1 (italic u and d) and at least six of italic r2 (italic v, j, l, k, w, z)..." (92) In the genealogical schema on the facing page, d and u are not italicized, nor in the explanatory sentence: "TH²ChD and RU each have an exclusive common ancestor (here called respectively 'd' and 'u')." Why italic in the first instance but not the second? Furthermore, in this sentence, TH²ChD, RU are in roman.

Earlier in the same paragraph, TH²ChDRU and VHJLKWN, are in boldface (93). Is this because TH²ChDRU (roman) is an abstraction based on the readings common to the group of manuscripts TH²CHDRU (bold)?

I am unable to distinguish possible errors in these statements from possible subtleties Schmidt intends. Yet the difference he is trying to express between readings in real manuscripts and conjectured readings in a tradition or in an imagined manuscript are crucial. I assume from the opening statement here that Schmidt concedes that no higher-level text can be constructed without first constructing the lower level text; that is, archetypes

---

40 Schmidt, *William Langland: A Parallel Text Edition*, 2:91. See also, such difficult formulations as the following: "But it seems reasonable to suppose that [Langland] showed a copy of the poem (here designated 'A-Ø') in its Pr-XI shape to personal acquaintances" (2:91). Does this refer to a textual form? or a physical manuscript?

41 I take all the following quotations from ibid., 2:92–93.

depend on readings found in sub-archetypes. But none of these reconstructed sub-archetypes or imagined manuscripts is in fact fully transcribed; with the exception of the highest editorially reconstructed text, and the lower extant manuscripts, they are little more than lists of lemmata.

Conclusion

You are asked to revise, and you do so piecemeal. In the early days of computing, you often did not know what version you were looking at. Each of us, doubtless, has had that Langlandian moment where we realize the copy we are so carefully revising today is actually older than the most recent revision that we completed yesterday or last week.

Jerome McGann claimed to be able to keep an entire book-length text in his mind at once; he did not begin writing until the entire book was mentally drafted. But I certainly cannot do this. I keep shapes of it, parts of it, and perhaps sentences of it in my mind. I recall them chaotically, and when I look at them in some print version, there are only a few pages on my screen at once. I could print out any of these, I suppose, and have a record of a something I could call a version, but that version is at best a late version of, say, the final paragraphs or pages, or maybe an early version of the early paragraphs, which take something of a different form in my head as I revise them abstractly to conform to what I have actually typed out today.

Manuscript production and print or typescript production embody slices of this production process in a fixed or static product. If professional scribes, typists, or typesetters are involved, those fixed versions are not entirely ours any more than the final printed version, corrupted by copy-editors (the modern version of that medieval bugaboo, the intelligent scribe) is ours. These manuscripts and these prints have material existence; at least, we can hold them and file them on library shelves. But once they are included in the editorial process, they undergo a transformation. They are changed from material things to texts;

that is to say, they are abstracted into repeatable transcribable units. The language editors and bibliographers use necessarily rationalizes and fixes this chaotic history: abstract texts and material supports are conflated and the objects of discussion shift, I think perniciously, from one to the other.

The basic entities of our textual-critical schemes, while seemingly trying to get beyond the belletristic mystification of an author's text by subjecting its reconstruction to some form of science (whatever that is), only multiply that belletristic entity and lend it a scientific veneer. Somehow, by surreptitiously performing radical acts of imagination in our textual-history schemata, the discredited act of divining an authorial original through *Fingerspitzengefühl* seems to have been obviated. But it is only reborn in a different form, and placed squarely at the heart of our theories.

In almost any textual-critical discussion, it is easy to see how these archetypal reconstructions move from their textual-critical base (which I call, a "modern editorial list" that in no sense constitutes a text) to the ontological status of a manuscript. It is given a date; a scribe is assigned to it (the "intelligent or editing scribe" or "Adam Pinkhurst" or perhaps the tinkering author working from a faulty copy). It assumes the same ontological status as real books and manuscripts. Shakespeare's inexistent "foul papers" become as important as extant quartos. Of course, editors of medieval texts and professional Shakespeareans are conscious of the difference between these things. But intelligent readers looking over one of these books or articles might reasonably conclude that Shakespeare's foul papers, the abstractions Q and F, or Chaucer's early versions of the *Canterbury Tales* are as real as any of the manuscript or early (or late) printed copies that are the basis of such notation.

In its strongest form, my argument is that textual critics have been able to construct their sophisticated schemes and theories only because they have sidestepped the most basic of editorial procedures: in *Blind Impressions* I pointed out one of these — editorial procedures have been developed to produce theoretically reasonable readings, but the question as to whether an editorial procedure produces historically correct readings has rarely been addressed. Here I point out another. All modern textual-critical projects rely to some extent on reconstructed or imagined *archetypes: an editorial "thing" or series of things lurking behind extant witnesses, lattices through which we somehow see the original authorial or archetypal manuscript. To reconstruct that requires filling in all the holes. But how we do that is anyone's guess. Textual criticism works in any of the more sophisticated forms developed in the last two centuries because it fails to account for or to define the ontological status of witnesses consistently in the edition-making process, and such failure is itself essential to the success of the editions that result.

CHAPTER 6

The Haunting of Suckling's *Fragmenta Aurea* (1646)

The Clark Library has multiple copies of what should be the same book, at least, under my definition of what a book is: Sir John Suckling, *Fragmenta Aurea* (London, 1646), consisting of his collected poems and plays. The three copies are listed in the Clark catalogue with modified LC numbers as PR3718.A1 1646, PR3718.A1 1646a, and PR3718.A1 1646a(2). This follows Clark cataloguing conventions (I think), in that "variant copies" are indicated with a letter (thus 1646 / 1646a) and second copies of the same variant copy are indicated simply by "[copy] 2." They differ in the order of their contents sections (1646a, copy 1 is eccentric); otherwise, the cataloguing distinctions are based on the standard distinctions in the Wing Catalogue regarding title-page variants, although Wing numbers, the basis for these edition distinctions, are not given in the electronic record.[1]

The difference that distinguished the principal bibliographical variants of this book in the latest Wing catalogue and in earlier catalogues is reflected in ESTC: the title is set either entirely in upper case or in conventional upper and lower case, easily represented on a keyboard as FRAGMENTA AUREA vs. Fragmenta Aurea.

---

1 PR3718.A1 1646a, copy 1, modern binding, has section I bound after sections II–IV. See detailed record at http://catalog.library.ucla.edu. Donald Wing, comp., *Short-Title Catalogue of books printed in England, Scotland, Ireland, Wales and British America and of English Books printed in other countries (1641–1700)*, 3 vols. (New York: Columbia Univ. Press, 1951) = Wing I; 2nd edn., 4 vols. (New York: MLA, 1972–98) = Wing II.

Fragmenta Aurea.

A Collection of all
THE
Incomparable Peeces,

WRITTEN
By Sir JOHN SVCKLING.

And published by a Friend to perpetuate his memory.

Printed by his owne Copies.

LONDON,
Printed for *Humphrey Moseley,* and are to be sold at his shop, at the Signe of the Princes Armes in St *Pauls* Churchyard.
MDCXLVI.

FRAGMENTA AVREA.

A Collection of all
THE
Incomparable Peeces,

WRITTEN
By Sir JOHN SVCKLING.

And published by a Friend to perpetuate his memory.

Printed by his owne Copies.

LONDON,
Printed for *Humphrey Moseley,* and are to be sold at his shop, at the Signe of the Princes Armes in St *Pauls* Churchyard.
MDCXLVI.

Figure 8a. Title Page of Suckling, *Fragmenta Aurea* (1646)
Figure 8b. Title Page of Suckling, *FRAGMENTA AUREA* (1646)

Basic cataloguing or collecting conventions require us to call these two separate editions or issues, even though they were clearly produced nearly simultaneously. A further title-page variant, identified in 1970, distinguished two forms of *Fragmenta Aurea,* with the result that there are now three Wing numbers for this book: S6126 (FRAG AUREA), S6126A (Frag Aurea), and S6126B.[2]

There is nothing out of the ordinary with this book or these copies; at least, there seemed to be nothing out of the ordinary when I first looked at them. The book is a collection of Suckling's works, bound together, with separate parts printed by different printers; it is one of a series of small literary editions printed by Humphrey Moseley, all in standard format, and it was reprinted two years later page for page. The four parts are at least potentially autonomous, in that they contain half-title pages, and new signature and pagination series. That the order of parts differs in individual copies is thus not surprising, nor should it affect cataloguing decisions. The book was included in Greg's scrupulously detailed *A Bibliography of the English Printed Drama to the Restoration*; copies exist in most major libraries; and it has also been subject to state-of-the-art scrutiny of ESTC bibliographers.[3] It should thus present few bibliographical problems. But that turns out not to be the case, and instead of the three (or perhaps two) Wing numbers that should account for this book, there are now seven that refer to the entire book or to parts of it; ESTC gives eight.

There are two simple features that seem responsible for this. (1) It is a collection of pieces, with sections individually signed; the order of sections is not necessitated by the pagination or

---

[2] See L.A. Beaurline and Thomas Clayton, "Notes on Early Editions of *Fragmenta Aurea,*" *Studies in Bibliography* 23 (1970): 165–70.

[3] David Scott Kastan, "Humphrey Moseley and the Invention of English Literature," in *Agent of Change: Print Culture Studies after Elizabeth Eisenstein,* eds. Sabrina Alcorn Baron, Erin N. Lindquist, and Eleanor F. Shevlin, 105–24 (Amherst: University of Massachusetts Press, 2000); W.W. Greg, *A Bibliography of the English Printed Drama to the Restoration,* 4 vols. (London: Bibliographical Society, 1957–59).

signature series, and thus the eccentric order of texts in Clark copy 1646a1. (2) The preliminaries contain both a blank leaf and a tipped-in author's portrait, whose location is not necessarily fixed. The purpose of this chapter is to discuss what this fairly routine case suggests for our tabulation of bibliographical evidence. While it is challenging to make abstruse technical jargon fit the real world situation (the task of most cataloguers), it is also amusing to describe that same situation in such a way that non-initiates can understand it, and that is the goal here.

Ideal Copy

To describe a book in a bibliographical sense is to give what is called ideal-copy description — not the form of any material book-copy (copy-specific description), but rather the standard or ideal form of the book, one which Fredson Bowers described as reflecting printers' intentions insofar as these intentions are manifested in actual books.[4] In practice, however, the distinction between ideal-copy description and copy-specific description is often difficult to maintain. For manuscript descriptions, which rely on the same formulae and conventions of description used for printed books, there is generally no difference, or the distinction might be defined in a different way: for example, a manuscript sophisticated or rearranged in the modern period might be described in the hypothetical form it had prior to that sophistication.[5] In the case of very rare books, or books with only a single surviving copy, there might be no difference even to define. Cataloguers might well be uneasy about constructing an ideal-copy description to which no surviving copy conforms,

---

4 Fredson Bowers, *Principles of Bibliographical Description* (Princeton: Princeton University Press: 1949), 37–42, 74, 113–23; see notes above.

5 See, e.g., relative to the Hengwrt MS, A.I. Doyle and M.B. Parkes, "Paleographical Introduction," in *Geoffrey Chaucer, The Canterbury Tales: A Facsimile and Transcription of the Hengwrt Manuscript with Variants from the Ellesmere Manuscript,* ed. Paul G. Ruggiers, xxii–xxv (Norman: University of Oklahoma Press, 1978).

since such a description would seem to oppose the material evidence on which it is based. The Gutenberg Bible poses a related problem. Although this book is very well studied and not particularly rare, individual descriptions in reputable catalogues vary so widely in their conventions that it is difficult to collate them. That is, there is no way to reference a page in one copy such that it is certain to be found in another. This is a point made by Paul Needham of the Scheide Library in numerous fora.

Another complicating issue is the dominance of single library collections, and the way copies are reported to large union catalogue projects. For incunable catalogues, individual libraries generally dominate: the most familiar example is the British Library catalogue of incunables (BMC); the form of the book-copy in the collection generally, and understandably provides the ideal-copy description for the book. For early English books, the STC project relied on a number of libraries, although again, privilege was necessarily granted to the particular copies in the British Library.[6] Because of this, copy-specific descriptions have a way of blurring into ideal-copy descriptions. Considered historically, this means that the bibliographical peculiarities or even the accidental history of one copy (its provenance) is projected onto the origin of all copies, that is, the one epitomizing "printers' intentions."

---

6 Catalogue of *Books Printed in the Fifteenth Century now in the British Museum*, 13 vols. (London: British Museum, 1908–). So, too, *Catalogue des Incunables of the Bibliothèque Nationale* (Paris: Bibliothèque Nationale, 1981–2006). Less confined to single copies is the union catalogue: *Gesamtkatalog der Wiegendrucke*, 10 vols. (Stuttgart: Hiersemann, 1928–), http://www.gesamtkatalogderwiegendrucke.de/. See, also, *Bayerische Staatsbibliothek Inkunabelkatalog*, 7 vols. (Wiesbaden: Reichert, 1988–), http://www.bsb-muenchen.de/inkunabeln.181.0.html. None of their four copies of Cicero, *Opera*, 1481 (BSB-INK C-358) exactly follows their ideal copy description.

General Description

Although it is customary in articles and notes such as this one to include a magisterial collation formula stating precisely the ideal form (in all senses) of the book, since that is at issue here, I will begin instead with a less technical description of the book. I follow that with a survey of the catalogues and descriptions that have dealt with this book and finally a discussion of the principal variants found in these copies.

The book is a collection of texts by Suckling, with part-titles for each of four sections. Individual sections (sometimes containing more than one work) were assigned to different printers, and these sections appear with independent signature series and independent pagination. Most of the title- and part-title-pages have variants. The general title page and preliminaries do not specify what is to be contained in the book, nor the order in which the sections should be bound.

The preliminaries consist of one quire of four leaves (octavo, from a half-sheet folded in quarto) and include an engraved author portrait. The engraving is usually tipped in facing the general title page, but individual copies show many variants in its placement. The general title page reads *Fragmenta Aurea: A collection of all the Incomparable Peeces written by Sir John Suckling*, 1646. This is followed by a four-page "To the reader." Following this initial quire, most copies contain the following potentially autonomous sections:

Section I:
Separate title page, printed by Ruth Raworth; Poems; Letters (full t-p); Account of Religion (full-t.p.), FINIS; A discourse (G4, p. 103; no tp.); "FINIS" (p. 119).

Section II:
Aglaura, separate title page, "printed for Tho Walkley" (this has variant forms); A2r/v prologues; epilogue FINIS; Aglaura (version performed at court) "printed Tho. Walkley"; "FINIS"

Section III:
Goblins ("private" version) separate title page, "Pr. for H. Moseley"; "FINIS"

Section IV:
Brennoralt ("private" version), separate title page "Printed for Humphrey Moseley"

The statements in the various title pages are straightforward and the printing history seems unproblematic. Moseley "has the book printed." Some of that printing is assigned to Walkley, who assigned it to Warren (sections II–IV, as well as general preliminaries). The first section (*Poems*) was assigned to Ruth Raworth. These printing stints were apparently more or less simultaneous or continuous, since sections of part-title pages were kept in type and reused for others.

The frequency of this order of texts in extant copies likely indicates how the book was ordinarily distributed and sold, and this could also be described in Bowers's terms as the form intended by Moseley. Other orders, however, are certainly possible, and nothing about the internal evidence suggests they are illegitimate (there is no feature in the book that alternative orders contradict). There might be some generic and aesthetic reasons to keep sections II–IV together (all are in the same type, and all are plays), but there is no reason, bibliographical or aesthetic, to keep these sections in the same order, and for this, descriptive bibliography must rely on the vague and problematic principle "majority rules."[7]

We thus know what the printer/publisher did, what the printing project entailed, and can predict the variants found in modern libraries. That is, analytical bibliography (defined as

---

7 This is not an uncommon situation for the earliest printed books; the series of pamphlet volumes printed by Ulrich Zell in the 1460s were clearly meant to be bound together, but in no set official combinations or order; see Severin Corsten, "Ulrich Zells frühste Produktion," *Gutenberg Jahrbuch* 2007, 68–76.

the recovery of printing procedures from the evidence of extant copies) and descriptive bibliography (the organization of copies into editions and states) has little more to say about this book. Given the number of books printed in the seventeenth century in England, it is, for the bibliographer, time to move on to the next one.

So to study this book beyond this is to focus not on printing history (imagined as a series of unmediated events that took place somewhere in the naive and unadulterated past), nor on a much grander cultural history, but rather on the means by which we speak of and understand that history. We are not looking at the moon; we are merely polishing lenses. And in that spirit, I am going to stay with this book a bit longer than most bibliographers, librarians, or cataloguers have the time or luxury to do. The problems I am finding seem not caused by the complexity or impenetrability of the history, but rather by the conventions of descriptive bibliography. Even simple, common, and expected variants have the effect of multiplying bibliographical variants (that is, entries in a catalogue) and confuse, if not the actual history of book, at least our conventional descriptions of this history.

Principal Catalogues

The relevant catalogues are W.W. Greg's *A Bibliography of the English Printed Drama to the Restoration,* Wing, ESTC, and EEBO.[8] Greg bases his catalogue on texts (plays), organized by date of first printing, and in a supplemental volume, "Collections," organized by author. All the others are based on books and editions. These are all, at least theoretically, descriptive catalogues, in that they are based on or incorporate ideal-copy description.

---

8 Early English Books Online, http://eebo.chadwyck.com; and English Short Title Catalogue, 1473–1800 (London, British Library), http://estc.bl.uk. For an overview and critique of these two catalogues, see Joseph A. Dane, *What Is a Book? The Study of Early Printed Books* (Notre Dame: University of Notre Dame Press, 2012), 218–27.

Each is nonetheless dependent upon the individual copies catalogued in individual libraries and these copies, however eccentric or inaccurately described, find their way erratically into the ideal-copy descriptions found in other catalogues.

Complicating this, Wing and ESTC are both union catalogues as well as descriptive catalogues. These two genres are not the same and their conflation occasionally leads to problems and inconsistencies: a union catalogue combines or lists the descriptions provided by the holdings of various libraries (there are far too many books for the bibliographers to have first-hand experience of all of them), and the provision of an item number at times tends to authenticate even faulty descriptions. A descriptive catalogue, on the other hand, is at least theoretically a critical catalogue; it relies on these individual descriptions (or the evidence they provide and sometimes conceal) in order to produce a standard that is itself reflective of what might be called original history (what took place in the printing house), not reception history (how the objects produced by that printing house behaved in history).

The most detailed of these is Greg's *Bibliography of the English Printed Drama to the Restoration*. The nature of the catalogue and its very detail helped legitimize certain types of errors. Greg was cataloguing texts, and he regarded these texts as being represented in various editions, which his bibliography catalogued. "Othello" is an entry for the play, but "the Folio of 1623" appears as an entry only in vol. 3 ("Collections"). Greg was not concerned here, as he might have been elsewhere, with sorting out bibliographical editions. Thus, individual plays such as *Brennoralt* and *Goblins* catalogued (wrongly) by individual libraries as separate bibliographical items rather than as parts of the collection *Fragmenta Aurea* would tend to find illusory support in Greg (they were given a unique reference number in his catalogue).

Greg identified two principal variants of *Fragmenta Aurea* based on differences in the title page and also provided entries for each play that appeared in it, leaving aside the question of whether that constituted an edition in the bibliographical sense.

He identified the two principal variants with an asterisk and a dagger (these are sometimes referred to as Greg 626 and Greg 626a). He also noted the absence of a rule under the date in the second variant, the basis for the variants noted by Beaurline and Clayton in 1970, although he did not classify that as constituting a bibliographical variant.[9]

Wing's *Short-Title Catalogue* came out in 1951. Wing did not take Greg into account and thus has only one entry for *Fragmenta Aurea*, but four items in all for this book and the sections within it. The entries for individual plays are the result of decisions and conventions of reporting libraries:

S6121 Aglaura (1646, 4o)
S6122 Brennoralt
S6126 Fragmenta aurea
S6129 The Goblins

The quarto designation for *Aglaura* is wrong, but legitimizes the notion that it is a separate edition from all the others.[10] In its second edition, Wing distinguished seven items, with the variant forms of *Fragmenta Aurea* determined by Greg and the 1970 article of Beaurline and Clayton:

S6121 Aglaura (Walkley var.)
S6121A Aglaura (T.W. var.)
S6122 Brennoralt
S6126 FRAG AUREA (large caps)
S6126A [anr. ed] Frag. Aurea
S6126B [anr. ed] date underlined
S6129 Goblins

---

9 Greg, *Bibliography of the English Printed Drama to the Restoration*, 3:1131.
10 Imposition by half-sheets, rather than full sheets, is always problematic in bibliography. Is a half-sheet folded once to be described as a folio (based on the folding), or a quarto (based on the relation to the original sheet)? Wing determines format by the the orientation of chainlines, thus by the relation of paper in the book to the original sheet of paper. A book formed of half-sheets folded once is thus a quarto.

Aglaura, Brennoralt, Goblins (items 6121, 6122 and 6129) are retained from the first edition and 6121A added as a variant of 6121.[11] They are considered independent, not based on analysis of production (internal evidence in books and external evidence in printing history), but because certain libraries contain independently bound copies of one of these units.

Wing I was intended at least in part as a finding guide, and Wing II expands the holdings section considerably for each entry. One of the consequences of this, at least for this entry, is that errors in Wing I are multiplied in Wing II, and thus inevitably find their way into ESTC. If Wing I considered a separately bound play (*Brennoralt,* for example) a separate edition based on the record in a reporting library, that entry reappeared, alongside copies reported by other libraries, even though the decisions of these libraries were likely based on different criteria of what constituted a real edition. S6121, S6122, and S6129 should be eliminated: they legitimize real or imagined variants, and because they are almost obligatory points of reference, they are or appear to be ineradicable in enumerative and descriptive bibliographies.

The most modern of catalogues, EEBO and ESTC, repeat (understandably) most of the errors of Wing, and (not so understandably) add more. In my most recent search, EEBO produced the following under the search "Suckling 1646":

1. Aglaura = S6121A (T.W.)
2. Aglaura S6121 = Greg 541b "Walkley"
3. Brennoralt S6122 = Greg 621b
4. FragAur S6126 (Yale copy — gives full pagination but images are only to Poems)
5. FRAG AR = S6126B (collation only to poems)
6. FRAG AUR = S6126A (Agl. t.p. Walkley)
7. Goblins (Yale) S6129, Greg 628a Collation says 64p (But images show this is bound in immediately following Aglaura.)

---

11 For *Goblins,* see discussion below.

These are the same seven items found, rightly or wrongly, in Wing II, and it may well be that the unstated principle behind the selection of these entries was simply to provide images for every item in Wing. This is certainly a reasonable and useful basis, but I do not find it stated directly.

ESTC has eight items:

1. Aglaura (Walkley) Greg 541b, S6121
2. Aglaura (T.W.) (var. missigned A3)
3. Brennoralt, date underlined; S6122 Greg 621b, Yale edition (which is in fact a copy of the complete FRAG AUR)
4. Frag Aur S6126A
5. FRAG AUR S6126
6. Frag Aur S6126B
7. Frag Aur S6126B "diff prelimns." Prologue after t.p., Harvard
8. Goblins

We recognize in ESTC all the variants noted in Wing; that is, all Wing numbers are confirmed. Editions continue to multiply, but at least one of these so-called editions is a pure ghost, as can be determined from catalogue entries alone: *Brennoralt* (Greg 621b, Yale) is not a real book or even a real book-copy: when you trace this book, what you get is Yale's FRAG AUR, and there is no reason to catalogue that separately, simply because some libraries happen to have a copy of a *Brennoralt* catalogued separately.[12]

These catalogues agree in most details, which ordinarily would indicate a consensus, particularly with a catalogue as good as ESTC. Here, however, the degree of consensus is just as likely to indicate a state of dependence. An error in one catalogue is given specious support as the same error reappears in others.

---

12 The same is true of #8 Goblins. On #7, see below. It is a ghost edition, based on a library catalogue. Yale seems to have five copies: all conform to ordinary descriptions (none contains the blank).

Variants Real and Imagined

There are two types of variants we should account for when dealing with this book and the catalogue entries for it: the first are variants created (perhaps inadvertently) at press. The second are variants of provenance, that is, different forms various book-copies took after they were printed. For descriptive bibliography, only the first class of variants should be of any importance. Descriptive bibliographers and the cataloguers who depend on them (enumerative bibliographers) are only concerned theoretically with ideal copy — what the printer intended to produce or could reasonably have hoped to produce, and what variants (or failures?) took place at press while the book was being printed. Yet the second class of variants (pure matters of provenance and later history) have created variants in description as well. Accidental forms of the book have become catalogued forms and have worked their way into standard catalogues (ESTC). These produce what are commonly known as ghosts or ghost editions: the book-copies that evidence such editions are very real; the editions themselves are not.

Ideally, I would try to distinguish or classify these variants more precisely than I do in the list below: flat-out errors, irrelevancies, inconsequential variant, possible bibliographical significance, matters to be determined by intent of catalogue, and so on. Unfortunately, as I attempt to construct this obvious hierarchy of variation or error, I run into problems, since even the most inconsequential of errors can quickly rise to bibliographical significance. Note in the imagined scheme here, it is not clear whether my word *error* refers to something done by the printer, the binder, or the bibliographer: the history of catalogue intentions subsequently bears upon the production of variation, both real and imagined.

1. Gen. title page FRAGMENTA AUREA vs. Fragmenta Aurea
2. part-title page for *Aglaura*; printed by T.W. for Humphrey Moseley and are to be sold at his shop / Printed for Tho.

Walkley, and are to be sold by Humphrey Moseley at his shop[13]

There are then some subsidiary variants, which may or may not be of bibliographical significance:

3. underline under imprint date of t.p.
4. the existence (real or inferred) of the initial blank
5. press variant allowrd/allowed on A3v of gen. prel.
6. state of the engraved author's portrait

These are all bibliographical variants, although in more or less descending order of importance: the state of the engraving would, in a bibliographical sense, be irrelevant.

Other more problematic variants include:

7. order of texts
8. the make-up of the preliminaries (prologue)
9. autonomy of individual parts

These last three variants are easily produced in the later history of the book: an individual copy might be broken up, parts re-ordered or bound separately, during which leaves might migrate from one location to another. If such things are unique to the later history of individual book-copies, they have no bibliographical significance. If they were produced deliberately at press (for example, the printer intended to distribute and sell sections individually), then they should be so catalogued. The two kinds of variants need to be distinguished, even though the evidence might not absolutely determine how to do so.

Certain variants are privileged: what is printed on the title page will generally lead to "bibliographical variants" (that is,

---

[13] Thomas Warren's name seems to be imported from 1648 edition: Letters t.p. (Printed by Tho. Warren for Humphrey Moseley). 93mm type is not the same as 92mm type used by Raworth. Tho. Warren in 1648 may be T.W. of 1646; I can't confirm the identity of type or ornaments, but I don't dispute it.

the things referred to or described in catalogues). A title-page variant will usually show up as two different entries in standard catalogues. A simple press variant (the variant on A3) is of no importance in and of itself to descriptive bibliography; that is, it does not result in a bibliographical variant, although it might constitute a point for a scrupulous collector. The word variant can refer confusingly to all these levels.[14]

I begin with the variants of the preliminaries. The most basic ones are those of the title page; according to the rules of descriptive bibliography, these rightly or wrongly define editions.[15]

Greg had identified two variants of the title page, easily distinguished typographically as FRAGMENTA AVREA vs. Fragmenta Aurea. Beaurline and Clayton's *Studies in Bibliography* article of 1970 described not two but three states, based on a detail earlier noted by Greg, but considered of no bibliographical import. These three states are unfortunately called A B and C, the same letters to be used in Wing II, but with entirely different meanings.

A: FRAG AUREA (most have error on A3v)
B: Frag Aurea (as above) without period after d, w/o rule under date (now = Wing 6216A)
C: Frag Aurea rule visible under date (now= Wing 6216B)

To Beaurline and Clayton, the "direction of variation" was A–C, and this is the opposite of what is implied in Greg and later in Wing's second edition. According to their argument, when "FRAGMENTA AUREA" was reset as "Fragmenta Aurea,"

---

14 STC2 simplifies the language through use of the terminology: ed., anr. ed., and var. This avoids the overuse of the problematic term "issue," or the even more bibliographically pernicious "re-issue."

15 Bowers, "Definitions," *Principles of Bibliographical Description*, 37ff., 113–15: the title page carries more weight in determining whether a "state" rises to the level of "issue" or "var. edition" than would a variant on any other page. But the reason is as much bibliographical as historical, in that individual copies are generally catalogued and thus defined primarily by what is on the title page.

slightly more space was required. The date was intended to be underlined on both pages, but this line moved below the frisket when the page was reset (the final d and final . were also obscured by the frisket). At some point in the print-run, this was corrected, and the error *allowrd* changed to *allowed*. Most copies thus show the underline.

Beaurline and Clayton claim they can see the uninked impression of the rule in the Huntington Library copy. I am certain they did: but I also say you can see almost anything when you have sufficient certainty it is there. I have the Huntington copy in front of me, and I cannot see what they claim is there; that may be because, certain though I am that the rule was indeed there on the forme (I agree with Beaurline and Clayton on this), I am less certain that such a rule would leave a visible impression on the printed paper through the frisket. I (thus?) see nothing.

Beaurline and Clayton do not discuss the implications of this for sorting out editions and catalogue entries (for example, the relation of this variant to the variation in part-title pages). Nor is there any direct statement as to how these title-page variants bear on the question of edition. Bibliographers usually refer to states as reflecting "what is on the typeset forme" and variation as indicated by a movement or change in type. I can't come up with another example quite like this, where typographical state is defined by matters of imposition rather than type, although I'm sure such books exist. If Beaurline and Clayton are correct that the Huntington copy is set from a forme containing the rule (whose impression they claim to see and which I divine), doesn't that mean it is typographically and thus bibliographically the same as S6126B? ESTC regards the variant title-page copies as variants of S6126B, but assigns them a new entry.[16]

---

[16] I do not understand (nor do the cataloguers I have consulted) why Beaurline and Clayton in 1970 do not refer to Wing's first edition at least in passing, which came out almost twenty years earlier. Contemporary reviews of the second edition referred to the first edition in much the same way — e.g., "an imperfect instrument but an indispensable one" (Robert Donaldson, rev. Donald G. Wing, *Short-Title Catalogue,* in *The Bibliotheck* 6, no. 5 (1973): 203–4, at 203.

The variants involving this real or phantom rule and even the variant title pages do not suggest significant facts about the printing history beyond the order in which these sheets were printed: they do not indicate an act of re-publication or re-issue. These variants thus have collecting value and define bibliographical editions, but they do not reflect on printing procedures the way variants in the part-title pages might do in other books. Preliminaries are conventionally printed last, and it is difficult to argue for any further motivation (for example, that changes were made in order to make the style reflect that of part-title pages).

Structure of Preliminaries

ESTC now employs in its physical descriptions only a pagination or foliation statement, not a full collation. It is difficult to determine from an ESTC description what the initial structure for a book with unpaginated preliminaries is or should be, and difficult also to determine how any particular copy described by a reporting library differs from an ideal copy; for example, the statement "[8]" describing a preliminary quire of four leaves (eight pages), doesn't tell us what to expect of those leaves. Greg provided a standard collation formula, yet his descriptions are occasionally so abstruse, it is no less difficult for cataloguers to follow or even to understand his conventions. Even Greg seems to have lost sight of their implications.

Greg collates the preliminary quire as follows: $A^4(A1 + 1)$. This means that the initial quire of the ideal copy is a four-leaf quire of a quarto (printed on a half-sheet) with the engraving tipped in between the first and second leaf. A1, under this collation, is blank.[17] Greg thus analyzes that quire as follows:

---

17 Complete statement: 8o. piA^4 (A1 + 1), A–G^8, H^4, 2A–E^8 F^4, 3A–D^8, 4A–C^8 D^4 [3C4 misprinted "4")], 169 leaves, paged (A2) 3–199, (2A4) 1–82, (3A2) 3–64, (4A3v) 2–52. Engraved portrait…pi A1 + 1V (recto and pi A1 blank) (Greg, *Bibliography of Restoration Drama,* 3: 1131).

pi A⁴(A1 + 1)

[A1 is an unsigned blank leaf, missing in most copies, theoretically conjugate with A4][18]

A1 + 1 — an inserted leaf with engraving ("A1 + 1" thus can refer to both a quire structure and a leaf, whereas "A1 +1v" refers to a specific page).

A2 — unsigned title page, theoretically conjugate (sewn) with A3 and part of same sheet as A1 and 4

A3 — signed "to the Reader"

A4 — end of "To the Reader"; verso blank

Since this is the standard description, any copy listed with no specific note to the contrary should conform to it. But this is not the case.

I believe Greg's collation is correct, but reporting libraries might well have difficulty understanding exactly what he is saying (as I did when I first encountered this description, and as I believe any cataloguer pressed for time might as well). For many such formulae, the only sure way to critique them or at times even to understand them is to have the book-copies on hand that are the bases for both the ideal-copy description and its variants.

The variants one would expect are: copies lacking the initial blank; copies missing the author's portrait; and author's portrait misplaced or pasted in. These might be legitimately described as follows: A⁴ or A⁴(-A1 + 1) or A⁴ (-A1), although one would be hard pressed to understand what these formulae mean without the books in hand (these would be used to describe the presence or absence of the initial blank and the tipped-in engraving). Greg lists three such variants, describing them as "(-pi A1, wants port.)" "-pi A1" "+pi A1" "wants port" "+pi A1." I believe this implies that every copy is described either as containing or as lacking the blank A1 (that is, every copy either is +A1 or -A1).

---

[18] A1 is required in Greg's formula even if no copies contain it, since under Greg's conventions, all quires must have even numbers, and all parts of original sheet (or half-sheet) must be accounted for, even if they don't exist.

But this is not the case. Most copies are simply listed without note, meaning that they conform to ideal-copy description. Does the note "wants port." mean that all other copies contain it? And what to make of this: "New York (2, one +pi A1)" that is, New York has two copies, one of which lacks the opening blank? Why is that not designated "-A1"? I believe I know what Greg means with all these distinctions, but without the books in hand, I cannot determine whether the reporting libraries agree with him.[19] I assume it is the complexity of collation statements that made ESTC opt for the easier pagination statements (pagination statements of reporting libraries are simply more reliable than collation statements). A common copy lacking the initial blank would have to be described by a cumbersome statement, such as, "A⁴(-A1, +A1 + 1) or simply (and ambiguously) -A1. A pagination statement could state: [8, lacks initial blank] [8, lacks portrait]. Note, however, that ESTC's pagination statements do not account for the structure of the preliminaries; all variants are listed as follows:

[8], 119, [7], 82, 64, [4], 52 p.

Any copy that was missing either the initial blank or the author's portrait would seem to fit this formula (the ideal copy descrip-

---

19 For example, the following: "BM (-pi A1, wants port.) [Why not: - A1, -(A1 + 1)?]

 Worc. 1 A1 Folger Harvard (one +A1, one wants port.) Hunt. Prince (+A1)."

 The Huntington copy does not have the blank; had Greg examined it (I assume the lack of a note suggests he had not), it should read (- A1). The second Huntington copy (under dagger 1) reads (+A1). I cannot determine from Greg the nature of Harvard copies: Houghton Reference tells me they have 3 copies: "A & B have second state t.p (=STC B); C is missing prelim. There is no portrait in B or C. A has two nineteenth-century blanks before portrait (thus missing A1). B and C have blank leaves, but also modern (thus also missing at least A1)."

tion), although as Greg's collation makes clear, we can see that they do not.[20]

A basic problem with all these formulae can be seen by looking at the 1648 edition and Greg's description. This is a page-for-page reprint of 1646 and is identical in structure (the paper is folded exactly the same way as in the 1646 edition). Nonetheless, Greg's description of the preliminaries is completely different: "1648:...8° pi A⁴." There are no references to variants in these preliminaries other than "wants port." According to a strict interpretation of this, there is no such thing as a copy with an initial blank, although you do not have to search far to find that such copies do, in fact, exist. Furthermore, even if those copies did not exist, by Greg's own rules, that blank would have to be accounted for. You cannot have a singleton unless it is pasted in or tipped in (+1). Any leaf that is letter-press must have a conjugate or must have once had one. And any copy without that conjugate must be listed as lacking it. The A⁴ designation of the preliminaries here implies that the portrait is engraved on the conjugate of leaf A⁴, not impossible, but not the way this book was made. The collation formula should be identical to that of the 1646 edition (ESTC's pagination statement is in fact the same, and the problems with that are of course the same ones as in the 1646 edition).

Ghost Variants

Among further variants in the preliminaries is what I'll call the ghost variant in a Harvard copy of S6126B producing ghost editions in both EEBO and ESTC. This presumed variant contains "different preliminaries": it contains the Prologue, signed A2 fol-

---

20 The initial blank also poses a problem; bibliographers have always had difficulty in noting the difference between an original blank, its absence, or a blank added by a binder, even for extremely valuable books. See Joseph A. Dane, "Wanting the First Blank: The Frontispiece to the Huntington Library Copy of Caxton's *Recuyell of the Historyes of Troye*," *Huntington Library Quarterly* 67, no. 2 (2004): 315–25.

lowing the unsigned title page, before "To the Reader," which begins (as in all copies) on A3. This copy thus appears to have the following structure:

[portrait]
[A1] title page
A2 Prologue
A3–4 To the Reader

But this structure is illusory. The so-called "Prologue" is not to *Fragmenta Aurea*. It is rather to *Aglaura,* and the leaf containing it follows (or should follow) the part-title page there.

I cannot explain how or when this leaf migrated from its correct position to the preliminaries, and the implication in ESTC that more than one copy actually has this variant, point, or defect is clearly false. It is nonetheless easy to see how this was missed, even at Harvard, where other copies are available. A book-copy with a four-leaf preliminary quire including the author's portrait, general title page, a prologue on a leaf signed A2, followed by a leaf marked A3, would be easily interpretable as a four-leaf quire with a tipped-in portrait. A2 would be interpreted (wrongly) as conjugate with A3. It is possible, although I don't know the evidence for this, that a book-dealer was unscrupulously creating "points" here (with the hypothetical description "Lot 823, *Fragmenta Aurea,* with the rare variant 'To the Reader' in the preliminaries"). By the time any dealer could have done this, or owner be fooled by it, the bibliographical resources were easily available to determine that this was a simple binding mistake. But to do so would have required time and effort, which no one involved would have had the incentive to expend.

Other ghost variants are less due to library mistakes than to their conventions. Even a cursory glance at the various catalogue entries reveals several of the presumed editions listed singly seem to have no or only tenuous bibliographical autonomy. This proliferation of ghost editions is due to the material holdings in individual libraries. The British Library in its general catalogue lists the two principal variants as one printed by "Walkley" and the other by "T.W.," described as "anr. copy, imperfect wanting portrait." These are the same two variants acknowledged in all modern catalogues, although the absence of the portrait is irrelevant. But the catalogue also lists an autonomous copy of *Goblins*: "another copy of pt. 3, containing 'The Goblins' ... (imperfect, wanting pp. 17–32)." This "copy of pt. 3" then receives an independent entry: "The Goblins ... 1646, wanting pp. 17–32" (shelfmark 644.c72).[21] The imperfect copy of *Fragmenta Aurea* becomes an imperfect copy of *The Goblins*, where there is no cross reference to the earlier entry. This may not be technically a ghost, although if there is no evidence that it differs from bound copies in any way, and no evidence for its originality, there would seem to be no reason to catalogue it separately, other than the shelving conventions of the library. The British Library catalogue is in the business of pointing to or directing its users to book-copies, and they thus acknowledge two book-copies with different titles: Suckling *Fragmenta Aurea* and Suckling *Goblins*.

Looking at numerous extant copies as well as descriptions of them, I see no evidence that any of these books were sold separately, or that contemporary booksellers or their customers constructed anything other than the standard copy. If these texts were distributed independently, they would likely appear in *Sammelband* with whatever other texts an owner happened to have. And there certainly ought to be copies of individual plays bound in with other plays not by Suckling. Yet what we see here, as a general rule, is that whenever one of these texts is bound in with another text, those other texts are invariably parts of this collection.

These texts (or books) came into existence as individual items recatalogued or rebound as single copies, perhaps due to a damaged copy of *Fragmenta Aurea*. Any library owning one of

---

21 "Explore the British Library," *British Library*, http://explore.bl.uk/, s.v. Suckling 1646. The on-line entry here repeats information from *British Museum General Catalogue of Printed Books to 1955*, 263 vols. (London: British Library, 1959–66).

these single texts certainly has to catalogue it that way: a holdings catalogue points to physical objects on shelves. This is fine for an individual library (provincial library X contains a complete copy of, say, *The Goblins,* not a partial copy of *Fragmenta Aurea*). Yet cataloguers or librarians are not justified in idealizing the copy in their collection (that is, moving from the level of enumerative to descriptive bibliography), just because history happened to put one there.

Conclusion

There are obvious complexities in this book, and when I first encountered it, I expected to find some of what I found here — a proliferation of editions based on the eccentricities and accidents of provenance. I assumed this would involve the order of parts, since the first copy I looked at had these parts misplaced, but that turned out not to be the case. There is nothing overly complicated about this book: its publication history is reasonably well stated by the internal evidence alone; it is re-edited, and it is part of a series of books (by Moseley) all in similar format. Given that, the errors in standard catalogues are somewhat surprising: Greg's collations, the ghosts in reporting libraries, the obvious errors in EEBO, and more surprisingly, in the state-of-the-art bibliography ESTC.

Editions of this book proliferate as variant forms in individual libraries are reported and as analytical bibliographers do the work they are supposed to do.

The dependence on real copies rather than principles of bibliography is problematic, as a brief thought experiment can show, one that is very real in the minds of bibliographers, cataloguers, and collectors. Suppose, for example, that a library contained a copy with the general title page ("Fragmenta Aurea"), the preliminaries, then the first part ("Poems"). This would be regarded as an incomplete copy of *Fragmenta Aurea,* and essentially valueless. If the owner then tore out the preliminaries and the general title page, that owner would now own a perhaps "rare and hitherto unrecorded" copy of Suckling's *Poems* (beginning with the seemingly correct quire A). Perhaps that same owner could seek through the torn out sections of other books to complete the set: *Poems, Aglaura, Goblins, Brennoralt.* Anyone who has looked through book or auction catalogues or even the notes of an eager seller is familiar with examples of this.

ESTC bibliographers were at a great disadvantage in comparison with Pollard and Redgrave in their 1926 STC, on which the revised STC and now the ESTC is based. We can assume, given the small number of entries (ca. 30,000 English books printed up to 1640), that Pollard and Redgrave saw, or could be reasonably expected to have seen, actual copies or facsimiles of the books they were cataloguing, including many of the reported variants. ESTC includes books printed up to 1800 (roughly 400,000); their bibliographers, consequently, have to rely to a large extent on the descriptions sent in by librarians (who were not necessarily bibliographers) working in individual collections. And, as we have seen in the case of Greg, it is not always easy to coordinate one's description of a physical book with the most detailed of bibliographical descriptions, a problem compounded by the use of simpler pagination statements.

The problems we encounter in enumerative and descriptive bibliography, trivial as they are, are simply too numerous to allow us to give enough attention to solve them. I can devote months to a single book if I am so inclined. A professional cataloguer or bibliographer, whose word carries much more authority than mine ever could, only has a few hours, if that, before being forced to move on to the next assignment. Furthermore, our bibliographical language often gets in the way of the things it is trying to describe, in just the same way as our historical narratives and theories get in the way of the material evidence that seems to support them. We already know as much as we would ever want to about the printing procedures of how this book came to be: history may be clear, yet our descriptions (the main source of my interest) remain murky. And yet even as this case shows, that murky tradition trumps the material details it is intended to describe; it is easier for all of us to accept and account for Wing's numbers (in fact, there seems little other choice) than to re-visit this corpus afresh.

CODA

T.F. Dibdin
The Rhetoric of Bibliophilia

I am thinking again of the date 1800, the crucial date in printing history: "ca. 1800," the hand-press period, the rise and progress of modern bibliography.[1] If we turn to English bibliography or book history of this period — the period of transition — one name dominates all others: Thomas Frognall Dibdin.

I have tried to write the history of Dibdin earlier, imagining a scholarly narrative to place him within history. That history would be understood as a history of type or typography, the very history Dibdin announces in the title of his four-volume revision of Joseph Ames's *Typographical Antiquities* of 1749, still a classic of English bibliography, written when typography was a synecdoche for what we now call printing.[2] But history is a complex thing, as is "a" history or "the" history. I settled instead for reproducing some of Dibdin's reproductions: images, type — the very idealizing of historical images that I discuss here and elsewhere — abstracting evidence to produce an image or version of evidence that is much more persuasive than the original. I set-

1 Joseph A. Dane, "'Ca. 1800': What's in a Date?" in *Blind Impressions: Methods and Mythologies in Book History*, 37–57 (Philadelphia: University of Pennsylvania Press, 2013).
2 Joseph Ames, *Typographical Antiquities: Being an Historical Account of Printing in England*, 3 vols. (London, 1749); rev. William Herbert and Thomas Frognall Dibdin, *Typographical Antiquities, or the History of Printing in England*, 4 vols. (London: Miller, 1810–19). See, further, Joseph A. Dane, *Out of Sorts: On Typography and Print Culture* (Philadelphia: University of Pennsylvania Press, 2011), 164–90.

tled, that is, for my own failure to write the narrative. I did not understand the reasons for this (or at least, I couldn't come up with a convincing reason for it).

A student studying the Romantics was referred to me by a colleague at the last stages of his dissertation. He had a chapter on Dibdin, I was told. (Is Dibdin Romantic?) I might be interested. I might help. The dissertation involved modern theory (my colleague likely implied this was lacking in my own work); there was a relation to queer theory, about which I knew not very much. I read the chapter. It was like a version of my own more professional chapter, and I could see too the history of my own dissertation there: drafts, false steps, the good days of insight and enthusiasm. I could calculate his days of work in the obvious seams between sections. This was exactly what I would have written as a graduate student, I thought, had I been directed to a topic as interesting as this one. It was similar to what I write today when I cannot get the narrative straight, as I cannot get this one straight.

"Queer? You say?" We are not talking about Dibdin's sexuality, of course. "Well have you read him?" I asked. "Dibdin's style. It's damn queer, wouldn't you say?" Why not a word on that? After all, Grad Student, you are not, say, a book historian, looking for amusing anecdotes about book prices and conditions in the early nineteenth century, so what else could possibly be interesting about Dibdin? As an example:

> The *Erudition* of Caxton appears to me to be deserving of better treatment than Bale and others have bestowed upon it. That he had a far greater claim to intellectual reputation than that of possessing the mere negative excellence of "not being downright stupid or slothful" must be allowed by the most fastidious reader of his numerous prologues and translations; and how a late "very learned" author of an amusing publication called "*Anonymiana*"* could so readily subscribe to the acrimonious censure of Bale, can only be accounted for from the supposition of his not having been conversant in Caxtonian lore. The reader will consult the numerous "*Testimo-*

nies" relating to the character and talents of our Typographer, which are selected in the preceding pages [vide p. lxiv to lxxi] and draw his own conclusion from the preponderating body of authority adduced. For my part, I should hope that the suffrages of commendation would be found more numerous than those of disapprobation....[3]

I could go on. I wish I could make this up. I employ the Sortes Dibdiniana method, and open the book at random:

The lover of rare old books, who has particularly turned his attention to the ancient specimens of the French presses, will probably call to mind the very singular and gigantic capital initial prefixed to the work, without date, entitled "*La Mer des Histoires*;" printed in the black letter....Although it has been my object to revive the use of the picturesque typographical ornaments, yet I should be unwilling to have it supposed that I encouraged the introduction only of such *bizarre* capital initial as are in these books, or in the above specimens, submitted to the reader's notice.[4]

I have no idea what qualification Dibdin is making here, or what he thought the image of the two animals, locked in what appears to be some kind of sado-masochistic sexual embrace forming a, to me, unreadable initial, might mean.

Another example, one littered with erudition:

While Herbert has equalled the industry of Bagford, and eclipsed the reputation of Ames, he has evinced such diligence, patience, and minute fidelity, as have scarcely been exhibited by the most distinguished *foreign* bibliographers; and if he does not display the liveliness of Chevillier, and the taste

---

3 Dibdin, *Typographical Antiquities*, 1:cxiv–cxv.
4 Ibid., 1:xxxii, n*).

> of Renouard he unites in himself all the accuracy of Audiffredi, and the perseverance of Panzer.[5]

As I read this, it becomes like a foreign language. I read with part of my attention, and perhaps a half-beat behind (or am I getting Dibdinesque?) translate what I have absorbed into an intelligible English sentence or thought. Do I know what is being said? And if I can follow the allusion to Renouard (book on Aldus? taste? I don't get it), even concur with the "perseverance of Panzer" (I think), who, then, is Audiffredi, or Chevillier, and do I have to stop to admit I don't know?

And I wonder too what Dibdin intended with all this impressive bibliography: was he interested in being remembered as a learned scholar of old books? Or as an eccentric old coot with a flair for style that he doubtless thought amusing for reasons utterly different from those we have for coming to the same judgment?

It is as if Dibdin has built an icon of the history he is describing, where we can pick out in the blur of his style a few "facts" as they would later be known, and put them in some usable, if not entirely intelligible order. Dibdin's style and technique become the very thing he is talking about, and we either throw our hands up in despair (I will never understand history; I will never get through Dibdin), or we just mine it for what we can, precisely the same thing we (or in this case, I) do when confronted with a card catalogue or heap of books in a rare book library, or the clutter of received or disconnected facts such as I find in Spurgeon, that allow us to construct a narrative or argument about "what happened" at some arbitrarily defined moment or period of history? How can we discover what those people were thinking if we are unable to find out what they were doing?

Dibdin is always in history, I then conclude, somewhat magisterially. But he is never a part of history. Damn queer, that Dibdin fellow!

---

5   Ibid., 1:91–93.

And why is it, I wonder, so many of those who followed him — those sober bibliographers like Samuel Sotheby, or Henry Bradshaw and his followers, or William Blades, who was certainly subject at times to the infections of Dibdin's style — why do they make no notice of this? And why does Grad Student pass over this as if it were the most natural thing in the world to sound like a crazy person? Have graduate students so assimilated what I call the Myth of Complete Competence that nothing sounds baffling to them anymore?

Again:

> I refer the student of ancient English literature to the elegant extracts given from this work by Warton and Mr. G. Ellis: but, as so much has been here said in commendation of it, he may probably not be displeased with the subjoined specimens....[6]

Or this:

> Homer, as the reader will naturally imagine, is the fountain head of it; but his pure stream has been so polluted by the absurdities of Dares and Dictys, and, in the 13th century, by the licentiousness of Guido de Colonna, that it has no pretensions whatever to a faithful historical legend....[7]

This is what Dibdin is, for better or for worse. And this is what connects him to the often quoted Thomas Warton, even though Warton is the soberest of scholars by comparison — reined in, I suppose, by the stylistic conventions of the late eighteenth century. And this is what distinguishes him from Blades or Bradshaw, whose styles often (not always!) seem to disappear in some kind of Addisonian transparency, I will say, in imitation of the very things I am both deriding and trying to discuss.

---

6 Ibid., 1:181.
7 Ibid., 1:9.

The following is typical of Blades in his more popular works, that is, those addressed to casual collectors rather than, say, professional scholars:

> The first edition of the *Canterbury Tales* is to them an ugly book and nothing more: they would prefer a volume of *Punch*. But convince them that a copy would fetch £1000 at public sale, and if there is the least chance of their shelves containing so rich a prize, no one will be more anxious and eager for a thorough examination. … Before stating the specific measurements of each type, I will give a few rules, which, in numerous instances, will, at a glance, enable the reader to "tell a Caxton" without even the trouble of measurement.[8]

Blades could be considered the second great descriptive bibliographer of the nineteenth century in England. I can claim this is a "breath of fresh air," or, having attuned oneself to Dibdin, or somehow allowed Dibdin to set the standard for style, I can simply shake my head and say I don't care a whit about the accuracy of his descriptions, the seminal nature of his work, the Caxton industry that owes so much to him: "The man's heart" I sadly say, "is just not in it."

To study Dibdin, then, is not to study what one imagines. We are not studying English literature or bibliography, not the history of English prose style or any prose style. Hardly the history of books, because the data Dibdin collected has been more or less transformed into the language of contemporary bibliography already. We are studying, then, a particular aberration in whatever history or subject we have defined. We were going to study books. We find ourselves instead within the aesthetics of prose style.

This, we could convince ourselves, is the difference between bibliography and what used to be called bibliophilia, the difference between collecting and cataloguing, dilettantism and true

---

8 William Blades, *How to Tell a Caxton, with some hints where and how the same might be found* (London: Sotheran, 1870), 6.

scholarship, or however we wish to define that. Yet even these categories are historically determined and only really apply to the period under discussion, which we alone would define, it turns out, in these terms. We try to put Dibdin within a dichotomy, and we end up again only projecting the modern categories we started with: history, we conclude, begins with dilettantism in the service of the aristocracy, and ends with the democratic meritocracy we imagine has privileged us.

part 3

CACOPHONIES
A BIBLIOGRAPHICAL RONDO

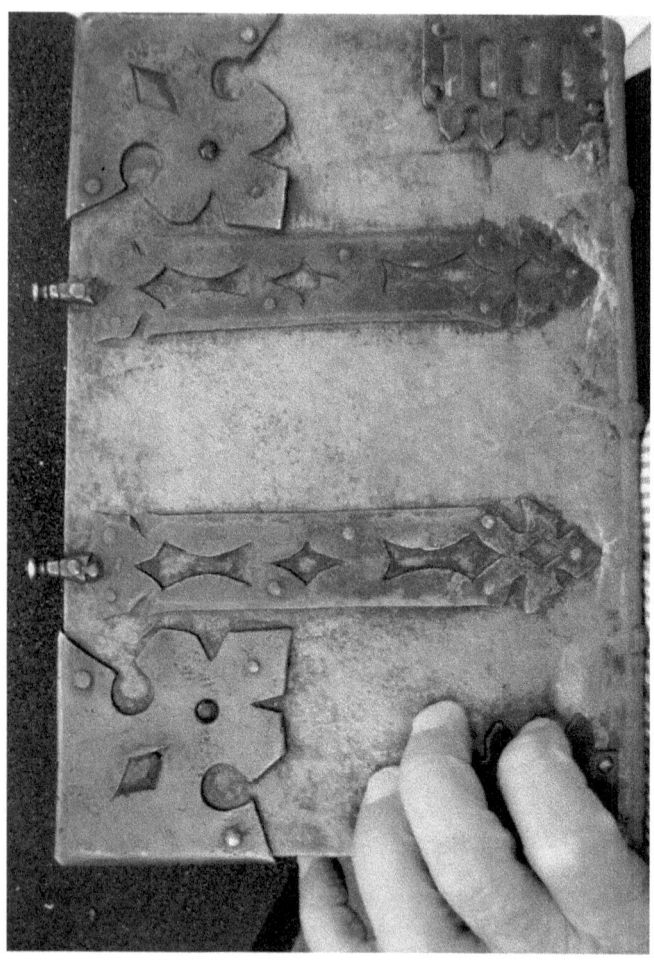

Figure 9. The Flewelling Antiphonary

SECTION 3.1

Fakes and Frauds
The "Flewelling Antiphonary" and Galileo's *Sidereus Nuncius*

I. The Flewelling Antiphonary

Doheny Special Collections at University of Southern California has a book (or a book object) catalogued as "The Flewelling Antiphonary." It is difficult to describe this, so I will provide a photo before proceeding.

It was recently restored and placed in a foam box. This restoration, as far as I can determine, consisted of rebacking (that is, replacing the spine) and possibly resewing of quires, although there are no detailed records of exactly what was done (and no reason such records should have been kept). I wish I could remember what this object looked like ten years ago when I first saw it. I remember that it was not noticeably fragile, and I assume it had not much changed since it came into the library in the 1920s. The question I had then, one I still have now, and one all my students ask when they see this is, "What exactly is this?" and, as a variant, "Is it genuine?" These are much like the questions students ask about the Voynich Manuscript or the Vinland Map. Are they genuine or authentic? Or are they fake? What is the difference between these two questions, and are they the only alternatives?[1]

Provenance

Ralph Tyler Flewelling was a professor of philosophy at USC in the early twentieth century, begetter of the "personalist" movement, which seems to have been complacent, Christian, and opposed to most things German, although steeped in that philosophical culture.[2] In his ambitions to form an important school of philosophy at USC, he also made many purchases for the library, often in philosophy (2000 volumes from the library of Theodor Gomperz in 1937) but also of early books and manuscripts. I had assumed, looking through the collection, that the incunables (some forty or fifty of them) had entered the library somewhat haphazardly. Most, however, were purchased by Flewelling himself on several European trips in the 1920s and from various local dealers in Los Angeles.[3]

What is now the "Flewelling antiphonary" is an oddity. It is not mentioned in Nethery's biography nor in Flewelling's own autobiographical *Forest of Yggdrasill*, even though this book is one of his more striking purchases. The book came from a cer-

---

1 As noted by Julian Brown, "Authenticity and fake are not the only possible verdicts": Julian Brown, *A Palaeographer's View: Selected Writings of Julian Brown*, eds. Janet Bateley, Michelle Brown, and Jane Roberts, chap. 11, "The Detection of Faked Literary Manuscripts," 253–62 (London: Harvey Miller, 1993).

2 Wallace Nethery, *Dr. Flewelling & the Hoose Library: Life and Letters of a Man and an Institution* (Los Angeles: University of Southern California Press, 1976), and, more extravagantly, Ralph Tyler Flewelling, *The Forest of Yggdrasill: The Autobiography of Ralph Tyler Flewelling*, ed. W.H. Werkmeister, with an introduction by Wilbur Long (Los Angeles: University of Southern California Press, 1962), e.g., "We pitch our camp in our symboled Jotunnheim and seek the wisdom of its waters in reflections upon memories past" (19). *The Personalist*, edited by Flewelling, was published until 1980, when it became *the Pacific Philosophical Quarterly*.

3 Nethery, *Dr. Flewelling*, 101–8, and Flewelling, *The Forest of Yggdrasill*, 88–93.

tain Meynial, whose letter of sale should provide some evidence as to the nature (or perceived nature) of this volume. But to me, it does not:

> Monsieur Ralph Tyler Fleweling
> Monsieur
> J'ai l'honneur de vous informer que la reliure avec ferrures que vous avez vue est du prise de 700 fr.
>   Veuillez agréer Monsieur mes salutations distingués
> M Meynial

The date (which I believe is 1929) is of some importance, since the reports of exchange rates vary from 25/1 in some sources to 1/1 in others. That is, between 70 and 700 USD in the late 1920s, roughly between 1,000 and 10,000 USD today. That range, unfortunately, is almost exactly the range distinguishing "cheap" from "expensive." And whether it was cheap or expensive might well inform what the word "reliure" means or was meant to mean: was this being sold simply for the clever binding? Or did this suggest a rebound manuscript that was itself "genuine"?

Once this book came into USC's possession, it seems always to have been regarded with suspicion (or bafflement) by librarians. It was never catalogued until very recently, although this was also true of much of their rare book collection.[4] I first saw it in the early 1990s when it was handed to me by a now retired rare book librarian, John Ahouse, who wondered what the library should do with it. Since then, it seems to have gained in prestige: the catalogue now has a "local note" suggesting it is "16th c." (the binding? the book block?) and it now has a new foam box in honor of a retired staff member.[5] Nonetheless, the official main-entry description contains little more. Even today,

---

[4] Until the Incunabula Short-Title Catalogue project, USC's incunables were more or less identified through whatever typed inscription they had when they came into the library.

[5] From USC public catalogue: "Publication info: 16th century Local note: USC Libraries Special Collections' copy restored in honor of Courtney Suri's service to USC, May 1, 2012."

no one seems to know how to describe this, and, as is the case with any book or art work, each restoration removes a bit more of the evidence required for reconstructing its history.

So I know "where it came from" — that is, the last stage of its provenance. On other basic questions, I am on shakier ground, and I find myself looking for experts: on paleography, bookbinding, clasps, vellum, painting, restoration, ink composition, musical notation, the liturgy (etc.). I do not have the competence to offer definitive judgments on any of these subjects. I certainly know those who could, but having dealt with many such experts in the past, I have learned that a good many of them pronounce with equal assurance on things they know well and things about which they are uncertain. You don't get the reputation of expertise by saying too often, "I really have no idea." (The default response seems to be, "I'll get back to you.")

I look at this book: I see bejeweled binding, probably visually "like" other such bindings (from where?) with, to me, extraordinarily large clasps in far better shape than others I have seen. At first glance, I would say this was a binding manufactured for some early film on Robin Hood. The vellum is discolored, and the colors unlike those I have seen elsewhere....I dream of having the radiological equipment that was used in the case of the *Sidereus Nuncius* (see discussion in part two of this section) to confirm whatever conclusion I might draw from this.

I would like to know more about the music notation in the manuscript, since I do not know whether it can be read at all. But this question too is not an easy one to deal with: to argue that the music is genuine (whatever that means) would likely require the assumption that it was copied from some other source (a manuscript of this same text?) and therefore reproduces an earlier representation of music which the manuscript creator may or may not have understood.

The same thing might apply to the writing, but here at least I have a few material notes to go on. The writing misuses the convention distinguishing round r from ordinary r (but so does, say, early printing). There are also numerous errors in Latin: p for the abbreviation *pro-*, for example. But none of that is period specific; scribes could misuse or misread or misunderstand Latin and basic writing conventions at any period of history. More amusing, comparing the opening to the later pages, it is as if one were viewing a summary history of medieval writing, from legible, late Carolingian (with clear letters, marked right slant), to a more formal textura. What we have is the record of a "scribe" (or workman or young child) working on imitating a textura hand during a period when no one was trained to write it. This version of paleographical history is constructed in a teleological fashion with textura as its goal, as if there had been no Renaissance or Enlightenment. But all this of course cannot be the case; the creator of this book was not a serious student of paleography. It's simply a projection of the way I am accustomed to view any series of differing hands that are used in real or faux medieval works.

I turn back to the minimal catalog notes, and see that what is dated as the sixteenth century is the manuscript, not the binding, and it is said to have possible eighth- or ninth-century illustrations. The first time I looked at this record, there were no notes available, but I state that only from memory. I distinctly remember that year (or was it two years later?) remarking in the presence of someone (who?) that those full-page illustrations were not characteristic of late liturgical manuscripts and that these were…did I say "like?" "in the style of?" illustrations from Carolingian manuscripts? Looking at this book today, I cannot help but wonder whether that remark is now embedded in this description. But the word "today," even in that last sentence, is a flexible thing: this very paragraph is based on notes taken in 2013/14. "Today" (now meaning "the summer of 2017"), all that remains is what I quote in footnote 5 above; the earlier notes have been expunged. And for good reason: for these illustrations are nothing at all like Carolingian ones. The figures are vertical; the faces are staid, completely unlike the curvaceous and brooding faces one finds in Carolingian manuscripts or their reproductions. They are reminiscent of the stodgy, spare reproductions of medieval manuscripts found in various publications of T.F. Dibdin. They copy something. And maybe that source was itself "genuine" in some sense. But the same thing could be said not only of late copies and reproductions, but of the vast majority of manuscript paintings and miniatures themselves.

II. [Galileo's] Sidereus Nuncius

About a decade ago, a copy of Galileo's *Sidereus Nuncius* came on the market. The Sidereus Nuncius is not a rare book: some eighty copies are known. But this one was unique in that it contained or purported to contain Galileo's signature and illustrations of phases of the moon drawn by Galileo himself. In other copies, these are etched; some ordinary paper copies leave blank spaces where these illustrations were to appear. The book became the subject of a number of scholarly projects; the most important was a two-volume work edited by Horst Bredekamp (2011). The Bredekamp volumes gave the scientific and bibliographical evidence authenticating the book; numerous skeptical studies and early reviews, as well as a 2013 *New Yorker* article by Nicholas Schmidle, provided the counterargument. Following the *New Yorker* article, a third volume of the Bredekamp project appeared (2014), renouncing the conclusions reached (or assumed) in the first two.[6]

---

6 Horst Bredekamp, gen. ed., *Galileo's O, Vol. 1: Galileo's Sidereus Nuncius: A Comparison of the Proof Copy (New York) with Other Paradigmatic Copies*, eds. Irene Brückle and Oliver Hahn (Berlin: Akademie Verlag, 2011), and Horst Bredekamp, gen. ed., *Galileo's O, Vol. 2: Galileo Makes a Book: The First Edition of Sidereus Nuncius, Venice 1610*, ed. Paul Needham (Berlin: Akademie Verlag, 2011). Horst Bredekamp (gen. ed.), *Galileo's O, Vol. 3: A Galileo Forgery (Galileo's O): Unmasking the New York Sidereus Nuncius*, eds. Irene Brückle and Paul Needham (Berlin: De Gruyter, 2014). See the skeptical review of Bredekamp's first two volumes and references by Stefano Gattei, Review of Horst Bredekamp (gen. ed.), *Galileo's O, Nuncius Newsletter* 6, December 10, 2012, http://www.museogalileo.it/en/newsletterslist/nunciusnewsletter_06_2012_eng/book_reviews_06_2012.html; Nicholas Schmidle, "A Very Rare Book: The Mystery Surrounding a Copy of Galileo's Pivotal Treatise," *The New Yorker*, 16 December, 2013, https://www.newyorker.com/magazine/2013/12/16/a-very-rare-book. The most important figure

What I am concerned with here is not the authenticity of the volume, but rather the process of authentication. The crowning achievement was Bredekamp's 2011 *Galileo's O,* involving a number of technological institutions with formidable titles,[7] and some of the best scholars I know. Their verdict, based on paper analysis, radiological analysis of the ink, bibliographical data, handwriting analysis, and binding was that the book was genuine, even though it required a great deal of ingenuity to make that case. The rhetoric of certainty in the Bredekamp volume is striking:

> This collaboration between specialists of various institutions, exemplary in its unbureaucratic and precise interplay....

> Through comparison of the NY copy with the two other paradigmatic copies from Graz and Washington and numerous other copies, a level of knowledge has been gained previously achieved only for the Gutenberg Bible...

> The New York copy was never removed from its seventeenth-century binding; it consists of proof-copy paper; it is the proof copy of the printed book; it has the stamp of Federico Cesi's personal library on its title page and elsewhere in the text; the title page carries the signature of Galileo; its writing and drawing materials are typical of the early seventeenth century; the black material on top of the drawings indicates a transfer process to the copperplate, and the style of the drawing is the same as that of Galileo's sunspots and the Florentine drawings.[8]

---

in the "unmasking" of this forgery is likely Nick Wilding of Georgia State University.

7 Stiftung Preussischer Kulturbesitz; Kupferstichkabinett Berlin; Staatliche Akademie der Bildenden Künst, Stuttgart; Bundesanstalt für Materialforschung und Prüfung, Berlin; Technische Universität Berlin; and Rathgen-Forschungslabor.

8 Bredekamp, *Galileo's O,* 1:11, 1:15.

This confidence is likely as much a product of editing as of the certainty of individuals, and scholars should not be criticized simply for stating their opinions in the strongest, most direct form. Yet even here, the shaky logic that led to the conclusions is visible in several rhetorical sleights-of-hand. For example, the book is in *Sammelband,* that is, bound with other contemporary books in a seventeenth-century binding. That the book "was never removed from its seventeenth-century binding" seems, when expressed that way, to confirm its authenticity. But those who claimed this, mis-described the evidence and did not formulate the correct question. It obviously does not matter whether the book was ever removed from an early binding; all that matters is when it was put there. In a similar fashion, those who investigated the ink concluded the ink of Galileo's supposed signature matched the ink of the drawings. But this again is the wrong question. It did not deal with the more important question of what the date of that ink was, and even more simply why it differed from other examples of seventeenth-century ink. In addition, some of those scholars (not all of them) who invoked paper evidence claimed their conclusions "matched other historical evidence."[9] Yet that "historical" evidence was not always from one of the impressive scientific organizations involved in the study; it was often purely aesthetic.[10] In 2011, even though many of the scientific instruments seemed to agree, the basis of that agreement seems now to be shared error.

This copy is unique in a number of bibliographical ways. The type impressions are deeper than in any other copy, the paper

---

9 Ibid., 1:127.
10 See, e.g., ibid., 1:38: "Each element of the inscription in the New York copy, including its whole ambience, is so inseparably connected to Galileo's style of writing that its authenticity is beyond doubt — No counterfeiter could have imagined it." Even in 2014, lapses in logic were not conceded: "on the one hand, nobody denied the logical rigidity of the newly presented facts. On the other hand, the conclusion that the SNML was authentic had been founded on such a firm basis that it seemed unimaginable suddenly to change one's mind" (ibid., 3:10).

differs from that in any other copy. At times, such contradictory evidence is cited as if it were supportive:

> In fact, the watermark shapes found in the sheets of the NY copy differ sufficiently enough from those in the regular copies to suggest that they stem from separate twin moulds.[11]

(They were "in fact" made from the same modern mould.) That very uniqueness, which should have raised suspicions, somehow contributed to the aura of authenticity (and of course value as well): *because* it was different from all copies known to be authentic, *therefore* it was even more valuable and thus by implication more authentic.

The most intricate explanation of these differences (given by Paul Needham) was that it was a proof copy; this conclusion, unfortunately, could both support the nature of the authenticity of the book as well as explain away any differences found between this and the other genuine copies of the book.[12] In order for such a copy to exist, it would have to result from a procedure such as the following: the printers created proofs sheet by sheet as they ordinarily would during the printing process, and the entire print run was printed off without illustrations. They kept these sheets, collated them, and gave them to Galileo, who then drew in the designs, and gave them back to the printers to be the basis of the engravings or etchings. After these illustrations were printed in most copies of the book, all these proofs were gathered up and given back again to Galileo. Did he sign it then? From there, it found its way into the modest seventeenth-century binding that contains it today. I believe I am summarizing this false argument correctly, but I am not certain of that. It is never explained with clarity and, given what are thought to be

---

11 Irene Brückle, Manfred Mayer, Theresa Smith, "The Paper," in Bredekamp, *Galileo's O*, 1:127–42, at 138.

12 These would be among the rarest of things in book history; Needham cites two others. I've never seen them. There may well be more. Needham, *Galileo Makes a Book*, 173–74.

the standard procedures of seventeenth-century printing, this would be difficult in the extreme to accomplish.[13]

The explanations are ingenious, but some of the arguments are easier to refute than to understand. The evidence concerning type impressions is basic. The depth of the impressions is clearly visible even in the reproductions provided in Bredekamp's volumes.[14] The way you fake a letterpress leaf is simple, as a Boston book dealer once explained to me. You go to the Widener or Houghton and get a photo of whatever page is missing from your copy. You then make from that a relief plate, and you print a copy from that using the ordinary procedures of letterpress printing. This particular dealer completed books in his shop by using stray seventeenth-century paper (this is likely why so many seventeenth-century books in reputable libraries lack blanks; see the various copies of Suckling's *Fragmenta Aurea* noted in chap. 6 above). The Galileo forger could have followed this standard procedure, but instead, he simply made his own paper; that way, at least, the paper would be consistent (the paradox is that genuine seventeenth-century paper that did not match would raise more suspicions than forged, twentieth-century paper that was consistent).

In standard letterpress printing, there is a lot of stray ink. Those who make a photographic copy either clean this up or they don't; that is, every area in the photograph shows black,

---

13 The procedure is easier for us to accept, since the notion of book-length proofs seem quite natural to us. But type was not kept standing through a complete print-run in the seventeenth century (typecases did not contain enough type to make this possible). See the contemporary description of the proofing process in Joseph Moxon, *Mechanick Exercises on the Whole Art of Printing (1683–4)*, eds. Herbert Davis and Harry Carter, 2nd edn., (London: Oxford University, 1962), 249. Retaining a complete "proof-copy" for most printing projects would have been pointless.

14 I had once assumed that "faked" leaves in early books were lithographic, and that genuine leaves would have the greatest "three-dimensionality." The only leaves I have seen so deeply impressed as the ones in the New York *Sidereus Nuncius* made me revise this erroneous opinion: they were forged leaves tipped in to a fifteenth-century St. Thomas. Needham's explanation is that the leaves, being used for proof only, were not sized, nor were they pressed together after collating in a book block.

or it does not. There are no shades and all areas to be printed in black will show impressions of equal depth, since the plate-making process interprets each area of black the same way. In an original copy, stray or unprinted ink sits on the surface, leaving no impression; if this is reproduced in a forgery, this ink will be deeply impressed. The telling detail in the Galileo involved stray ink left by the shoulder of type sorts at the edge of the forme. In an original copy, these marks (if they were there) would be lightly impressed; in the forgery, they are as deeply impressed as everything else.

A second piece of evidence concerns supposed press-variants and corrections, this one involving a broken typesort. If a bibliographer can identify a particular typesort, it is possible to follow its history through the printing process. I'm skeptical about this, since those typesorts are not as clearly defined as is claimed by the sometimes enthusiastic researchers who have found them.[15] And I imagine a similar skepticism must have pervaded Needham's mind, who did not notice that the typesort evidence he had painstakingly assembled absolutely contradicted his proof-copy theory.

A broken sort is visible in three places in all copies of the book. Yet in the proof copy, there are no broken typesorts. If there were only one instance of this, it would be easy to explain: a sheet of the proof copy was printed, a typesort then broke, and the broken sort appeared in all other copies of that sheet. Here, that same broken sort re-appears in subsequent sheets; it should, by all rights, appear in the proof copy sheets as well (since it was presumably created during in the printing of the first sheet in which it appears). But it never appears in the proof copy. You would have to imagine a perfectly good sort printed clean in a sheet of the proof copy; it then was damaged; when that same broken sort appears again, it is a second sort that happened to

---

15 The most convincing studies in this area have been by Adrian Weiss, e.g., "Reproductions of Early Dramatic Texts as a Source of Bibliographical Evidence," TEXT: *Transactions of the Society for Textual Scholarship* 4 (1988): 237–68.

be damaged in exactly the same way following the printing of the second perfect proof sheet. It was then replaced, and after the third proof-sheet was printed, remarkably enough, it broke again, precisely as it had after printing earlier sheets of the proof copy. Obviously, this explanation is absurd: the broken typesort is the same in all three places. The reason it appears unbroken in the forged copy is that that copy was made from the Graz facsimile and in that facsimile, the impressions of this broken sort (which appears in all other copies) have been retouched.

The Retractions

Paul Needham's extensive "Final Thoughts" in the third Bredekamp volume is a model of scholarly introspection: to understand how errors are possible requires understanding the process by which they took place, which often is detailed, personal, and not at all in the genre of evidence allowed by most scholarly discussion.[16] But Needham's introspection is not shared by all contributors. The same rhetoric of certainty I noted earlier pervades Bredekamp's volume of retractions as well, where several of the scholars who confidently authenticated the Galileo copy now condescendingly take the forger to task for misunderstanding the details of, say, paper construction, and for arrogantly assuming he could fool professionals like themselves (Bredekamp's volumes 1 and 2 prove, of course, that he had done just that!):

> Given the effort of making of the forged paper, what led the forgers to use a fibre [cotton] that was all but unheard of in the seventeenth century? A lack of real understanding of his-

---

16 Paul Needham, "The Evidence of the Forged Printing," in Bredekamp, *Galileo's O,* 3:25ff., and Paul Needham, "Final Thoughts," in Bredekamp, *Galileo's O,* 3:95–98.

torical papermaking and a confusion of terminology are two probably explanations.[17]

Professional hand papermaking requires expert skills, even though a reasonable sheet can be made after a short introduction to the process. We can safely say that the forger did quite well in this respect. To make a sheet that looks old requires more specialized knowledge, and here the forger became creative. He closely matched the laid and chain pattern of the mould surface with respective watermarks. But to fully imitate a stock as it would be found in a historic book requires more knowledge than single sheet forgery, and this is where the forger made mistakes.[18]

The poor forger! Think what he could have done had he had the same modern scholarly knowledge and expertise that led to the authentication of his work only three years earlier. In other sections, scholars are more circumspect:

> The forgers' knowledge of which areas of a book should be dirty was originally convincing....Awakened, as our eyes were in the latest examinations, we saw what was unnoticed before. The surface soiling through is the result of a manual manipulation of the page surfaces.[19]

Finally, the forger's motives come into question:

> The fake restorations were probably done in an attempt to distract from the crude look of the forgery.[20]

---

[17] Irene Brückle, Theresa Smith, Manfred Mayer, "The Evidence from the Forged Paper," Bredekamp, *Galileo's O*, 3:35–60, at 38–39.

[18] Ibid., 39.

[19] Ibid., 58.

[20] Irene Brückle and Manfred Meyer, "The Evidence of the Forged Compasso Book Structure," Bredekamp, *Galileo's O*, 3:71–88, at 75.

And from there, a new set of conclusions is formed. The forger has met his match, and that must have been what motivated him. Because finally, this isn't about making money, and it isn't about the challenge of making an object of art; like everything else, it is all about us:

> Taking all elements together, it seems as if the forger…was working against a fictive enemy, an enemy that might incorporate the combined knowledge of specialists. It is our thesis that the book is a projected duel with the community of specialists. The hidden agenda of the making of the book might have been a clandestine satisfaction regarding the incapability of specialists to detect the forgery as such.[21]

---

21 Horst Bredekamp, "Towards a Psychology of the Forger," Bredekamp, *Galileo's O*, 3:89–95, at 89.

SECTION 3.2

Modernity and Middle English

Science is the belief in the ignorance of experts.
— Richard Feynman, "What is Science?"

We are reading a book of criticism by a poet, who is reading and interpreting a medieval poem. One would expect that the humanist approach to this (my own) would adopt one of the lines of criticism of the past few decades (New Criticism, Deconstruction, New Historicism, the New Philology), whereas the scientific response (here by a particle physicist) would insist on an older more conservative approach, arguing on the basis of lexical information, old philology, material evidence from the manuscripts (and so on). At least, this is what one of us speculates. But in fact, our arguments and assumptions are exactly the opposite of what we expect: the humanist adopts a quasi-scientific approach, the physicist a more literary-critical one.

The poem is a simple one, read in this case by Susan Stewart.[1] And the interpretation turns on the following lines:

Nou goth sonne vnder wod —,
me reweth, marie thi faire Rode.
Nou goth sonne vnder tre, —
me reweth, marie thi sone and the.

---

1 Susan Stewart, *Poetry and the Fate of the Senses* (Chicago: University of Chicago Press, 2002), 202.

This is quoted from a standard anthology by Carleton Brown, *English Lyrics of the XIIIth Century*.[2] Stewart's note (I'm not sure she authored it) adds: "Brown has taken the text from the Bodl[eian]. Ms. Arch. Selden."[3] One of us rather unkindly points out the irrelevance of this note: "Bodl." cannot be expanded to "Bodl[eian]." The period is also otiose once the abbreviation is expanded, wrongly here. To identify the manuscript as from the Selden collection is not really meaningful, since there is no number. It would be more responsible, from a scholarly perspective, simply to quote Brown directly.

Of course, when we are doing or performing literary criticism, we rarely understand the full meaning or function of technical notes in a critical edition. And there ought to be a way to acknowledge that responsibly: "See note in Brown" (that is, "I do not fully understand its significance, nor if it bears on the present argument"). Yet modern literary criticism does not permit such statements: instead, we follow the Myth of the Full Presence, not only of the text, but of all information about the text. For a moment, reading and writing literary criticism or perhaps any scholarship in the humanities, we are in that magical world where we have access to all knowledge concerning the present subject and are only arguing about how everything fits together or perhaps debating the political and social implications of it all. But surely we know we are speaking from the grandest ignorance. We do not know the author of this poem, its background; we might not even know the language it is written in. And our scholarship, if it can be called that, consists of gerrymandering a topic of discussion in such a way that no one other than ourselves can be conversant with it. Here is Stewart again:

> In one of the earliest English lyrics on Christ's passion, the anonymous poem, or perhaps fragment of a longer work, beginning "Nou goth sonne under wod," the possibilities of

---

2 Carleton Brown, *English Lyrics of the XIIIth Century* (Oxford: Clarendon Press, 1932).

3 Stewart, *Poetry and the Fate of the Senses*, 365.

parallel times occurring within a deictic 'now' that is itself taking time truly structure the entire work.

> Nou goth sonne under wod, —
> me reweth, marie thi faire Rode.
> Nou goth sonne under tre —
> me reweth, marie, thi sone and the.

The poem is in the pure stress four-beat meter we last read in Caedmon's "Hymn," but it is also in couplets....The sone that goth under wod is both the sun setting behind a wood on the horizon and the son Christ, going under the wood of the cross...."I pity this faire rode's rosy complexion, the color evoking the sunset's reflection." and "I pity thy fair rood" or cross, as well as "scion" or "offspring"....the "tre" is both the wood of the rood and the place of Christ in the Trinity.[4]

The "tre" suggests to Stewart other groups of three ("thrie") besides the Trinity — for example, the three Marys — also trust (*treow*).

The reading is dazzling, but many of the particular suggestions are philologically suspect. The Caedmon hymn is not written in "pure stress," nor related to this poem metrically. The sound *th-* (three) is not *t-* (tree), nor are the vowel sounds in *tre, treowe,* and *thrie* the same, as even their spelling indicates. "Tree" and "truth" are no more puns in Middle English than they are today. *Rode* does not sound the same as *rood* nor is it related to *ruddy*; *son* and *sun* are only phonetically equivalent in their modern English cognates. Many professional medievalists, however, provide support for these readings.[5]

---

4 Ibid., 202.
5 See, e.g., Edmund Reiss, "A Critical Approach to the Middle English Lyric," *College English* 27, no. 5 (1966): 373–79, often reprinted. For Reiss, *sonne, wod, Rode,* and *tre,* "all ambiguous," are key words, and it hardly matters, say, "whether or not *sonne* and *sone* are homophonic" (375). This seems to mean that if a reader with only minimal fluency in Middle English might confuse them, that confusion is a legitimate feature of the poem.

The most important point concerns the pair *wod* and *rode*. Stewart's interpretation "evoking the sunset's reflection" is put into quotations, as if her voice and the voice of the poet were merged. I am not sure whether Stewart is here paraphrasing the poet, or her own reading of the poet:

> And that interior expression in turn breaks into two referents: "I pity Marie, thi faire rod (or rosy complexion, the color evoking the sunset's reflection)" and "I pity thy fair rood" or cross, as well as "scion" or "offspring."[6]

The question is a philological one: in Middle English, can *wod* ("wood") rhyme with *rod* ("cross")? And the answer under the rules of Old Philology is no. There is no more relation between the sounds of these words in Middle English than there is between modern English *rode* and *wood*. There might be a convention of rhyming (visual? part-rhymes?) where these words rhyme, but such a convention was never operative in early English literary history.

Brown's textual note is important here: one scribe had the same thought that Stewart expanded into a literary-critical reading of the lines, seeing in *rode*(?), or whatever might have been written in the source, the word for cross. But to communicate that meaning to a contemporary reader required changing the rhyming word from *wood* = "wood" to *wod* = "mad." A sound argument thus could be advanced that since a near contemporary saw a confusion of words there (that is, they saw, as we do, the word rode as meaning "cross"), then why shouldn't we? Yet even the supporting scribe provides evidence that refutes the possibility of the modern reading: a medieval reader who interprets *rod* as meaning "cross" cannot accept the rhyme *wod* = "wood."

This inspired reading, which is not unique to Stewart, is a reflection of modern philological training. It is also a reflection of modern teaching of historical poems. One of the few Old Eng-

---

6 Stewart, *Poetry and the Fate of the Senses*, 202.

lish poems read or anthologized is "The Dream of the Rood," a poem (or title) every schoolchild of English literature knows (or once knew!), one so familiar it is rarely translated as "The Dream of the Cross." Thus, modern readers of literature come to this Middle English poem prepared to pass a vocabulary quiz: rod = rood = cross. And they can apply here their knowledge of Old English, however minimal that may be.

My friend the particle physicist is unconvinced by this logic, but refuses to concede that Stewart's reading is valid solely on its own impressionistic terms; to be accepted, it must be valid in historical terms as well, at least, as history is and must be understood by humanists. I believe my friend is projecting onto the humanities what seems to me (naively) a scientific assumption: a statement is valid insofar as it corresponds to a state of affairs, here defined philologically. I am willing to let Stewart's statements pass (in the end, what difference does it make?); the particle physicist is suddenly less generous.

Humanities vs. Science

Having beaten this argument to death, the particle physicist and I began to consider why we were arguing at all. I don't criticize her credentials in humanities, and she does not in turn deride my ignorance of basic principles of physics. To what extent do the divergent ways we approach the problem of this poem and Stewart's reading reflect our training, or even the nature of our fields? Is my reading (which turned out to be dodderingly conservative) better than the reading of the scientist? Or was that reading simply a reflection of my own anxiety as a humanist — that is, my attempt to imitate science, or a humanist's version of it? Or as the humanist in this discussion, am I longing to be a poet (as Geoffrey Hartman and Harold Bloom once claimed critics to be), and resentful of the readings of a real one?

The question (for me) is not what science is or how science is opposed to the humanities, since I am not sure these entities are defined well enough to be opposed, even in popular polemics.[7] Those divisions seem in large part the result of arbitrary (but socially material) divisions in the history of American and British educational systems of the late twentieth century, divisions then projected onto the presumed objects and methods of their respective fields.

Perhaps the question should be rephrased: what is meant by "science" (the concept) when it is invoked by a self-styled member of the humanist camp? That is, how does the invocation of science (or scientific method) function in the language of humanists? Examples from my early training are unsettling: many articles of mid-twentieth-century criticism claimed to be scientific, as does D.F. McKenzie's classic bibliographical article on "Printers of the Mind."[8] In this case, scholars assume without comment that there is something rigorous about scientific study or method, and they wish their own humanistic arguments to partake of that. Something is worthy of being called science, the same way as something is worthy (whatever that means) of being called, say, "history" or "philology" or "criticism," perhaps further qualified by a word such as "genuine," "true," or "new." Under this verbal system, a field such as science or a medium-hard history becomes an undefined Other that opposes or humiliates all one's enemies.

Yet according to my friend, citing Feyerabend, "facts" (whatever they are) will not solve the problem: "science is much more

---

[7] This is the way the question is phrased or understood in Stephen Jay Gould's arguments with E.O. Wilson: there is a thing called science, and something else called humanities, both givens. See Stephen Jay Gould, *The Hedgehog, the Fox, and the Magister's Pox* (New York: Harmony Books, 2003); E.O. Wilson, *Consilience: The Unity of Knowledge* (New York: Knopf, 1998); and E.O. Wilson, *The Social Conquest of Earth* (New York: Liveright Books, 2013).

[8] D.F. McKenzie, "Printers of the Mind: Some Notes on Bibliographical Theories and Printing-House Practices," *Studies in Bibliography* 22 (1969): 1–75; see my critique "Bibliographers of the Mind," in *Blind Impressions: Methods and Mythologies in Book History*, 58–72 (Philadelphia: University of Pennsylvania Press, 2013).

sloppy and irrational than its methodological image,"[9] and there is really no such thing as science, anyway. The word *science* may be a single word, but there is no single concept, method, or institution that corresponds to that word.[10]

When I first got to graduate school, I pretended to be serious. The first seminar I took was of a then familiar genre that administrators still encourage faculty to develop — one based on a concept or argument, rather than subject matter. This one was in medieval literature, and the topic or theme was "The Creator." We would read a number of texts, literary, philosophical, even glosses, all interesting in and of themselves, and see how they reflected this theme.[11] The crux of the course was that the word creator meant that any medieval writer was like God, insofar as each was "creating"; their activity was itself "like" any medieval work on the seven days of creation, or any medieval work about any other medieval work on the seven days of creation. This seemed even then a clear case of *petitio principii* (I didn't know the principle then), and given my antipathy to authority, it was, I imagined naively, us (if indeed I had an ally) against them.

A Canadian student presented a completely irrelevant report on Northrup Frye's *Anatomy of Criticism*, which even then (1976) was twenty years old and more than a decade out of fashion. This was the first report that did not consist of unfunny, graduate school puns on the word *create* and seemed to me a great coup: it was invoking science (or something called science) against what seemed then nothing more than a form of humanistic belletrism. When I read Frye today, and recall that I once considered his admirable discourse as exactly what he claims it to be — a form of science — I am amazed at my earlier self. Today, the only relation to science I see in Frye is his own invocation of the term. Yet convinced as I was by his assertions

---

9 Paul Feyerabend, *Against Method* (London: Verso, 1975), 157–58.
10 Ibid., 238.
11 More accurately, we were "assigned" a number of texts, since few of the students bothered to read them.

then, I can only suspect that that is why I have become so skeptical of them since.[12]

---

12 Northrup Frye, *Anatomy of Criticism: Four Essays* (Princeton: Princeton University Press, 1957); see Polemical Introduction: "It seems absurd to say that there may be a scientific element in criticism when there are dozens of learned journals based on the assumption that there is, and hundreds of scholars engaged in a scientific procedure related to literary criticism. Evidence is examined scientifically; previous authorities are used scientifically; fields are investigated scientifically; texts are edited scientifically. Prosody is scientific in structure; so is phonetics; so is philology. Either literary criticism is scientific, or all these highly trained and intelligent scholars are wasting their time on some kind of pseudo-science like phrenology" (8).

SECTION 3.3

The Quantification of Readability

We have no reliable indicators of the relative legibility of good hand-writing and typeset text even today, so there is no likelihood that we shall ever know how easy or otherwise it was for people in the nineteenth century to read handwritten lithographed books.
— Michael Twyman, *Early Lithographed Books*

According to the clichés often used to describe them, certain typefaces, those by Nicolas Jenson, Aldus, or even John Baskerville, are more beautiful, less fatiguing, and finally more readable than their typographical alternatives.[1] All of these terms are problematic, and much of it is similar to that once used to promote high-end stereo equipment, whose virtues are too nuanced to be revealed in such vulgar experiments as double-blind studies. I focus here on one of those seemingly impressionistic terms: the notion of readability or *lisibilité*, which I cannot state confidently are precisely the same thing. Although it is an easy and

---

1 There are many examples in Daniel Berkeley Updike, *Printing Types: Their History, Forms, and Use: A Study in Survivals*, 2 vols., 2nd edn. (Cambridge: Harvard University Press, 1937; Updike's language is often repeated by those who follow him. Quantification of typographical evidence can support quite various conclusions, but attempts were made as early as the eighteenth century: see Giacomo Sardini's claims (erroneous, it turns out) of the "economy" of Jenson's blackletter, or the equally false claims, often made, about the "efficiency" of Aldus italics; Joseph A. Dane, *Out of Sorts: On Typography and Print Culture*, chap. 3: "The Voodoo Economics of Space: From Gothic to Roman," 57–71 (Philadelphia: University of Pennsylvania Press, 2011); and Joseph A. Dane, *What Is a Book? The Study of Early Printed Books* (Notre Dame: University of Notre Dame press, 2012), 124–25.

simple matter to count the number of letters a typeface of similar height can cram into a line or page, and easy as well to define that by a word such as "efficiency," determining whether the result is more "readable" than an alternative is much more complicated.

The most detailed studies of this that I have seen are by Ezio Ornato.[2] Ornato is one of the most serious promoters of quantifiable studies in book history. He is attempting not simply to define and classify observable data from printed books and manuscripts, but to use that as an index of psychological facts.[3] I fully expected Ornato's article to suggest or design an experiment in which readability could be studied. Such a study would require that readability be clearly enough defined so that other scholars could discuss and test the same thing. Considering this question further, I realized that such a definition might not be necessary. We might not need to know what readability is, or even understand the difficulties involved in studying such a thing, as long as we can construct a study that measures or tests a reader's ability to do something or perform a task in regard to script or print in a way that can be measured. It hardly matters in the end what we call that activity, and "readability" might serve as well as anything.

Research on "readability" might thus proceed roughly the way an optometrist proceeds with eye charts. How many mistakes do competent readers, however defined, make when faced with different styles and sizes of typefaces? We would simply place different texts in front of particular readers under whatever conditions we chose. And if we could not recreate precisely or accurately the medieval or early modern ambience of reading, we would at least have made a start.

---

2 Ezio Ornato and Réjean Bergeron, "La lisibilité dans les manuscrits et les imprimés à la fin du Moyen Age: Preliminaires d'une recherche," *Scrittura e Civiltà* 14 (1990), 151–98; repr. *La face cachée du livre médiéval: L'histoire du livre vue par Ezio Ornato, ses amis et ses collègues* (Roma: Viella, 1997), 521–54.

3 Cf. the more narrow use of quantification in codicological studies of Albert Derolez, *Codicologie des manuscrits en écriture humanistique sur parchemin*, 2 vols. (Turnhout: Brepols, 1984).

All this occurred to me before I began reading the article, and discovered that Ornato and Bergeron's study does not involve real readers at all — neither past, historical readers, nor modern subjects of experiments. What is called "lisibilité," translated here as "readability," then, has nothing directly to do either with reading or with readers.

Readability and "Readability"

Ornato does not provide a test or even suggest how one might be designed. Instead, the material evidence he defines and quantifies seems connected to the abstraction he discusses only through a leap of faith (or here, through the introduction of another abstraction — "functionality"):

> S'il est aisé d'observer des permanences et des changements dans la structure du livre et la presentation de la page écrite d'une époque à l'autre, voire d'un volume à l'autre; il est impossible de faire apparaître la cohérence sous-jacent à des phénomènes relevant en apparence du libre arbitre de l'artisan sans faire appel à la notion de fonctionnalité.[4]

> [It may well be easy to observe what is permanent and what changes in the structure of the book and the presentation of the written page from one epoch to another, or even from one volume to another; it is impossible to show the underlying coherence of what the artisan does without appealing to the notion of functionality.]

"Readability," it turns out, does not involve anyone's ability to read. The questions Ornato and Bergeron formulate here are as follows: What are the factors that we can use to determine an early scribe's concern with readability (however defined)? What quantifiable features of a book might support the abstract and

---

4   Ornato and Bergeron, "La lisibilité," 521.

malleable notion of historical readability? Such questions seem matters of speculative psychology. It remains to be seen or theorized whether these factors actually do affect a text-copy's "ability to be read or deciphered" and so affected readers contemporary with that text's production.

One of the more ingenious definitions of evidence involves the distribution of word-breaks in a given manuscript or printed book: how many word-breaks occur in a column of writing or print? That evidence also depends on the establishment of a base or control. Ornato and Bergeron detail the difficulties involved: word-breaks are determined or affected by column length, genre, vocabulary, and (although they do not really deal with this) resources in the typecase. Unlike scribes, typesetters do not produce and invent what they can use; they could not, say, compress text beyond the limits of the typesorts they have.[5]

Genre, hand, manuscript space, white space — all these factors are incorporated into the results. Yet these results, mystifying and complex as they finally appear to be, are not directly and clearly connected with the main topic; or rather, the subject of the study has changed: the article provides not "evidence of readability," but rather "details of layout in a manuscript that can be quantified" and a list of considerations why not everything that can be seen or measured or counted can be quantified in a significant way. What Ornato and Bergeron do not come up with is an answer to the most pressing question: what is the link between this quantifiable evidence and the abstraction that we are considering? No amount of manipulation of data can make that step.

Every solution proposed requires an additional assumption: for example, given that word-breaks are difficult to read, *if* the scribe shows an effort to avoid word-breaks, that scribe is *therefore* concerned with what we call "reader ease," which in turn

---

[5] The limitations of a typecase, e.g., the number of sorts available for a particular letter, has been a basic consideration in the discussion of early typefonts since the early twentieth century. See, e.g., Gottfried Zedler, *Die älteste Gutenbergtype mit 13 Tafeln in Lichtdruck* (Mainz: Gutenberg Gesellschaft, 1902), 18.

shows a concern for "readability" as understood by that scribe, leaving the question open as to whether this is what we ourselves might consider readability, or whether the scribe was correct in this assessment. These logical steps seem reasonable, but the conclusions are not necessary. A scribe's effort may be meaningless: perhaps the scribe is merely playing a game. How would we know if this were the case? Perhaps the scribe is attempting to economize; again, we have no way of knowing this. Perhaps the scribe is more concerned with the particular task assigned; for example, the text has been cast off in some way, and the scribe thus must fit x amount of text within the page, leaf, or quire provided. Perhaps the scribe has aesthetic concerns and tastes we know nothing about.

Most important, even if we could determine scribes' motives, we still are far from determining the effect of their actions. Most human beings likely want to do good in the world, and most human beings act in accordance with what they believe to be ethics. But what we are interested in here is not motives but results, not what human beings think of themselves and their actions, but what effect those actions have. These are obviously two different things. Most human endeavors result in failure. So do the workings of, say, evolution. Why should a perfect scribe's efforts be exceptional?

McKenzie's "Printers of the Mind" were printers imagined by analytical bibliographers rather than printers evidenced by historical documents. They were efficient, reasonable, and purposeful, quite unlike those who lived in the real world. The scribes and typesetters we must imagine here are no different, since we have to define each of their actions as in the service of their readers. Each act we can measure serves the very ideals we imagine those workers to hold, even though we ourselves have never experienced anything comparable in life or thought.

Conclusion

There are a number of experiments that could be conducted to test the relevance to real readers of evidence such as is collected here. One is of course the eye chart. One could test type by comparing random letters with words (that is, a foreign language against a known one) adjusting sizes and brightnesses, etc. until one established some sort of control. Having set this control, one might then begin to test Type A against Type B, format A against format B, the frequency of word-breaks (can a reader recognize a hyphenated word quickly enough to justify its use?), again adjusting contrasts and even sizes against the control type. We should be able to determine something from this, but until we do the experiment, it's not clear what we should call that "something." We would then be in the position to claim, perhaps without foundation, that a reader's behavior and preferences today are comparable to those of readers more than a half millennium earlier, even though, given a contemporary reader's experience with digital reproduction of texts, I would not be confident that how readers react or perform today would be the same as how they perform even a year from now.

There might also be ways to control such things as the way a real reader holds a real book, and what the effect of physical distance might be, that is, whether a large typeface seen at arms-length is the same as a small typeface seen held close. A Missal was seen from several feet away (we think), a breviary or book of hours within less than an arm length. Is "readability" a function of that distance? Missals, for example, cannot be read efficiently, we might assume, if held close to one's face. Or is this too much to claim: can we ignore the technology of lenses that control all our experience of the way we hold books? And even here, we have not risen to the level of what "readability" is in any significant sense, since that involves not the recognition of letters (as in a reading test at the DMV), but rather knowing what the words say and moving through the text in an efficient way. Few persons today, if any, have sufficient experience with medieval texts and handwriting to serve as test subjects. And if such readers exist, they could hardly be said to be comparable to ordinary readers of the past.

Historical printers might experiment or imagine versions of all this, given that they likely had some concern with the abstraction "readability" comparable to what Ornato wishes to test. But there is no hard evidence that they did. They likely relied on some version of the same banalities we do (type A is "fatiquing") or simply judged what was available in terms of aesthetics or fashion (type B is old-fashioned and ugly). In addition, printers had no reliable feedback. All the printer can do is privilege those books and book-forms that sell, but there is, of course, no way to know for certain what factors are involved. Even today, no one knows what really sells books, as I am assured by a colleague who sells far more than I do. "Readability," however defined, is only one factor and a very unstable one: it likely improves as readers wish to read certain texts — that is, you will read Aldine italics or Baskerville's "transitional" typefaces much better once you decide that the texts associated with them are of value. Each may well become more "readable" (to early or recent readers) the more readers accept the nostalgic view of the Renaissance they embody. But if so, we have another case of a dubious abstraction producing the material evidence that supports it.

SECTION 3.4

The Elephant Paper and the Histories of Medieval Drama

In "Disillusionment at 10 O'Clock," the American poet Wallace Stevens tells of a haunted house with colors that are not there. There are rings. Many scholars claim the poem is about ghosts, or that creative people live much richer and more colorful lives than ordinary dull people, represented by the colorless nightgowns. The purpose of this paper is to argue that "Disillusionment at 10 O'Clock" is really about an elephant.

The opening paragraph above is in a genre that most of us have confronted so many times that we are incapable of recognizing a parody, even one we ourselves have constructed. The gratuitous naming of the poem, the poet, often a reference to the date, details from Wikipedia or the introduction to whatever text we have forgotten we have assigned — all coming to a crushing end in the topic sentence closing the first paragraph, exactly where we have been taught and have taught that a writer should insert a thesis.

The poem is about an elephant.

Once we have an idea, we are ready to imagine a coherent argument and to begin constructing a coherent paper. As I have taught many times, after writing the opening paragraph, you don't really need to do much else: the paper more or less writes itself. Whether refereeing journal articles or reading student papers, I have made nearly all my evaluations after that first paragraph. I know whether I will recommend it for publication or give it an A-: the rest of my time will be spent marshaling the evidence and rhetoric to support that decision. All that remains is determining which sections I will highlight, which sentence or expression I will quote directly, what "minor points" I will make at the end of my report.

"Disillusionment at Ten O'Clock" is about an elephant.

The poem is an elephant.

The paper is an elephant.

To begin with, Stevens's poem is not overly small, nor are the points it makes small; and elephants, as we all know, are large.

[I draw an elephant on the board; it is stylized, mannered, large, and with luck, I will make it not appear to be a cartoon mouse. Ears, tusks, looking straight ahead, with one giant foot raised.]

Note that this elephant, mannered on the chalkboard, consists entirely of lines, much like the poem. In fact, referring to elephants in the real world, rather than in the imaginary two-dimensional one (and Stevens, as we know, was constantly comparing the real to the poetic world) we see that the relationship is even stronger. The lines of the poem are like the lines in the skin of the elephant, the folds of the skin. Note too, that the very lines of the poem are written in feet (elephants have four) and many poems (this one is the exception that proves the rule) are written in octosyllables, that is, four feet!

There are as many words for poems as there are words for elephants: hephalumps, pachyderms, Dumbo. The poem is entirely of words, and in fact, some of the more imaginary elephants, as well as the scientific classification of them, are largely(!) dependent on words, as are the sailor and baboon here. Stevens's poem is far from an easy one; elephants too can be difficult. There are many grey areas in the poem, ambiguities, just as there are grey areas in the elephant. Arguably, there is a key to the poem, and the tusks of the elephant, as everyone knows, were once, back in Stevens's day, made into the keys for the piano. Coincidence?

One of the more striking features of the poem is the baboon. Although some scholars have noted the blue and red face and posterior of the baboon, aligning itself in various mysterious but unknown ways with the planet-like rings of color preceding this, it should not be forgotten that baboons are first and foremost wild animals associated with a (real? mythological?) jungle environment, as are, of course, elephants.

Elephant is three syllables, as are the first three words of the Stevens's poem.

Elephants I believe eat bamboo (the similarity in sounds to baboons is noteworthy). The reference to bamboo is unaccountably repressed in the poem, although the allusion in the absence of form more than makes up for this.

The contrast of color to the surface of the elephant could not be more obvious.

The poem is an elephant. The poem is about an elephant. The paper is an elephant. All papers are elephant papers.

I used to demand that students incorporate a thesis statement in their papers, unconsciously channeling my own high school teacher: it was how I did things myself. It all seemed so obvious: you just say directly and clearly that Shakespeare sonnets are about, oh, dark ladies, elephants, or even what they say they are about. What could be clearer than that? Yet one day, I was drawing a familiar chalk elephant on the board, pretending to amuse my students, asking them, for my sake, to do anything other than write the elephant papers they had been taught to write. To do anything other than to take poem X and announce that it was not really poem X, but rather an elephant. I began laughing at myself although no one heard me. It was on that day that I began to take my own advice. Or at least, try. And that is why there are no thesis sentences here.

Groupe Annales

The Annales Group of historians built their enterprise on a polemic: history should not be written top-down, but from the bottom up. This particular metaphor could be read in at least two ways. First and foremost, it meant that history would not be limited to court-gossip, kings and queens, conquests, battles. It would rather be written of labor, ordinary people, peasants, food production, the elimination of horse excrement from the trenches of a siege in the Middle Ages, and so on. The slogan could be read another way as well: history would not be written down from grand abstractions such as historical periods, centuries, or nations. That is, it would no longer be written uncritically, or even according to the critical methods of Karl Popper, starting with a hypothesis which all the facts would then put to the test.[1]

As if to enforce the renunciation of abstractions, many in this school developed a formal writing tic: articles and studies would begin, not with a grand thesis, but rather a small and specific anecdote (an example most familiar to English readers is Robert Darnton's *Great Cat Massacre*)[2] from which the scholarly work would develop. A large portion of the articles in literature or the humanities I read in English today have adopted this model. On the one hand it is maddening. On the other, is epitomizes the theory: basic to the argument is not a thesis, but a set of facts — an anecdote.

There is a noticeable difference between early work in this school — work such as Marc Bloch's *Feudal Society* (1939-40), and later works, such as Georges Duby's *Trois Ordres* (1978) or Fernand Braudel's *Civilization and Capitalism* (1955-79).[3] Bloch's *Feudal Society* seems in search of its organizing principles, and even important concepts and categories: the first feudal age, the second feudal age, and of course feudalism itself are difficult to discover, define, or even critique, as they are lost, it seems, in

---

[1] See, among many summaries, Peter Burke, *The French Historical Revolution: The Annales School 1929-1989* (Stanford: Stanford University Press, 1990); Roger Chartier, "History and Social Science: A Return to Braudel" (2002), in *The Author's Hand and the Printer's Mind*, trans. Lydia G Cochrane, 44-55 (Cambridge: Polity Press, 2013).

[2] Robert Darnton, *The Great Cat Massacre: And Other Episodes in French Cultural History* (New York: Basic Books, 1984).

[3] Marc Bloch, *La société féodale*, 2 vols. (Paris: Michel, 1939-40); Fernand Braudel, *Civilization and Capitalism, 15th-18th Century*, 3 vols. (New York: Harper, 1982-84); Georges Duby, *Les trois ordres, ou L'imaginaire du féodalisme* (Paris: Gallimard, 1978); Emmanuel Le Roy Ladurie, *Montaillou, village occitan de 1294 à 1324* (Paris: Gallimard, 1976).

some pattern of plowing furrows or evidence of crop rotation. Emmanuel Le Roy la Durie's *Montaillou* (1975) is similar; here the scholar defines a body of seemingly amorphous evidence (inquisitorial records) and asks a question of that evidence that it was never intended to address, taking from it facts it recorded with uninterest and thus disinterest: the events of everyday life. The categories that finally control this evidence are no more than chapter headings, and there is no attempt to reproduce or critique the patterns of thought that either existed in the witnesses or were projected there by scholars. Under this method, it doesn't really matter whether the witnesses are biased, afraid, making excuses, or confessions, since the data in their testimony consists of facts neither they nor their inquisitors cared at all about: the nature of the doorstep they were sitting on when a certain heretical conversation took place inside; what were their working hours that gave them the leisure to eavesdrop on others. All this serves as evidence of grander things—privacy, sexual mores, the concept of the Truth, the economics of the village.

But these methods and the assumptions underlying them soon became tangled in other, quite contradictory assumptions, and the kind of history that Annales historians rejected began to appear in their own writings in different form. Rather than a ruling monarchy or nation controlling the movement of evidence, a large abstraction takes over, such as Duby's notion of *mentalités*, a version of the more creaking and obsolete notion of *Zeitgeist*: there are certain mental patterns, and mental forms that produce a series of variant structures in the real world (most notably for Duby, the notion of Three Estates). For Braudel, the notion of *la longue durée* invites us to see nothing but continuities beneath the cacophony of evidence. *Le grand récit* of the nineteenth century reappears in a new guise.

History is continuity. Events are *really* manifestations of abstract mental patterns.

And suddenly, it is elephants again, all the way down.

Book History

If the world were a coherent, rational, and intelligible place, then scholarly methods would be well suited to describing it. But the world is not such a place, and scholarly methods, particularly in the humanities, are much better at articulating their own truths.

What I am contrasting here are two primary and competing interests: (1) the "heaps of books" that we might find on a library shelf, with a dealer, or even in our homes, vs. (2) the catalogue — that is to say, a coherent statement of what those books are: this could be an enumerative bibliography (that is, a book list), the electronic card catalog of a particular library, or a descriptive bibliography (that is, a catalogue of definitions of editions that enables us to define individual copies of those editions as essentially "the same" (see Chapter 6 above).

Catalogues and their entries are most amusing and interesting because they are full of mistakes, and the discovery of those mistakes is a rewarding and not particularly difficult task. The catalogue adopts the omniscient tone I have spoken about in my introduction: on this basis of omniscience, it then describes the individual object. And the individual object, in my experience, always and inevitably resists (referring again to Stevens) "almost successfully."

There is thus always work to be done in this area of cataloguing by non-cataloguers — a note, an article, a chapter. Scholars have the luxury of devoting far more time to individual cases than any cataloguer could. And there is always a reason for such work: the resistance of the single object calls into question the principles of the much grander thing — the catalogue, the bibliography, the entire industry of book history.

The Growth and Progress of Growth and Progress

Nineteenth-century scholars developed a theoretical model in which to organize material: in the areas I have worked in, a most noteworthy example was in medieval drama. Medieval drama was well suited to this model; it is vast, repetitious, largely unreadable. After going through Arnoul Gréban's 30,000-line *Mystère de la Passion,* we might be excused from thinking that if you have read one of these Passion cycles, you have read them all. Much scholarship in this area was consequently designed to relieve other scholars from the basic business of reading it.[4] The most useful example of this in English is Karl Young's *Drama of the Medieval Church,* where centuries of Latin drama are organized in such a way as make it possible not only to find examples of these plays, but to place new discoveries within his categories and implied histories.[5] Young's theory organizing these plays is that medieval drama evolved within set genres from simple to complex. This theory (or principle of organization) was often challenged but never really tested by going through the evidence. A simple and obvious way to do this might have been to line up forms defined in Young with the dates assigned to individual texts: does the pattern support or refute Young's thesis.

That is what I attempt below.

In order to perform this test, I limited myself to Young's vol. 1 and the genre or play-type Visit to the Sepulchre, where Young's theory is most prominent. I did not second-guess any of the dates assigned to manuscripts, but simply accepted what his notes claim, for example "saec. xii" (most of his examples are dated only by century, and obviously they were not so dated using the same criteria). Young defines a progression of five steps, grouped into two "Stages." The Table below indicates the number of manuscripts Young cites in his text (that is, for Stage IA, two thirteenth-century manuscripts, eleven fourteenth-century

---

4   For example, Louis Petit de Julleville, *Les Mystères,* 2 vols. (Paris: Hachette, 1880), in series Histoire du Théâtre en France.
5   Karl Young, *The Drama of the Medieval Church,* 2 vols. (Oxford: Clarendon Press, 1933). See, as an example in the same area, the series Records of Early English Drama (http://reed.utoronto.ca/), whose individual volumes, presenting presumably unmediated evidence, are far less useful than the fully organized summary by Ian Lancaster, *Dramatic Texts and Records of Britain: A Chronological Topography to 1558* (Cambridge: Cambridge University Press, 1984).

ones). When a manuscript is given a range (such as late twelfth-/ early thirteenth-century), I have in most cases classed it in the later century.

	Stage IA	IB	STAGE IIA	IIB	IIC
10th c	1				
11th c	5				
12th c	8		1		
13th c	2	7	4	1	5
14th c	11	6	2	3	5
15th c	4	6	8	9	2
16th c			7	3	
17th c	1			1	
18th c					

Table 1. Manuscripts cited in Young's text.

Looking at this, the difficulties in Young's theory are apparent. The table supports the notion that Stage IA is early; it has several examples from the tenth through twelfth centuries, which the other forms do not. Beyond that, there is very little one can conclude from this, other than that fifteenth-century manuscript and printed versions of all types (except for the early type IA and fully developed type IIC) are more common than others.

Arranging the examples given in Young's extensive and systematic notes in volume 2 gives similar results, suggesting I think that the examples chosen by Young to include in his text were representative of those available to him: [6]

---

[6] The tables are very rough. Many references are doubtless repeated in Young's notes, which I have not attempted to eliminate. I am also certain I made several embarrassing errors, quickly reducing "saec. xii," "thirteenth-century," and "1487" to my arabic listing here. Printed service books also skew these results, as Young notes, *Drama,* 2:637n2. I am not sure what to

	Stage IA	IB	STAGE IIA	IIB	IIC
10th c					
11th c	2				
12th c	8	1	3		1
13th c	8	4	6	4	3
14th c	13	14	17	4	4
15th c	10	18	22	20	6
16th c	2	9	12	8	1
17th c	2	2			
18th c		2			

Table 2. Manuscripts cited in Young's notes.

The pattern claimed by Young again is supported in some cases: IA is the simplest form and found in the earliest manuscripts. But there is no obvious progression that is supported by the numbers: fourteenth- and fifteenth-century manuscript versions are more common than others, which tells us almost nothing.

This is only a first step. It does not settle the matter of Young's theories. It only sets out the relationship between the evidence and the theory of dramatic development, that is, the chronological relationship between various forms. Any argument for or against this theory needs to confront the ambiguity of these figures and determine how that is to be accounted for (I would likely account for it by arguing that the chronological argument is false, or at least unsupported by evidence). Yet this simple and obvious procedure is one that neither Young's critics nor Young himself seemed to choose. Young likely developed his theory before collecting all his evidence (the theory was a useful way to organize that evidence). But Young's critics developed no test of this theory. Instead, his book led simply to counter-theories,

do with certain examples, e.g., those in Young's note 2:677–78n1 and have not included them.

often ones with far more speculation than put forward by Young himself.[7]

When I last moved, I decided to throw out five large loose-leaf notebooks, each page with notes on scholarly books, all arranged in an arbitrary set of categories I got from an undergraduate "Guide." One of those was on Maurice Sepet's *Les Prophètes du Christ: Etude sur les origines du théâtre au Moyen Age* (Paris: Didier, 1878). I cannot remember many of the details from Sepet, who argued that the Prophet Plays (the *Ordo Prophetarum*) were at the origin of all medieval drama.[8] What I can remember is my summary statement (I wrote these at the end of each notecard, knowing that some day in the future I would have to cite the book it summarized, and would have to do so in a single-sentence note). What I focused on was Sepet's use of the word *loi* to describe his own organizational scheme, a word that, at least to a late-twentieth-century reader, had to be taken as a metaphor with the same meaning as the word *law* in such phrases as "Boyle's Law." It refers less to the workings of a mysterious force in literature or nature than to the schemes observers can use to organize their results.[9] The simple-to-complex model thus was not history, but rather the way to organize one's view of history.[10]

Again, my memory fails: I know that Sepet gave evidence of having read all the Prophet Plays, and at the time, I was naive

---

7 O.B. Hardison, Jr., *Christian Rite and Christian Drama in the Middle Ages: Essays in the Origin and Early History of Modern Drama* (Baltimore: The Johns Hopkins Press, 1965).

8 These are most familiar to medieval students from the variant in the twelfth-century Jeu d'Adam. They are included also in Young, "The Procession of Prophets," *The Drama of the Medieval Church*, 2:125–71.

9 See, however, Steven Shapin, *A Social History of Truth: Civility and Science in Seventeenth-Century England* (Chicago: University of Chicago Press, 1994), critiquing the entire notion of disinterested observation.

10 Although I did not know this then, nineteenth-century dramatic scholars did not invent this model of "growth and development"; they rather began with the genial narrative histories of earlier scholars, such as Luigi Riccoboni's *Histoire du théâtre italien* (Paris: Cailleau, 1730), a history translated and included in the introductions to several English dramatic anthologies of the eighteenth century.

enough to discover from personal diligence that this is not at all an interesting intellectual exercise. But after that, it is all a jumble. It would have been better, perhaps, to have read Sepet and left the plays alone, since reading them took all the energy I could more profitably have spent on critiquing the way Sepet presented them. Most contemporary scholars are not in a position to respond to this statement; and until they do what I did, and attempt to reconstruct what Sepet once did to form his *grand récit,* they will just have to take my word for it.

SECTION 3.5

The Pynson Chaucer(s) of 1526
Bibliographical Circularity

The Pynson edition (or editions) of Chaucer in 1526 is (are) either a mainstream example of fifteenth- and sixteenth-century Chaucer editing, squarely within the tradition of Chaucer folio editions, or an outlier. It (or they) consist(s) of three parts, each with an autonomous signature series (that is, each could be sold as an individual item with quires signed A, B, C…): the *Canterbury Tales, Troilus and Creseyde,* and the *House of Fame* with other texts. Each is printed in the same format and in the same type. The colophon for the *Canterbury Tales* contains the date 1526; the colophons for the other two contain only a reference to the printer. The Short-Title Catalogue (STC) assigns three numbers — 5086, 5088, and 5096 — although in all extant copies but one, the three items are bound together in some way.[1]

The main question I ask here is simply whether descriptive bibliography should consider this one or three items (the bib-

---

1 There are three versions of the STC/ESTC: A.W. Pollard and G.R. Redgrave, *A Short-Title Catalogue of Books Printed in England, Scotland and Ireland, and of English Books Printed Abroad, 1475–1640* (London: The Bibliographical Society, 1926); a three-volume second edition of the same title revised by W.S. Jackson and F.S. Ferguson (London: The Bibliographical Society, 1976–91). When necessary, these are conventionally distinguished STC1 and STC2, although (without qualification) an "STC number" refers to the one assigned in STC2. The online English Short-Title Catalogue (ESTC) is based on these, but includes books to 1800, http://www.bl.uk/. Early English Books Online (EEBO) contains images of many of these books, as well as bibliographical descriptions (not yet fully incorporating everything in ESTC), http://eebo.chadwick.com/.

243

liographical version of whether it actually *is* one or three items). The related questions I brought to this problem seemed rather simple ones to me, and I had hoped I could deal with them without referring to the books themselves or even to images of them. There was no advantage, bibliographical or ethical, to working this way; it was simply an arbitrary choice. But this method proved difficult. The language used to describe copies in standard bibliographies and in library catalogues is equivocal, and even the simplest questions I addressed to competent librarians produced ambiguous results: libraries that were said to hold the books did not; the order of texts implied by the catalogues was incorrect. And despite my familiarity with the ESTC, even the simplest of its conventions often baffled me.

This section will show why these simple questions proved difficult and what obstacles presumably authoritative bibliographical references place in the way.

Early Descriptions

By the time Pollard and Redgrave made the decisions regarding this book, now embodied in their *STC* of 1926, the most important bibliographical authorities had spoken and their conclusions were various. Ames, *Typographical Antiquities* (1749), noted Pynson's early edition of *Canterbury Tales* of 1492 (STC 5084), but made no reference to this one. Herbert, in his revision of Ames, had a copy of the 1526 edition, but Dibdin, in his revision, noted that Herbert's "description, it must be confessed, is not quite so clear and methodical as could be wished."[2] The full entry in Dibdin is as follows:

CHAUCER'S WORKS. Imprinted at London in fletestrete, by me Rycharde Pynson, printer vnto the kynges noble grace:

---

[2] Joseph Ames, *Typographical Antiquities* (London, 1749), rev. William Herbert (1793–95); Thomas Frognall Dibdin, *Typographical Antiquities, or the History of Printing in England,* 4 vols. (London: W. Miller, 1810–19), 2:519.

and fynisshed the yere of our lorde god a. M.CCCCC. and XXVI. the fourth day of Iune.[3]

"Chaucer's Works" is Dibdin's addition, since that inclusive title is not found in the books themselves. Dibdin proceeds, describing the texts in the order they appear in his copy: *Troilus and Criseyde, Boke of Fame,* and *Canterbury Tales.* He quotes Herbert's description:

> Chaucer's Canterbury Tales, with the following poems, The boke of Troylus and Cryseyde, the boke of Fame, the assemble of Foules....What other pieces it may contain is uncertain at present, since the copy that the writer of the preface to Urry's Chaucer had the use of, was imperfect, containing only the pieces above-mentioned; and my own copy more so, having nothing beyond La bele Dame sans mercy; however, I shall describe such as I have, in the order they stand. Of the Canterbury tales I have two copies, but unluckily neither of them have the title leaf, or the prohemye, as mentioned in the preface to Urry's Chaucer. Indeed that other copy seems to have wanted the title also, as no mention is made whether the said title was general, or only for the Canterbury Tales.[4]

I assume that by "missing the prohem," Herbert means missing the first leaf of the *Canterbury Tales,* which contains on its recto a full page with the title, "Here begynneth the boke of Caunterbury tales…" (A1r), on its verso, a Prohem, based loosely on Caxton's preface to the second edition of *Canterbury Tales,* and a list of tales (A1v). The following page begins The Prologue of the Authour, meaning the General Prologue (A2).

This description is certainly in error, as Dibdin realized: the general title page was not "missing"; it simply did not exist except in its invocation. And the question of concern here — whether the three sections were intended as one book or three — was not

---

3 Ibid.
4 Ibid.

yet formulated.⁵ T. Thomas's preface to Urry's edition of 1721, referenced by Dibdin, describes it as Pynson's "Second Edition" (the first was the edition of 1492 containing only the *Canterbury Tales*). Thomas clearly considered it a single edition; he did not distinguish the three sections, but simply listed the texts without reference to the tripartite structure of the book indicated by the signature series.⁶ Skeat, in his edition of Chaucer, was not much interested in the history of editions as a subject, since his own would supplant all of them. To him, the first "complete works" was Thynne's 1532 edition (STC 5068), which initiated a series of folio editions to 1687, each re-editing and supplementing those before it. His introductory section, "The Complete Works," states unequivocally: "the first collected works was that edited by W. Thynne in 1532."⁷ The first scholar who seemed even to imagine the problem was Eleanor Hammond in her 1908 *Chaucer: A Bibliographical Manual*.⁸ Hammond's *Manual* described editions under two headings: Complete Works, and Copies of Individual Works. The first item in Hammond's list of complete works is Pynson, 1526:

> The copy in the Grenville Library of the British Museum has as titlepage for the first of the three parts, which are there bound together: Here begynneth the boke of Troylus and Creseyde newly printed by a trewe copy.
> Titlepage to the second part:...boke of Fame....
> Titlepage to the third part....
> Colophon Thus endeth the boke of Caunter | bury tales. / Imprinted at London in flete- | strete / by me Rycharde Pynson | printer vnto the kynges no- | ble grace: and fynis= | hed the

---

5 I assume the two copies referred to by Herbert are the two referenced in Pollard and Redgrave in the 1926 STC: L (a complete copy) and O (containing only the *Canterbury Tales*).

6 John Urry, ed., *The Works of Geoffrey Chaucer* (London, 1721), sig. l2r.

7 Walter W. Skeat, *The Complete Works of Geoffrey Chaucer*, 7 vols. (Oxford: Clarendon Press, 1894–97), 1:xvii.

8 Eleanor Prescott Hammond, *Chaucer: A Bibliographical Manual* (New York: Macmillan, 1908).

yere of our lorde god a M. CCCCC. | and xxvi. the fourth | day of June. [9]

The most important pronouncement was that of Pollard and Redgrave in the 1926 STC. Pollard and Redgrave assigned three separate STC numbers (apparently following Skeat, rather than Hammond) and these numbers would necessarily be the basis of all bibliographical discussion, if not bibliographical decisions, to follow.[10] I quote these in full, respecting as well as I can the typographical conventions they use. Note that Pollard and Redgrave place what they consider editions of *Troilus* among other editions of *Troilus* and editions of the *Canterbury Tales* with other editions of that title. Thus even though these three parts generally appear together in individual book-copies, they are separated in STC:

5086 [Anr. ed.] [Here begynneth the boke of Canterbury tales, dilygently corrected and newly printed.] fol. R. Pynson, 1526 (4 jn.) L. O. This with nos. 5088 and 5096 may be called the first edition of Chaucer's works.

5088 Here begynneth the boke of fame, made by G. Chaucer. With dyuers other of his workes. fol. R. Pynson, [1526?] L

5096 [Anr. ed.] Here begynneth the boke of Troylus and Creseyde. fol. R. Pynson, [1526?] L[11]

STC 5086 is preceded by the two Caxton editions of *Canterbury Tales* (CT) and the Pynson edition of 1492. STC 5088 is preceded by the Caxton edition of *House of Fame* (HF). STC 5096 is then

---

9 Ibid., 114.

10 The most extensive and detailed base for STC descriptions was George Watson Cole, *Check-list or Brief Catalogue of the Library of Henry E. Huntington (English Literature to 1640)* (New York, 1919). Unfortunately, this is the one major early Chaucer edition that the Huntington Library does not possess.

11 Pollard and Redgrave, STC 1926. The abbreviations L and O here refer to locations of copies, e.g., London (now British Library) or Oxford.

preceded by editions of *Troilus* by Caxton and De Worde. The entry for 5088 does not read [Anr. ed.]; this might be an error, but I assume it means that Pynson's supposed edition contains works in addition to the *House of Fame*; earlier editions of *House of Fame* (which immediately precede this) contain only the single text. I think the brackets in 5086 ("[Here begynneth....]") are a mistake, although there might be a convention justifying them. Only two copies are noted: the British Library copy and the Oxford copy, and from this, we might guess that other British libraries do not have the work, which is not the case.

The revised STC of 1976 (STC2) expands these entries and expands the holdings list. But Pollard and Redgrave's decisions in the 1926 STC (based on two copies) remain the basis of these descriptions:

> 5086 [Anr. ed.] Here begynneth the boke of Caunterbury tales, dilygently corrected, and newly printed. fol. (*R. Pynson*, 1526 (4 jn)). L L2. LEEDS.G2.Blackburn Pl. +; HD, TEX (frag.). Y.) [1526]
>
> This, 5088, and 5096 may be called the 1st ed. of Chaucer's Works
>
> 5088 [Anr. ed., w. additions.] Here begynneth the boke of fame, made by G. Chaucer; with dyuers other of his workes. fol. (*R. Pynson,*) [1526?] L(imp.), L2. C2. LEEDS. Blackburn PL.; HD.Y.
>
> Issued w. 5086
>
> 5096 [Anr. ed.] Here begynneth the boke of Troylus and Creseyde, newly printed by a trewe copye. [Anon.] fol. (*R. Pynson,*) [1526?] L.C4.G2.LEEDS. Blackburn PL +; HD. Y. (Blackletter A)

Comparing these descriptions with those from the 1926 STC raises a few questions. (In the paragraphs below, I distinguish the STC of 1926 from the 1975 revision with the abbreviations STC1 and STC2.) Was HF in STC1 not called "Anr. ed." because it contained additions (my thought above)? Or was that simply an error? The "Oxford" copy of CT seems to have disappeared (I believe it is now in Texas). The brackets for "Here begynneth" in STC1's entry for the CT have disappeared. (What were they supposed to have meant?) Further problems emerge: STC1's statement "may be called the first edition of Chaucer's works" is retained in STC2 under 5086. But there is no reference to that in the two other volumes. In STC2, the entry under 5088 contains the additional statement, "Issued w. 5086." No such statement occurs under 5096.

The information is now contradictory and misleading. First of all, STC2 introduces the ambiguous notion "issue."[12] To say a book was "issued" with another must mean, if anything, that it was produced at the same time and was intended to be sold with that second book. If such a statement is not qualified (for example, "may have been issued...") then the conjectured date 1526 should also not be qualified: read [1526] not [1526?]. Furthermore, if 5086 is "issued" with 5096, then 5096 must of course be "issued" with 5086, but there is no note to that effect. That seems obvious, but in catalogues whose conventions are as strict as those in STC2, nothing can be imagined to be obvious.[13]

Let us now look at entries in ESTC as constituted online today (meaning "the last time I checked it").

Here begynneth the boke of C[a]nterbury tales, dilygently [and] truely corrected, an[d] newly printed
[Imprinted at London: In fletestrete, by me Rycharde **Pynson**, printed vnto the kynges noble grade: and fyuished [sic],

---

12 See also, STC2 on the 1602 edition: 5076 "Anr. issue, w. gen. tp reset" for one of the copies 1561, whereas 5076.3 is "A variant, w. colophon:..." I don't understand the difference between "issue" and "variant." See further STC2 entries 5078, 5079, 5081, and my discussion in Joseph A. Dane, *Who is Buried in Chaucer's Tomb? Studies in the Reception of Chaucer's Book* (East Lansing: Michigan State University Press, 1998), 5–8.

13 Joseph A. Dane, *What Is a Book? The Study of Early Printed Books* (Notre Dame: University of Notre Dame press, 2012), 196, and references.

the yere of our lorde god. a. M.CCCCC. and xxvi. the fourth day of Iune. [1526]

The cryptic note "Anonymous. By Geoffrey Chaucer." must be saying that an anonymous prologue precedes the *Canterbury Tales*, but it would be hard to determine that without the book in hand. References include STC (2nd edn.), 5086 and Duff 89. This is Duff's detailed catalogue of fifteenth-century English books, although I'm not certain of its relevance here.[14] The section "Holdings" (meaning, extant copies) lists 5 British copies, 3 American.

ESTC's entries for the other sections are as follows. For the *House of Fame*:

> Here begynneth the boke of fame, made by Geffray **Chaucer**, with dyuers other of his workes.
> [Imprinted at London: In fletestrete, by Richarde **Pynson**, printer to the kynges most noble grace, [1526?]
> Place of publication and printer's name from colophon; publication date conjectured by STC.
> Edited by William Caxton. — STC
> Issued with STC 5086
> 5 British holdings; 2 American.

And finally, for *Troilus and Criseyde*:

> [Emprynted at London: In Fletestrete by Rycharde **Pynson** printer vnto the kynges noble grace, [1526?]
> Note : Anonymous. by Geoffrey **Chaucer**

As in *House of Fame*, there are 5 British copies, and two American copies (these are the same seven copies, of course, although the note does not state that).

---

14 E. Gordon Duff, *Fifteenth-Century English Books* (London: Oxford University Press, 1917).

From this, without investigating the entries in individual catalogues, I can only conclude that the Oxford copy of the *Canterbury Tales* noted in STC1 ended up in Texas, and that all other listed copies are copies containing all three works. I don't understand the use of brackets around publication information that is clearly quoted from the actual books (does this mean, strangely, that that information is not on the title page?). The problem with "issue," raised in STC1, reappears. And as is often the case, when a statement like this reappears in a later catalogue, it is not simply "repeated"; it is, rather, "confirmed."

Under modern cataloguing conventions, the three sections must either constitute "one edition" intended to be sold and bound together, or they are "three editions" that could like any other books be bound together by a bookseller or by an owner. If the claim that they were "issued" together is at all meaningful, that likely means they constituted one edition, but it almost certainly means that the publication dates are the same: 1526 indeed needs to be in brackets (as in the ESTC entry for *Troilus*) that is, it is conjectured, but it does not need to be in brackets with a question mark — what does that mean? that it is "sort of" questioned?

Finally, although it is doubtless churlish to criticize cataloguers for making no more mistakes than I myself will introduce trying to copy their entries, it seems to me that the more scrupulous the conventions, the more problematic the details become. Why, for example, are letters in the title bracketed, but the preposterous turned letter n transcribed as a u followed by "[sic]"? This is pedantry. A turned n is not a u to begin with. It is a mis-set n. Our "Anonymous" reappears. Why are names in bold? (Generally, any change in typeface in these bibliographies represents something of bibliographical concern: but note how the italics used in STC2 to distinguish actual text from paraphrased or conventional text have disappeared.) The bold-face, as far as I can tell, is no more than a highlight; that is, it is bibliographically meaningless.

Putting these together we can come to some tentative conclusions, which have nothing to do with facts or early printing history, but only with the history of STC from its origins in 1926 to the present-day on-line ESTC. Pollard and Redgrave made their decisions on the basis of two copies: the British Library copy had all three works bound together; another (the Oxford copy) had only one. Furthermore, because there was no extant general title page, there was, on Skeat's authority, no complete edition. The 1526 Pynson, like the early Caxton volumes, had failed to represent adequately the ideal form of the "complete edition" which was found in the 1932 Thynne edition and in the folio editions that followed it.

STC2 and ESTC are stuck with the decisions of STC1. They could hardly renumber the books, even though their examination of the many individual copies now recorded almost certainly leads to the opposite conclusion: that the copy O (now Tex) is an outlier (much like pamphlet copies of later Chaucer editions that are found bound singly) and that the three sections (*Canterbury Tales, Troilus,* and *House of Fame*) were intended as one book. Again, none of these decisions may be wrong, but this shows how difficult it can be to eradicate errors once introduced into standard bibliographical history.

Order of Sections

All but one of the extant copies contains all three STC items (STC 5086, 5088, and 5096), and no copy exists that binds only two of them together.[15] Does the ordering in the extant book-copies tell us anything about how the printer Pynson conceived these books?

The most important copy bibliographically is the British Library copy, the basis for STC descriptions and also the only copy described in detail in Hammond's *Bibliographical Manu-*

---

15 One advantage of the STC's decisions is that it should enable me to refer to the three "items"/"works"/"parts"/"sections"/"books"/"pamphlets" by STC numbers rather than a word that implies bibliographical status. But as even the introductory sentence above shows, it is almost impossible to do this.

al of 1908. This copy places the *Canterbury Tales* last; the now standard ordering of texts in "complete works" editions places the Tales first, a tradition which begins in 1532 and continues through modern editions. For the Pynson Chaucer, the placement of the *Canterbury Tales* last makes sense, since its colophon is the only one of the three to include a date.

Other copies have different orders for these sections, which I will distinguish as CT (*Canterbury Tales*), HF (*House of Fame* and other texts), and TC (*Troilus and Criseyde*). Harvard has the order CT, HF, TC; the Yale copy also has this order. Leeds has TC, HF, CT. Glasgow has CT, TC, HF.[16] A logical explanation can be given for any of the extant orders: CT is first because it was first in the 1532 edition (the argument could then be made that it was "later" bound to conform to complete-works editions, but another argument could be made that the later order was based on this one). CT is last because it contains a colophon; HF is last because it concludes with "minor works" following the *House of Fame*. But such arguments may be specious: there is no argument that would place HF before TC, as in the Harvard and Yale copies, unless it would also justify HF as the first of three (a placement that does not appear in any copy).

It seems to me I could reasonably conclude one of two things: (1) that the order of these texts "makes sense" to any binder, even though the orders are different, and (2) that the order of the texts is completely random and the only reason for certain orders not appearing is that too few copies exist. The fact that either of these arguments can be made tells me that we are back at square one: there is nothing to be concluded at all.

Descriptive bibliographers might well feel they do not have the luxury to carry on such discursive discussions: ideal copy description should, if possible or feasible, reflect the printer's intentions (at least, that was how Fredson Bowers conceived it)[17];

---

16 Blackburn PL and Lambeth Palace, despite what ESTC says, claim not to have copies. I cannot confirm whether ESTC's assertions or the librarians' denials are true.

17 Fredson Bowers, *Principles of Bibliographical Description* (Princeton: Princeton University Press, 1949), e.g., 113.

yet since printers may have been as wishy-washy or vague as the rest of us, there will be some situations where conventional bibliographical distinctions, meant to be clear and decisive, cannot possibly reflect the historical facts that are the subject of a catalogue. There is no bibliographical room for a situation where neither printer nor distributor had any opinion or preference on section order, or perhaps, even whether the books should be bound together in the first place.[18]

Alexandra Gillespie, who has studied and thought about the 1526 Pynson edition(s) as much as anyone, started at a different place in Chaucer history, beginning with the notion of a complete-works edition, and working not forward but backward. Not only is Pynson's edition a complete works, but precedent for both this edition and Thynne's 1532 edition can be found in Caxton and De Worde's early quarto editions of individual works. The individual items now found bound separately in almost all copies (for example, de Worde's 1498 *Canterbury Tales*, STC 5085, and his *Troilus*, STC 5095) were once intended to be bound together, at least potentially. Customers who imagined a "complete works" in the early sixteenth century would have one available to them at a bookseller, by combining any of the quartos of Caxton or De Worde that happened to be available. But even Gillespie's thoughts on this matter run afoul of Hammond's note: "No collection, even partial, of the Minor Poems was brought together until the ed. by Pynson in 1526. In subsequent prints of the Works or Poems the minor poems are included."[19] In other words, Pynson is the only printer to produce any "collection" of Chaucer works (in this case, the "minor poem") in an edition with a single signature series (STC 5088). His 1526 edition is thus more easily seen as a precedent for the edition series

---

18 Precedents for this situation are not uncommon. The pamphlets printed by Ulrich Zell (the first printer from Cologne) in the 1460s were clearly meant to be bound together (or foreseen that way), but not in any particular order or number. Zell's own notes exist in a presentation copy, whose order and selection occurs in no other extant copy. See my *What Is a Book?*, 175–76.

19 Hammond, *Chaucer*, 350.

of 1532–1687 than as an endpoint in Chaucer editions by Caxton and De Worde.

Conclusion

In their book *The Ants*, Bert Hölldöbler and E.O. Wilson describe a rather terrifying predator of a particular species of ant. This predator gains access to the ant colony easily, even though to us, it seems not to resemble these victims at all. Hölldöbler and Wilson then imagine an unsettling scenario to explain how this is possible:

> When the crickets [who prey on ant eggs] are newly introduced into an ant nest,... they are usually treated in a hostile manner by the worker ants. They are then able to escape death only through swift and nimble running. But the ant aggression usually subsides as soon as the crickets adjust their locomotory pattern to the movement patterns of the undisturbed host ants....Although the cricket does not look like an ant overall, portions of its body resemble parts of the ants' bodies. Hölldobler [in a 1947 study] elaborated his tactile mimicry concept with a metaphor. Suppose, he said, that we live in a completely dark room and orient primarily by means of the tactile sense in our hands. Among hundreds of us dwells one creature that is very differently constructed but has appendages resembling human hands, and it also manages to mimic our body movements and to touch us with a humanoid caress. This creature is perceived by us as a fellow human being until some crucial behavioral mistake unmasks it as an alien.[20]

This entomological variant of Plato's cave has kept me up at night, imagining shaking hands in a dark room with an alien

---

20 Bert Hölldobler and Edward O. Wilson, *The Ants* (Cambridge: Harvard University Press, 1990), 513.

predator or food source, while mistaking it for a possible sexual partner. I can extend this metaphor again, with the alien STC-creature extending its apparently book-like hands into the closed and protective field of book-copies and their histories. As long as the appendages are properly constructed, and the caresses appropriate, all seems fine. And this is the world in which scholars and bibliographers are more or less content to live. But the world perceived may well be far different — what appears to be the "fit" of bibliography to the objects of the bibliographers' study is simply the ant-like appendages, mimicking the books. We can only hope they will be fellow-ants (the subject of Holldöbler's metaphor) rather than predatory invaders, who of course would use precisely the same technique.

SECTION 3.6

Margaret Mead and the Bonobos

Anthropologists working in specific fields have challenged the details of this study; in a sense its inaccuracies in terms of ethnology make it all the more valuable as a created structure through which men see history, a myth like those of the Greeks.
— Page DuBois, *Centaurs and Amazons*[1]

The following pages look at two controversies in the so-called soft sciences that at least claim to be understood or constructed according to the methods of the hard sciences; they are based on the observation and definition of facts, and the presentation of those facts within a coherent scientific narrative. My association of these two subjects could be dismissed as arbitrary, an example of the humanistic "juxtology" that I criticized in Chapter 4 of this volume. Yet I don't associate these simply to "see what happens." I know what happens; these two subjects have always seemed to me to be the same.

The two subjects are (1) Margaret Mead's now classic 1928 study *Coming of Age in Samoa,* along with its recent critiques, led by Derek Freeman's *Margaret Mead and Samoa,* and (2) the bonobos along with their attendant mythology. Bonobos were discovered or defined in 1919; what I call their mythology developed in the 1950s and 1960s, when Mead's book reached the

---

1 DuBois is here referring to Claude Levi-Strauss, *The Elementary Structures of Kinship* (1949).

height of its popularity, and culminated in a series of studies by Frans de Waal.[2]

The sets of facts on which these arguments are based would seem to be these: the sexual lives of young girls in Samoa at the time of Mead's interviews, and the social lives of the bonobos in the twentieth century. Yet even as I describe these, the limits of those things become problematic. Mead's subject — the sexual lives of Samoans — was redefined as Mead's study became controversial. What is at issue is (or should be) "the sexual lives of the Samoans when Mead was there"; Samoans either were or were not as she describes, or more or less as she describes. They aren't that way today, and therefore there can be no retesting or confirmation of what Mead reported. Both Mead's supporters and her detractors agree on this. Researchers affect and at times effect what they intend to study. Because the experiment is unrepeatable, what it claims as facts (whether right or wrong) are beyond normal scientific critique. For the bonobos, things are different or at least seem to be. We assume their behavior is genetically determined except in the most extreme of cases (confinement to a prison). Bonobo society, whether today or in the not very distant past, whether wild and undocumented or closely studied, either in nature or in a modern zoo, is a constant. The popular understanding of them depends on this assumption.

Unlike the human subjects of Mead's study, bonobos have evolved through history and without this evolutionary assumption there would likely be little interest in them; but they do not,

---

2 Frans de Waal, *Bonobo: The Forgotten Ape* (Berkeley: University of California Press, 1997), *Chimpanzee Politics: Power and Sex among Apes* (Baltimore: Johns Hopkins University Press, 1982), and "Sex as an Alternative to Aggression in the Bonobo," in *Sexual Nature/Sexual Culture*, eds. Paul R. Abramson and Steven D. Pinkerton, 37–56 (Chicago: University of Chicago Press, 1995); Derek Freeman, *Margaret Mead and Samoa: The Making and Unmaking of an Anthropological Myth* (Cambridge: Harvard University Press, 1983); Margaret Mead, *Coming of Age in Samoa: A Psychological Study of Primitive Youth for Western Civilisation* (New York: Morrow, 1928), and many re-editions; see Mary Pipher, Introduction in the Penguin Perenniel Classics edition (New York: Morrow, 2001), xvi: "Everyone in college read Mead in the 1960s."

as we do, possess a history: we speak of them as if they are static — that is, "bonobos as presently evolved" rather than "bonobos as presently evolving." Mead's society, by contrast, evolves very quickly, although the meaning of the word *evolve* is not quite the same here. Whatever naive/native state the Samoans once enjoyed (and even stating that makes the assumption seem shaky) was corrupted by their association with Westerners. The Samoans were not just observed — they were imprisoned within the language and conventions of early to mid-twentieth-century Europeans, as surely as bonobos were often confined to zoos.

There are further paradoxes involved in these assumptions. One of the reasons we are interested in the bonobos is the evidence they provide about evolution, specifically, our own evolutionary history. They are, perhaps, more "like" the ancestor of the bonobo/chimpanzee/human than are either chimpanzees or humans. And this may or may not tell us something about ourselves, just as could our assumption that humans uncorrupted by modern technology are spared distinctly modern neuroses. Either our ancestors were the violent, murderous beings we see among us today (and now see in chimpanzees), or a gentler, kinder race, corrupted by whatever one wants to put at the origin of corruption (civilization, say, or evolution itself).

The Bonobos

If we define an animal species through DNA, the bonobos have been around as long as we have. But "bonobos," in the sense we understand that word, have existed for less than a century. The now standard behavioral description is from a study by Eduard Paul Tratz and Heinz Heck conducted in the early twentieth century, published only in 1954. The study is brief, only a few pages, and presented in a summary version by de Waal "in slightly compressed form." De Waal summarizes the characteristics identified in Tratz and Heck as follows:

1. Bonobos are sensitive, lively, and nervous, whereas chimpanzees are coarse and hot-tempered.
2. Bonobos rarely raise their hair; chimpanzees often do so.
3. Physical violence almost never occurs in bonobos, yet is common in chimpanzees.
4. Bonobos defend themselves through aimed kicking with their feet, whereas chimpanzees try to pull attackers close to bite them.
5. The bonobo voice contains a and e vowels, whereas the chimpanzee uses more u and o vowels.
6. Bonobos are more vocal than chimpanzees.
7. Bonobos stretch their arms and shake their hands when calling, whereas chimpanzees do not.
8. Bonobos copulate more hominum and chimpanzees more canum.[3]

The outlines of the full-blown bonobo myth are here, supported even by the kind of phonetic analysis one might see in freshman essays. Points 1, 3, and 8 involving violence and sex are the key components of the myth. This is the basis for the full sexual myth found in de Waal: female dominance over males; no jealousy or competition for females; non-nuclear families; and indiscriminate sexual play: male/male, male/female, female/female:

> [In chimpanzees and baboons] male superiority remained the "natural" state of affairs. In both chimpanzees and baboons, males are conspicuously dominant over females... Enter the bonobo, which is best characterized as a female-

---

3 de Waal, "First Impressions," *Bonobo*, 9, referring to Eduard Paul Tratz and Heinz Heck, "Der afrikanische Anthropoide Bonobo: Eine neue Menschenaffengattung," *Säugetierkundliche Mitteilungen* 2, no. 3 (1954): 97–101. Another early notice is H.J. Coolidge, "*Pan paniscus*: Pygmy chimpanzee from South of the Congo River," *American Journal of Physical Anthropology* 18, no. 1 (1933): 1–57. See also: H.J. Coolidge, "Historical Remarks Bearing on the Discovery of *Pan paniscus*," in *The Pygmy Chimpanzee*, ed. R.L. Susman, ix–xiii (New York: Plenum Press, 1984); E.S. Savage-Rumbaugh and B. Wilkerson, "Socio-sexual Behavior in *Pan paniscus* and *Pan troglodytes*: A Comparative Study," *Journal of Human Evolution* 7, no. 4 (1978): 327–44.

centered, egalitarian primate species that substitutes sex for aggression... Sexual encounters of the bonobo kind are strikingly casual, almost more affectionate than erotic.[4]

And quoting Tratz and Heck, de Waal writes, "The bonobo is an extraordinarily sensitive, gentle creature, far removed from the demoniacal primitive force of the adult chimpanzee."[5]

It is almost too good to be true. At the same time a society was described by Mead freed of such modern neuroses as jealousy and competitiveness, a new species was discovered that seemed to exhibit much the same thing. The Samoans expose our own neuroses and thus suggest a possible avenue to free ourselves from them; the bonobos expose the violence in both human and chimpanzee society, and again, suggest that this is not something to which we are doomed genetically. These are presented not as mere utopian projections, but as "facts."

Coming of Age in the 1960s

The story of Mead's Samoa, the late-twentieth-century attack on her, and the counter-attack is well-known. The purpose of Mead seemed always satiric in the classic sense, as its very sub-title indicates: "A Psychological Study...for Western Civilisation." Like classical bucolic poetry, her Somoan research was more about "us" than "them," a commentary and critique of our society rather than a description of a supposedly more primitive one:

> If it is proved that adolescence is not necessarily a specially difficult period in a girl's life...then what accounts for the presence of storm and stress in American adolescents?[6]

---

4 de Waal, *Bonobo*, 3–5.
5 Ibid., 9. Cf. Desmond Morris, *The Naked Ape* (New York: Dell, 1967) or with Konrad Lorenz, whose books (like those of Mead) were required reading for undergraduates in the 1960s. According to de Waal, the notion of "the killer ape" prepared him for his "discovery" of the bonobo in 1978 (*Bonobo*, 153).
6 Mead, *Coming of Age in Samoa*, 137.

Reading such statements in the twenty-first century makes it easy to see why they were critiqued at the end of the last:

> The life of the day begins at dawn, or if the moon has shown until day light, the shouts of the young men may be heard before dawn from the hillside. Uneasy in the night, populous with ghosts, they shout lustily to one another as they hasten with their work.
>
> Romantic love as it occurs in our civilisation, inextricably bound up with ideas of monogamy, exclusiveness, jealousy, and undeviating fidelity does not occur in Samoa.
>
> Familiarity with sex, and the recognition of a need of a technique to deal with sex as an art, have produced a scheme of personal relations in which there are no neurotic pictures, no frigidity, no impotence, except as the temporary result of severe illness, and the capacity for intercourse only once in a night is counted as senility.[7]

These statements, some singled out by Freeman, are at odds with even the general descriptions by Mead that document them. Contrary evidence is simply explained away:

> Cases of passionate jealousy do occur but they are matters for extended comment and amazement.[8]

In nine months, Mead recorded only four cases:

> a girl who informed against a faithless lover accusing him of incest, a girl who bit off part of a rival's ear, a woman whose husband had deserted her and who fought and severely in-

---

7   Ibid., 12, 73, and 105.
8   Ibid., 111.

jured her successor, and a girl who falsely accused a rival of stealing.[9]

Jealousy does not occur. If testimony indicates it does, then that testimony calls for "extensive comment": the more extensive the testimony, the less factual the event that elicited it.[10]

Because of the nature of Mead's research, the facts, if understood as the sexual habits of the Samoans at the time she interviewed them, are irrecoverable. All that can be in dispute is the quality of Mead's testimony. And an important aspect of this is Mead's later response to critiques. Mead's book went through several printings and revisions: 1939, 1947, 1953, 1961....And Mead had many opportunities either to revise it, to provide a self-reflective critique of what she had done, insofar as she remembered the particulars, or to respond seriously to critics. Derek Freeman, the most important of these, did not call upon her to renounce her thesis, or even to revise her findings — that is to say, rewrite the interviews. He only asked that she respond to recent objections. Yet instead of defending the quality of her interviews, Mead redefined what constitutes fact by shifting it from the object of research to the research itself. What seems to be placing her research in historical context is actually a sleight-of-hand making it invulnerable to critique:

> It must remain, as all anthropological works must remain, exactly as it was written true to what I saw in Samoa and what I was able to convey of what I saw; true to the state of

---

9 Ibid., 112.
10 Utopian descriptions of South Pacific society are common in early travel writings: e.g., *Pacific Journal of Louis-Antoine de Bougainville 1767–1768*, trans. and ed. John Dunmore (London: Hakluyt Society 2002), 60–63, and Louis-Antoine de Bougainville, *Voyage autour du monde par la frégate La Boudeuse et la Flûte l'étoile* (1772), ed. Michel Hérubel (Paris: Le Monde, 1966), 205–15, where many of the same motifs appear.

> our knowledge of human behavior as it was in the mid-1920's; true to our hopes and fears for the future of the world.[11]

What Freeman claims is that Mead misrepresented a set of facts (sexual behavior) because she took as valid the oral testimony of her witnesses. Mead never even addresses this question. Instead, she turns the question away from "a set of facts" (behavior) to "evidence" (a contemporary summary of behavior). What is in dispute now is not how Samoans behaved, but rather her own words in the earlier monograph — that is, her own testimony, not that of her witnesses. And the question seems now, not whether that testimony (her own) reflects the testimony of her witnesses, but simply whether it "exists." With that, the set of facts she seems to uphold is irrefutable. In the 1930s, she transcribed and analyzed a set of witness statements in a way that became the book. Those are the facts, she states, and they will last longer than the currency of the language it took to create them. No one has a scientific basis to demand that she revise and thus "falsify" (that is, "change") what she wrote or said in 1928.

Mead's preface thus turns on a mischievous use of the word TRUE. In the first sentence, the word "true" means that her statement corresponds to "what I saw" (immediately qualified as true to "what I was able to convey of what I saw"); this qualification is not really a qualification at all but a simple tautology. In the second case, it means something quite different: "an accurate expression of what we thought of human behavior in the 20s" (is this before or after the study of the Samoans?) and finally "true" to our vision of the future, a vision which can hardly be the same or even coherent over time. The society Mead described no longer can be observed; the experiment cannot be reproduced. The scholar's own words and analysis, by contrast, are fixed, and thus factual, and thus eternal. Mead the anthropologist has become Mead the Shakespearean sonneteer. And

---

11 Margaret Mead, Preface, *Coming of Age in Samoa: A Psychological Study of Primitive Youth for Western Civilization* (New York: American Museum of Natural History Press, 1973), xxiv.

if all statements, like poems, are facts, then it is meaningless to claim any of them are.

In both cases, a set of facts could easily have been defined: what were, or are, the social habits of the bonobos? What were the social habits of the Samoans in 1928? Those facts could then have been interpreted and used for a number of purposes: as anthropological data, as a critique of scientific or social scientific method, or legitimately as a form of social satire. The bonobos and primitive societies tell us, in our own Eurocentric ways, something about ourselves. Even though most of us know little to nothing about any of these topics, we could at least take such imagined scientists seriously enough to distrust them.

SECTION 3.7

Reading My Library

It is the end of the year, and today I am reading my library. It's a simple exercise, consequent upon moving too many times, twice in the last decade. There were once more than seventy book and record boxes, and next time, there will be fewer. Reading my library is in part a metaphor, or more exactly, a negative synecdoche. I am deaccessioning. Today I am reading my library. And tomorrow, I will be giving much of it away.

It is part of the elimination of books, book-copies, I should say (those with the banality of my annotations still in them), since the texts will be readily available on line or in libraries as long as I feel any need of them. I am being as systematic as I can, and there are a number of books and categories that will likely be spared: books in a foreign language, early printed books, books on books, books on Chaucer, books on metrics, books I have written, textbooks for courses I may one day teach again, books written by those friends and colleagues who may one day find themselves in my living room. A year ago, I had included here books on art or on music, but "what cannot be given away," I find, is a steadily narrowing category.

That leaves too many to own, and still too many to move. I realize some will likely end up in the dumpster or in the garage of whoever cleans up after me and can't bear to throw them away. But that also leaves books for reading, and that is what I am doing now.

There are a number of books I bought when I was a graduate student. In those days buying books was like mastering them, and a professor in the humanities who pretended to a wide range of intellectual interests ought to own as many as possible. There is philosophy, most of Wittgenstein, *Madwoman in the Attic,* novels (a special category), architecture, mathematics, history. I am now reading them all, and when I am done with them, they will go to the "Free Books" bench outside the main English office. There they will stay, closely observed, far longer than they would have stayed had such a bench existed years ago. Students now pick them up, and think as I do, but never thought before: "Do I really want to move *that* in a year or two?"

It makes for an interesting read, my personal version of the low-brow Harvard Library of Civilisation.

Locke, *Essay on Human Understanding,* complete, paper, vol. 1
Wittkover, *Architectural Principles in the Age of Humanism*
Frank, *Dostoevsky*
Pottle, *Boswell: Early Years*
Clifford, *Dictionary Johnson*
Clifford, *Hester L. Pozzi*

....

It turns out the only way I could force myself to read all these was to threaten myself to give them away unread. I am now done, and thus they won't be missed.

These, with others, go also to the Free Bench. *Tom Jones* sits for several weeks. Braudel's *Civilization and Capitalism* lasts four days. Wilson's *Patriotic Gore* and everything in imposing red wrappers by Marx last nearly two weeks. Yet Kojeve's *Introduction à la lecture de Hegel* is gone within an hour. A lavish catalog of Daumier lasts a week.

What has gone to this shelf must be as good a reflection of my interests as what I retain: what I've read is who I am, or once desired to be; what I plan to read, study, re-read, or simply own is something else altogether. Books of both categories reflect my economic status, enthusiasms, simple greed, obsessions, and happenstance. But the self I will have constructed when my deaccessioned books are gone may well be much more coherent, consisting only of what is valuable and professional: bibliography, anything printed before 1800, Chaucer, French books, novels and now-dated criticism, Greek and Latin (the remnant of my father's profession), German books of all genres (because I have the least competence in this language, oddly or thus it is the only one I read for pleasure). I will be left with a streamlined core or version of something, my academic self perhaps, an illusion of coherence, visible to anyone, despite my inability ever to find it myself.

Bibliography

Alderson, William L. and Arnold C. Henderson. *Chaucer and Augustan Scholarship.* Berkeley: University of California Press, 1970.

Annotated Books Online: A Digital Archive of Early Modern Annotation, http://www.annotatedbooksonline.com.

Bahr, Arthur. *Fragments and Assemblages: Forming Compilations of Medieval London.* Chicago: University of Chicago Press, 2013.

Beadle, Richard. "The Virtuoso's *Troilus*." In *Chaucer Traditions: Studies in Honour of Derek Brewer,* eds. Ruth Morse and Barry Windeatt, 213–33. Cambridge: Cambridge University Press, 1990.

Beaurline, L.A. and Thomas Clayton. "Notes on Early Editions of Fragmenta Aurea." *Studies in Bibliography* 23 (1970): 165–70.

Beesemyer, Irene Basey and Joseph A. Dane. "The Denigration of John Lydgate: Implications of Printing History." *English Studies* 81, no. 2 (2000): 117–26.

Benson, Larry D., gen. ed. *The Riverside Chaucer,* 3rd edn. Boston: Houghton Mifflin, 1987.

Bergeron, Réjean and Ezio Ornato. "La lisibilité dans les manuscrits et les imprimés à la fin du Moyen Age: Preliminaires d'une recherche." *Scrittura e Civiltà* 14 (1990): 151–98. Repr. *La face cachée du livre médiéval: L'histoire du livre vue par Ezio Ornato, ses amis et ses collègues,* 521–54. Roma: Viella, 1997.

Binns, J.W. *Intellectual Culture in Elizabethan and Jacobean England: The Latin Writings of the Age.* ARCA Classical and Medieval Texts, Papers and Monographs, 24. Leeds: Cairns, 1990.

Blades, William. *How to Tell a Caxton, with some hints where and how the same might be found.* London: Sotheran, 1870.

Boffey, Julia and A.S.G. Edwards. "Chaucer's Chronicle,' John Shirley, and the Canon of Chaucer's Shorter Poems." *Studies in the Age of Chaucer* 20 (1998): 201–18.

Bowers, Fredson. *Principles of Bibliographical Description.* Princeton: Princeton University Press, 1949.

Bradshaw, Henry. *Collected Papers.* Cambridge: University Press, 1889.

Braudel, Fernand. *Civilization and Capitalism, 15th–18th Century,* trans. Siân Reynold. 3 vols. New York: Harper, 1982–84.

Bredekamp, Horst, gen. ed. *Galileo's O.* 3 vols. Vol. 1: *Galileo's Sidereus Nuncius: A Comparison of the Proof Copy (New York) with Other Paradigmatic Copies,* eds. Irene Brückle and Oliver Hahn. Berlin: Akademie Verlag, 2011.

———. *Galileo's O,* Vol. 2: *Galileo Makes a Book: The First Edition of Sidereus Nuncius, Venice 1610,* by Paul Needham. Berlin: Akademie Verlag, 2011.

———. *Galileo's O,* Vol. 3: *A Galileo Forgery (Galileo's O): Unmasking the New York Sidereus Nuncius,* eds. Irene Brückle and Paul Needham. Berlin: De Gruyter, 2014.

Brewer, Derek. *Chaucer: The Critical Heritage.* 2 vols. London: Routledge and Kegan Paul, 1978.

British Museum General Catalogue of Printed Books to 1955, 263 vols. London: British Library, 1959–66.

Brown, Carleton. *English Lyrics of the XIIIth Century.* Oxford: Clarendon Press, 1932.

Brown, Julian. *A Palaeographer's View: Selected Writings of Julian Brown,* eds. Janet Bateley, Michelle Brown, and Jane Roberts. London: Harvey Miller, 1993.

Brusendorff, Aage. *The Chaucer Tradition.* London: Oxford University Press, 1925.

Burke, Peter. *The French Historical Revolution: The Annales School 1929–1989*. Stanford: Stanford University Press, 1990.

Catalogue of Books Printed in the Fifteenth Century now in the British Museum, 13 vols. London: British Museum, 1908–.

Chartier, Roger. *The Author's Hand and the Printer's Mind*, trans. Lydia G. Cochrane. Cambridge: Polity Press, 2013.

Cole, George Watson. *Check-list or Brief Catalogue of the Library of Henry E. Huntington (English Literature to 1640)*. New York, 1919.

Cook, Megan. "How Francis Thynne Read His Chaucer." *Journal of the Early Book Society for the Study of Manuscripts and Printing History* 15 (2012): 215–44.

Coolidge, H.J. "Historical Remarks Bearing on the Discovery of Pan paniscus." In *The Pygmy Chimpanzee*, ed. R.L. Susman, ix–xiii. New York: Plenum Press, 1984.

———. "*Pan paniscus*: Pygmy chimpanzee from South of the Congo River." *American Journal of Physical Anthropology* 18, no. 1 (1933): 1–57.

Corsten, Severin, "Ulrich Zells frühste Produktion," *Gutenberg Jahrbuch* 2007, 68–76.

Crotch, W.J.B. *The Prologues and Epilogues of William Caxton*. EETS 176. London: Oxford University Press, 1928.

Dane, Joseph A. *Abstractions of Evidence in Manuscripts and Early Printed Books*. Aldershot: Ashgate, 2009.

———. *Blind Impressions: Methods and Mythologies in Book History*. Philadelphia: University of Pennsylvania Press, 2013.

———. "A Ghostly Twin Terence (Venice, 21 July 1475; IGI 9422, 9433)." *The Library*, ser. 6, 21 (1999): 99–107.

———. *The Long and the Short of It: A Practical Guide to European Versification Systems*. Notre Dame: University of Notre Dame Press, 2010.

———. *The Myth of Print Culture: Essays on Evidence, Textuality, and Bibliographical Method*. Toronto: University of Toronto Press, 2003.

———. *Out of Sorts: On Typography and Print Culture*. Philadelphia: University of Pennsylvania Press, 2011.

———. "Toward a Description of Chaucer's Verse Forms." *Studia Neophilologica* 81, no. 1 (2009): 45–52.

———. "Wanting the First Blank: The Frontispiece to the Huntington Library Copy of Caxton's *Recuyell of the Historyes of Troye*." *Huntington Library Quarterly* 67, no. 2 (2004): 315–25.

———. *What Is a Book? The Study of Early Printed Books.* Notre Dame: University of Notre Dame Press, 2012.

———. *Who Is Buried in Chaucer's Tomb? Studies in the Reception of Chaucer's Book.* East Lansing: Michigan State University Press, 1998.

Darnton, Robert. *The Great Cat Massacre and Other Episodes in French Cultural History.* New York: Basic Books, 1984

de Ricci, Seymour. *English Collectors of Books and Manuscripts (1530–1930).* Cambridge: Cambridge University Press, 1930.

Derolez, Albert. *Codicologie des manuscrits en écriture humanistique sur parchemin.* 2 vols. Turnhout: Brepols, 1984.

de Waal, Frans. *Bonobo: The Forgotten Ape.* Berkeley: University of California Press, 1997.

———. *Chimpanzee Politics: Power and Sex among Apes.* Baltimore: Johns Hopkins University Press, 1982.

———. "Sex as an Alternative to Aggression in the Bonobo." In *Sexual Nature/Sexual Culture,* eds. Paul R. Abramson and Steven D. Pinkerton, 37–56. Chicago: University of Chicago Press, 1995.

Dibdin, Thomas Frognall. *The Bibliographical Decameron.* 3 vols. London: Shakespeare Press, 1817.

———. *Typographical Antiquities, or the History of Printing in England.* 4 vols. London: Miller, 1810–19.

Donaldson, Robert. Rev. Donald G. Wing, *Short-Title Catalogue.* *The Bibliotheck* 6, issue 5 (1973): 203–4.

Doyle, A.I., and M.B. Parkes. "The Production of Copies of the *Canterbury Tales* and the *Confessio Amantis* in the Early Fifteenth Century." In *Medieval Scribes, Manuscripts and Libraries: Essays Presented to N.R. Ker,* eds. M.B. Parkes and A.G. Watson, 163–210. London: Scolar Press, 1978.

Duffell, Martin J. "Chaucer, Gower and the History of the Hendecasyllable." In *English Historical Metrics,* eds. C.B. McCully and J.J. Anderson, 210–18. Cambridge: Cambridge University Press, 199

Dryden, John. *Fables Ancient and Modern; translated into Verse, from Homer, Ovid, Boccace, & Chaucer.* London, 1700.

DuBois, Page. *Centaurs and Amazons: Women and the Pre-History of the Great Chain of Being.* Ann Arbor: University of Michigan Press, 1982.

Duby, Georges. *Les trois ordres, ou L'imaginaire du féodalisme.* Paris: Gallimard, 1978.

Duff, E. Gordon. *Fifteenth-Century English Books.* London: Oxford University Press, 1917.

Duffell, Martin J. "Chaucer, Gower and the History of the Hendecasyllable." In *English Historical Metrics,* eds. C.B. McCully and J.J. Anderson, 210–18. Cambridge: Cambridge University Press, 1996.

———. "'The Craft so long to Lerne': Chaucer's Invention of the Iambic Pentameter." *The Chaucer Review* 34, no 3. (2000): 269–88.

Early English Books Online, http://eebo.chadwyck.com/.

Echard, Siân. *Printing the Middle Ages.* Philadelphia: University of Pennsylvania Press, 2008.

Ellis, Alexander J. *On Early English Pronunciation with especial reference to Shakspere and Chaucer, Part III: Illustrations of the Pronunciation of the XIVth and XVIth Centuries.* London: N. Trübner & Co., 1871.

Elwert, W. Theodor. *Traité de versification française des origines à nos jours.* Paris: Klincksieck, 1965.

English Short Title Catalogue. London: British Library, http://estc.bl.uk/.

Estill, Laura. "The Urge to Organize Early Modern Miscellanies: Reading Cotgrave's *The English Treasury of Wit and Language." Papers of the Bibliographical Society of America* 112, no. 1 (2018): 27–73.

Febvre, Lucien and Henry-Jean Martin. *The Coming of the Book: The Impact of Printing 1450–1800,* trans. David Gerard, eds. Geoffrey Nowell Smith and David Wooton. London: Verso, 1976.

Feyerabend, Paul. *Against Method.* London: Verso, 1975.

Feynman, Richard. "What Is Science?" *The Physics Teacher* 7, no. 6 (1966): 313–20.

Flewelling, Ralph Tyler. *The Forest of Yggdrasill: The Autobiography of Ralph Tyler Flewelling,* ed. W.H. Werkmeister. Los Angeles: University of Southern California Press, 1962.

Forni, Kathleen. *The Chaucerian Apocrypha: A Counterfeit Canon.* Gainesville: University of Florida Press, 2001.

———. "'Chaucer's Dream': A Bibliographical Nightmare." *Huntington Library Quarterly* 64, nos. 1/2 (2001): 139–49.

Freeborn, Dennis. *From Old English to Standard English: A Course Book on Language Variation Across Time.* 3rd edn. Houdmills: Macmillan, 2006.

Freeman, Derek. *Margaret Mead and Samoa: The Making and Unmaking of an Anthropological Myth.* Cambridge: Harvard University Press, 1983.

Frye, Northrup. *Anatomy of Criticism: Four Essays.* Princeton: Princeton University Press, 1957.

Furnivall, F.J. *A Temporary Preface to the Six-text Edition of Chaucer's Canterbury Tales,* Chaucer Society Publ., ser. 2, pt. 3. London: N. Trübner & Co., 1868.

———. *Trial Forewords to my Parallel-Text Edition of Chaucer's Minor Poems for the Chaucer Society.* Chaucer Society Publ., ser. 2, pt. 6. London: Trübner & Co., 1871.

Galloway, Andrew. "Reading Piers Plowman in the Fifteenth and the Twenty-First Centuries: Notes on Manuscripts F and W in the Piers Plowman Electronic Archive." *Journal of English and Germanic Philology* 103, no. 2 (2004): 232–52

Gascoigne, Bamber. *How to IdentifyPrints: A Complete Guide to Manual and Mechanical Processes from Woodcut to Ink-Jet.* New York: Thames and Hudson, 1986.

Gaskell, Philip. *A New Introduction to Bibliography.* New York: Oxford University Press, 1972.

Gaylord, Alan T., ed., *Essays on the Art of Chaucer's Verse.* New York: Routledge, 2001.

Gillespie, Alexandra. *Print Culture and the Medieval Author: Chaucer, Lydgate, and Their Books, 1473–1557.* Oxford: Oxford University Press, 2006.

Godwin, William. *Life of Geoffrey Chaucer the Early English Poet.* 2 vols. London: Davison, 1803.

Gould, Stephen Jay. *The Hedgehog, the Fox, and the Magister's Pox.* New York: Harmony Books, 2003.

Grafton, Anthony J. *The Footnote: A Curious History.* Cambridge: Harvard University Press, 1999.

Greetham, David. "Phylum—Tree—Rhizome." *Huntington Library Quarterly* 58, no. 1 (1995): 99–126.

Greg, W.W. *A Bibliography of the English Printed Drama to the Restoration.* 4 vols. London: Bibliographical Society, 1939–59.

———. *The Calculus of Variants: An Essay on Textual Criticism.* Oxford: Clarendon Press, 1927.

———. *Collected Papers,* ed. J.C. Maxwell. Oxford: Clarendon Press, 1966.

Grierson, H.J.C., ed. *Poems of John Donne.* 2 vols. London: Oxford University Press, 1912.

Halle, Morris and Samuel Jay Keyser. "Chaucer and the Study of Prosody." *College English* 28, no. 3 (1966): 187–219.

Hammond, Eleanor Prescott. *Chaucer: A Bibliographical Manual.* New York: Macmillan, 1908.

Hanna, Ralph. *Introducing English Medieval Book History: Manuscripts, their Producers and their Readers.* Liverpool: Liverpool University Press, 2013.

———. *London Literature, 1300–1380.* Cambridge: Cambridge University Press, 2005.

———. *Pursuing History: Middle English Manuscripts and their Texts.* Stanford: Stanford University Press, 1996.

Harner, James L. MLA *Literary Research Guide: An Annotated Listing of Reference Sources in English Literary Studies,* 6th edn. New York: MLA, 2014.

Hardison, O.B., Jr. *Christian Rite and Christian Drama in the Middle Ages: Essays in the Origin and Early History of Modern Drama.* Baltimore: The Johns Hopkins Press, 1965.

Hind, A.M. *Engraving in England in the Sixteenth and Seventeenth Centuries: A Descriptive Catalogue with Introduction,* 3 vols. Cambridge: Cambridge University Press, 1952–64.

Hölldobler, Bert and Edward O. Wilson. *The Ants.* Cambridge: Harvard University Press, 1990.

Jackson, H.J. *Marginalia: Readers Writing in Books.* New Haven: Yale University Press, 2001.

Jardine, Lisa and Anthony Grafton. "'Studied for Action': How Gabriel Harvey Read his Livy." *Past and Present* 129, no. 1 (1990): 30–78.

Johns, Adrian. *The Nature of the Book: Print and Knowledge in the Making.* Chicago: University of Chicago Press, 1998.

Johnston, Hope. "Readers' Memorials in Early Editions of Chaucer." *Studies in Bibliography* 59 (2015): 45–69.

Kane, George. *Piers Plowman: Evidence for Authorship.* London: Athlone Press, 1965.

Kane, George and E. Talbot Donaldson. *William Langland's Piers Plowman: The B-Version.* London: Athlone, 1975.

Kastan, David Scott. "Humphrey Moseley and the Invention of English Literature." In *Agent of Change: Print Culture Studies after Elizabeth L. Eisenstein,* eds. Sabrina Alcorn Baron, Erin N. Lindquist, and Eleanor F. Shevlin, 105–24. Amherst: University of Massachusetts Press, 2000.

———. *Shakespeare and the Book.* Cambridge: Cambridge University Press, 2001.

Kastner, L.E. *A History of French Versification.* Oxford: Clarendon Press, 1903.

Kerby-Fulton, Kathryn and Maidie Hilmo, eds. *The Medieval Professional Reader at Work: Evidence from Manuscripts of Chaucer, Langland, Kempe, and Gower.* Victoria: University of Victoria, 2001,

Kerby-Fulton, Kathryn, John Thompson, and Sarah Baechle, eds. *New Directions in Medieval Manuscript Studies and Reading Practices: Essays in Honor of Derek Pearsall.* Notre Dame: Notre Dame University Press, 2014.

Kinney, Claire R. "Thomas Speght's Renaissance Chaucer and the Solaas of Sentence in Troilus and Criseyde." In *Refigur-*

ing Chaucer in the Renaissance, ed. Theresa M. Krier, 66–86. Gainseville: University Press of Florida, 1998.

Knight, Jeffrey Todd. *Bound to Read: Compilations, Collections and the Making of Renaissance Literature.* Philadelphia: University of Pennsylvania Press, 2013.

Kren, Thomas and Scot McKendrick, eds. *Illuminating the Renaissance: The Triumph of Flemish MS Painting in Europe.* Los Angeles: J. Paul Getty Museum, 2003.

Lancaster, Ian. *Dramatic Texts and Records of Britain: A Chronological Topography to 1558.* Cambridge: Cambridge University Press, 1984.

Lerer, Seth. *Chaucer and His Readers: Imagining the Author in Late Medieval England.* Princeton: Princeton University Press, 1993.

———. "Latin Annotations in a Copy of Stowe's Chaucer and the Seventeenth-Century Reception of *Troilus and Criseyde.*" *Review of English Studies* 53, no. 209 (2002): 1–7.

Le Roy Ladurie, Emmanuel. *Montaillou, village occitan de 1294 à 1324.* Paris: Gallimard, 1976.

Lounsbury, Thomas R. *Studies in Chaucer: His Life and Writings.* 3 vols. New York: Harper, 1892.

Macauley, G.C., ed. *The Complete Works of John Gower, edited from the Manuscripts with Introductions, Notes, and Glossaries.* 4. vols. Oxford: Clarendon Press, 1899–1902.

Machan, Tim William. "Kynaston's *Troilus,* Textual Criticism and the Renaissance Reading of Chaucer." *Exemplaria* 5, no. 1 (1993): 161–83.

Madan, Falconer. *The Early Oxford Press: A Bibliography of Printing and Publishing at Oxford, 1468–1640.* 3 vols. Oxford: Clarendon Press, 1895.

Manly, John and Edith Rickert. *The Text of the Canterbury Tales.* Chicago: University of Chicago Press, 1940.

Mazaleyrat, Jean. *Elements de métrique française.* Paris: Armand-Colin, 1974.

McGann, Jerome J. *A Critique of Modern Textual Criticism.* Chicago: University of Chicago Press, 1983.

McKenzie, D.F. "Printers of the Mind: Some Notes on Bibliographical Theories and Printing-House Practices." *Studies in Bibliography* 22 (1969): 1–75.

McKerrow, Ronald B. *Introduction to Bibliography for Literary Students.* Oxford: Clarendon Press, 1927.

McKitterick, David. *Old Books, New Technologies: The Representation, Conservation, and Transformation of Books Since 1700.* Cambridge: Cambridge University Press, 2013.

McLeod, Randall. "*Gon.* No more, the text is foolish." In *Division of the Kingdoms: Shakespeare's Two Versions of King Lear,* eds. Gary Taylor and Michael Warren, 153–93. Oxford: Clarendon Press, 1983.

McMurtrie, Douglas C. *The Book: The Story of Printing and Bookmaking, Illustrated.* New York: Dorset Press, 1989.

Mead, Margaret. *Coming of Age in Samoa: A Psychological Study of Primitive Youth for Western Civilisation.* New York: Morrow, 1928.

Minkova, Donka and Robert Stockwell, "Emendation and the Chaucerian Metrical Template." In *Chaucer and the Challenges of Medievalism: Studies in Honor of H.A. Kelley,* eds. Donka Minkova and Theresa Tinkle, 129–39. Frankfurt am Main: Peter Lang, 2003.

———. "The Partial Contact: Origins of English Pentameter Verse: The Anglicization of an Italian Model." In *Language Contact in the History of English,* eds. Dieter Kastovsky and Arthur Mettinger, 337–62. Frankfurt am Main: Peter Lang, 2001.

Morris, Desmond. *The Naked Ape.* New York: Dell, 1967.

Morris, Richard, ed. *The Poetical Works of Geoffrey Chaucer.* 3 vols. London: Bell, 1866.

Moxon, Joseph. *Mechanick Exercises on the Whole Art of Printing (1683–4),* eds. Herbert Davis and Harry Carter. 2nd edn. London: Oxford University, 1962.

Needham, Paul. "The Paper of English Incunabula." In *Catalogue of Books Printed in the XVth Century Now in the British Library (BMC), XI: England,* ed. Lotte Hellinga. Houten: Hes & De Graaf, 2007.

———. *The Printer and the Pardoner*. Washington, DC.: Library of Congress, 1986.

Nethery, Wallace. *Dr. Flewelling & the Hoose Library: Life and Letters of a Man and an Institution*. Los Angeles: University of Southern California Press, 1976.

Newton, Judith May. *Chaucer's Troilus: Sir Francis Kynaston's Latin Translation, with a Critical Edition of his English Comments and Latin Annotations*. PhD dissertation. University of Illinois, Urbana-Champaign, 1967.

Osberg, Richard. "False Memories: The Dream of Chaucer and Chaucer's Dream in the Medieval Revival." *Studies in Medievalism* 19 (2010): 204–25.

Owen, Charles A., Jr. *The Manuscripts of the Canterbury Tales*. Cambridge: D.S. Brewer, 1991.

Pace, George B. and Alfred David, eds. *The Variorum Edition of the Works of Geoffrey Chaucer, 5: The Minor Poems*. Norman: University of Oklahoma Press, 1982.

Pacific Journal of Louis-Antoine de Bougainville 1767–1768, trans. and ed. John Dunmore. London: Hakluyt Society, 2002.

Parkes, Malcolm B. "The Influence of the Concepts of Ordinatio and Compilatio on the Development of the Book" (1976). Rpt. Malcolm B. Parkes, *Scribes, Scripts, and Readers: Studies in the Communication, Presentation, and Dissemination of Medieval Texts*, 35–70. London: Hambledon, 1991.

Pearson, David. *Provenance Research in Book History*. New Castle: Oak Knoll, 1998.

Percy, Thomas. *Reliques of Ancient English Poetry: Consisting of Old Heroic Ballads, Songs, and other Pieces of our earlier Poets*. 3 vols. London: J. Dodsley, 1765.

Petit de Julleville, Louis. *Les Mystères*. 2 vols. Paris: Hachette, 1880.

Petrucci, Armando. *Writers and Readers in Medieval Italy: Studies in the History of Written Culture*, ed. and trans. Charles M. Radding. New Haven: Yale University Press, 1995.

Piers Plowman Electronic Archive. Society for Early English and Norse Electronic Texts. 1994–2017, http://piers.chass.ncsu.edu/.

Poiron, Daniel, ed. *Le Roman de la Rose.* Paris: Flammarion, 1974.

Pokorny, Julius. *Indogermanisches etymologisches Wörterbuch.* 2 vols. Bern: Francke, 1959–69.

Popper, Karl. *Objective Knowledge.* Oxford: Clarendon Press, 1972.

Prothero, G.W. *A Memoir of Henry Bradshaw, Fellow of King's College, Cambridge, and University Librarian.* London: Kegan Paul, Trench & Co., 1888.

Raby, F.J.E. *A History of Christian Latin Poetry.* 2nd edn. Oxford: Clarendon Press, 1953.

Ramsey, Roy Vance. *The Manly-Rickert Text of the Canterbury Tales: A Revised Edition with a foreword by Henry Ansgar Kelly.* Lewiston: Edwin Mellen, 1994.

Reiss, Edmund. "A Critical Approach to the Middle English Lyric." *College English* 27, no. 5 (1966): 373–79.

Riccoboni, Luigi. *Histoire du théâtre italien.* Paris: Cailleau, 1730.

Robinson, F.N., ed. *The Complete Works of Geoffrey Chaucer.* 2nd edn. Boston: Houghton Mifflin, 1957.

The Romance of the Rose, ed. Charles Dahlberg. Norman: University of Oklahoma Press, 1995.

Ruggiers, Paul G., ed. *Editing Chaucer: The Great Tradition.* Norman: Pilgrim Books, 1984.

Ryan, Lawrence V. "Chaucer's Criseyde in Neo-Latin Dress." *English Language Renaissance* 17, no. 3 (1987): 288–302.

Saintsbury, George. *A History of English Prosody from the Twelfth Century to the Present Day.* 3 vols. London: Macmillan, 1906–10.

———. *Minor Poets of the Caroline Period.* 3 vols. Oxford: Clarendon Press, 1905–21.

Savage-Rumbaugh, E.S. and B. Wilkerson. "Socio-sexual Behavior in *Pan paniscus* and *Pan troglodytes*: A Comparative Study." *Journal of Human Evolution* 7, no. 4 (1978): 327–44.

Schmidle, Nicholas. "A Very Rare Book: The Mystery Surrounding a Copy of Galileo's Pivotal Treatise." *The New Yorker*, 16 December, 2013, 62–73, https://www.newyorker.com/magazine/2013/12/16/a-very-rare-book.

Schmidt, A.V.C., ed. *Piers Plowman: A Parallel-Text Edition of the A, B, C, and Z Versions*. 4 vols. London: Longman, 1995–2008.

Scholderer, Victor. *Fifty Essays in Fifteenth- and Sixteenth-Century Bibliography*, ed. Dennis E. Rhodes. Amsterdam: Hertzberger, 1966.

Sepet, Maurice. *Les Prophètes du Christ: Etude sur les origines du théâtre au Moyen Age*. Paris: Didier, 1878.

Seymour, M.C. "Chaucer's Legend of Good Women: Two Fallacies." *Review of English Studies* 37, no. 148 (1986): 528–34.

Shapin, Steven. *A Social History of Truth: Civility and Science in Seventeenth-Century England*. Chicago: University of Chicago Press, 1994.

Sharpe, Kevin. *Reading Revolutions: The Politics of Reading in Early Modern England*. New Haven: Yale University Press, 2001.

——— and Steven N. Zwicker, eds. *Reading, Society and Politics in Early Modern England*. New York: Cambridge University Press, 2003.

Sherman, William H. *Used Books: Marking Readers in Renaissance England*. Philadelphia: University of Pennsylvania Press, 2007.

Shoaf, R. Allen. "'For there is figures in all things': Juxtology in Shakespeare, Spenser, and Milton." In *The Work of Dissimilitude in Renaissance Literature: Essays from the Sixth Citadel Conference on Medieval and Renaissance Studies*, eds. David G. Allen and Robert White, 266–85. Newark: University of Delaware Press, 1992.

Skeat, Walter W. *The Chaucer Canon, with a Discussion of the Works Associated with the Name of Geoffrey Chaucer*. Oxford: Clarendon Press, 1900.

———. *The Complete Works of Geoffrey Chaucer*. 7 vols. Oxford: Clarendon Press, 1894–97.

———. *An Etymological Dictionary of the English Language.* Oxford: Clarendon Press, 1884.

———. *The Vision of William concerning Piers Plowman with Vita de Dowel, Dobet et Dobest, and Richard the Redeles, by William Langland.* 2 vols. London: Oxford University Press, 1885.

Spurgeon, Caroline F.E. *Five Hundred Years of Chaucer Criticism and Allusion, 1357–1900.* 3 vols. New York: Russell and Russell, 1960.

Stallybrass, Peter and Roger Chartier, "Reading and Authorship: The Circulation of Shakespeare (1590–1619)." In *A Concise Companion to Shakespeare and the Text*, ed. Andrew Murphy, 35–56. London: Blackwell, 2007.

Stamatakis, Chris. "'With diligent studie, but sportingly': How Gabriel Harvey Read His Castiglione," *Journal of the Northern Renaissance* 5 (2013). http://www.northernrenaissance.org/with-diligent-studie-but-sportingly-how-gabriel-harvey-read-his-castiglione/.

Stewart, Susan. *Poetry and the Fate of the Senses.* Chicago: University of Chicago Press, 2002.

Stoddard, Roger E. *Marks in Books.* Cambridge: Harvard University Press, 1985.

Sutton, Dana F. Sir Francis Kynaston, *Amorum Troili et Creseidae Libri Quinque* (1639), http://www.philological.bham.ac.uk/troilus/.

Ten Brink, Bernhard. *The Language and Metre of Chaucer (1884).* 2nd edn., rev. Friedrich Kluge, trans. M. Bentinck Smith. London: Macmillan, 1901.

Thynne, Francis. *Animadversions Uppon the Annotacions and Corrections of some Imperfections of Impressiones of Chaucers Workes (1598),* ed. G.H. Kingsley, rev. F.J. Furnivall. London: N. Trübner & Co., 1875.

Tratz, Eduard Paul and Heinz Heck. "Der afrikanische Anthropoide Bonobo: Eine neue Menschenaffengattung." *Säugetierkundliche Mitteilungen* 2, no. 3 (1954): 97–101.

Travis, Peter. *Disseminal Chaucer: Rereading The Nun's Priest's Tale.* Notre Dame: University of Notre Dame Press, 2010.

Twyman, Michael. *Early Lithographed Books: A Study of the Design and Production of Improper Books in the Age of the Hand Press*. London: Farrand Press, 1990.

Tyrwhitt, Thomas. *The Canterbury Tales of Chaucer. To which are added, an Essay on his language and versification, an introductory discourse, and notes.* 4 vols. London, Payne 1775–78.

Updike, Daniel Berkeley. *Printing Types: Their History, Forms, and Use: A Study in Survivals*. 2nd edn. 2 vols. Cambridge: Harvard University Press, 1937.

Urry, John, ed. *The Works of Geoffrey Chaucer*. London, 1721.

Utz, Richard. "The Colony Writes Back: F.N. Robinson's *Complete Works of Geoffrey Chaucer* and the *Translatio* of Chaucer Studies to the United States." *Studies in Medievalism* 19 (2010): 160–203.

Wagner, Bettina and Marcia Reed, eds. *Early Printed Books as Material Objects: Proceedings of the Conference Organized by the IFLA Rare Books and Manuscripts Section, Munich, 19–21 August 2009*. Berlin: De Gruyter Sauer, 2010.

Warner, Lawrence. *The Lost History of Piers Plowman: The Earliest Transmission of Langland's Work*. Philadelphia: University of Pennsylvania Press, 2011.

Warton, Thomas. *The History of English Poetry from the Close of the Eleventh to the Commencement of the Eighteenth Century*. 3 vols. London: Dodsley, 1775–78.

Weiss, Adrian. "Reproductions of Early Dramatic Texts as a Source of Bibliographical Evidence," TEXT: *Transactions of the Society for Textual Scholarship* 4 (1988): 237–68.

Wilson, E.O. *Consilience: The Unity of Knowledge*. New York: Knopf, 1998.

———. *The Social Conquest of Earth*. New York: W.W. Norton, 2012.

Wimsatt, W.K., ed. *Versification: Major Language Types, Sixteen Essays*. New York: MLA, 1972.

Wolf, Helmut. *Sir Francis Kynastons Übersetzung von Chaucers Troilus and Criseyde: Interpretation, Edition und Kommentar*. Frankfurt am Main: Peter Lang, 1997.

Wing, Donald, comp. *Short-Title Catalogue of books printed in England, Scotland, Ireland, Wales and British America and of English Books printed in other countries (1641–1700)*. 3 vols. New York: Columbia University Press, 1951. [2nd edn., 4 vols., New York: MLA, 1972–98.]

Yerkes, David. "Chaucer's Twelve 'Long' and 'Short' Vowels: The Evidence from Rhymes in *Troilus and Criseyde*." *The Chaucer Review* 45, no. 3 (2011): 252–74.

Young, Karl. *The Drama of the Medieval Church*. 2 vols. Oxford: Clarendon Press, 1933.

Zedler, Gottfried. *Die älteste Gutenbergtype mit 13 Tafeln in Lichtdruck*. Mainz: Gutenberg Gesellschaft, 1902.

Zumthor, Paul. *Essai de poétique médiévale*. Paris: Le Seuil, 1972.

www.ingramcontent.com/pod-product-compliance
Lightning Source LLC
Chambersburg PA
CBHW072040160426
43197CB00014B/2568